Sport and Identity
in the North of England

Sport and Identity
in the North of England

edited by Jeff Hill and Jack Williams

KEELEUNIVERSITY**PRESS**

First published in 1996 by
Keele University Press
Keele, Staffordshire

© The contributors

Typeset by Carnegie Publishing Ltd
18 Maynard St, Preston
Printed by Hartnolls
Bodmin, Cornwall, England

ISBN 1 85331 082 4

Contents

Notes on contributors   vii

1.   Introduction
     Jeff Hill and Jack Williams   1

2.   Sport and community: a case study of the mining
     villages of East Northumberland, 1800–1914
     Alan Metcalfe   13

3.   Football, sport of the North?
     Tony Mason   41

4.   'The making of the healthy and the happy home':
     recreation, education, and the production of
     working-class womanhood at the Rowntree
     Cocoa Works, York, c. 1898–1914
     Catriona M. Parratt   53

5.   Rite of spring: Cup Finals and community in the
     North of England
     Jeff Hill   85

6.   Churches, sport and identities in the North, 1900–1939
     Jack Williams   113

7.   Heroes of the North: sport and the shaping of
     regional identity
     Richard Holt   137

8.   Sport and racism in Yorkshire: a case study
     *Brian Holland, Lorna Jackson, Grant Jarvie
     and Mike Smith*   165

     Index   187

Notes on contributors

Jeff Hill teaches in the Department of International Studies, Nottingham Trent University. He has written articles on aspects of both sport and the labour movement in the nineteenth and twentieth centuries, and is currently writing a book on the Lancashire cotton town of Nelson.

Brian Holland has presented a number of papers to national and international conferences on the issue of sport and racism. He works for the Commission for Racial Equality and is completing a PhD on racism and British football.

Richard Holt was for several years a member of the History Department at the University of Stirling. More recently he has taught at the University of Leuven, Belgium, and De Montfort University, Leicester. He is the author of *Sport and Society in Modern France* (1981) and *Sport and the British* (1989). He has written several articles on the social history of sport as well as editing *Sport and the Working Class in Modern Britain* (1990).

Lorna Jackson teaches at Moray House Institute, Heriot-Watt University, Edinburgh.

Grant Jarvie teaches at Moray House Institute, Heriot-Watt University, Edinburgh. He is the author of *Highland Games: The Making of the Myth* (1991), co-editor of *Scottish Sport in the Making of the Nation* (1994) and co-author of *Sport and Leisure in Social Thought* (1994).

Tony Mason teaches at the Centre for Social History, University of Warwick. He is the author of several books and articles on nineteenth- and twentieth-century social and labour history, including *Association Football and English Society, 1863–1915* (1980), *Sport in Britain* (1988) and *Passion of the People? Football in South America* (1995).

Alan Metcalfe teaches in the Departments of Kinesiology, History and Sociology at the University of Windsor, Ontario, Canada. In the recent past his research interests have been focused on the recreational activities of miners in Northumberland, on which he has written chapters and articles. He is the author of *Canada Learns to Play: The Emergence of Organised Sport in Canada, 1807–1914* (1987), and since 1970 he has published and edited the *Canadian Journal of the History of Sport*.

Catriona Parratt teaches undergraduate and graduate courses in sports history in the Department of Sport, Health, Leisure and Physical Studies at the University of Iowa, Iowa City, USA. Her research interests are in working-class women's sport and leisure in nineteenth- and twentieth-century Britain, on which she is currently writing a book. She is a native of Lincolnshire.

Mike Smith teaches at the University of Warwick. Born in Yorkshire, his knowledge of sport in the county is coupled with research interests in management of the outdoors and the sports sciences.

Jack Williams teaches in the School of Social Science, Liverpool John Moores University. He has written on the social history of cricket and is currently preparing a study of cricket and culture in England between the wars.

1. Introduction

Jeff Hill and Jack Williams

'With Slomer ... gone you'll find all the big combines finding it easier to move into town. You mark my words. There'll be no king pin anymore. We'll become like all the other big towns – socialist, impersonal, anonymous. The only thing we'll be known by' – he waved his gloved hand at me – 'will be the standard of our football team.'[1]

'Sport', says Tony Mason, 'often contributes to an enhancement of the individual's sense of identity with or belonging to a group or collectivity. It can be district, village, town, city or county. It can be class, colour or country.'[2] This process can take curious forms. When, in late 1994, the newly-enriched Blackburn Rovers embarked on their attempt to conquer European football by way of the UEFA Cup competition, their ambitions were dashed at the first hurdle by Trelleborg, a club virtually unknown outside Sweden. The setback stunned Blackburn but was greeted with amusement in neighbouring Lancashire towns. Ten miles away in Burnley unofficial additions appeared on road signs announcing: 'Burnley – twinned with Trelleborg'. Longstanding local rivalries now fostered new international liaisons.

It is with the capacity of sport to generate these kinds of allegiances that this collection of essays is primarily concerned. Its appearance, we feel, is timely. In the mid-1990s the problem of identity is becoming a central, even fashionable, one among historians and other social scientists. Much of the attention given to this issue is explained by the continuing development of feminist theory and studies, which have succeeded in establishing the idea of gender as a key concept in understanding the social process. At the same time, the resurgence of nationalism in many parts of Europe since the 1980s has re-focused analysis on the nature of national identity and its associated questions of race and ethnicity. Moreover, the development of the interdisciplinary terrain of cultural studies has called attention to the importance

1

of language and non-verbal forms of communication as determinants of our perceptions of the world and has served to reinforce concern with how we think about ourselves. Whatever the precise reasons for this concern with identity might be, there can be little doubt as to its importance. It is a fundamental issue in human societies. As Anthony D. Smith points out, it was embedded in Greek myth. In Sophocles' play *Oedipus Tyrannos* 'the question of identity, collective as well as individual, broods over the action. "I will know who I am": the discovery of self is the play's motor and the action's inner meaning.'[3] Smith goes on to echo Mason's point that the self is composed of layers of identity and allegiance – gender, territory, religion, ethnicity, class and so on. It is through the cultural activities of our everyday lives, many of which, such as sport, are apparently trivial, that identity is being constantly produced, that in the words of Clifford Geertz, 'man is an animal suspended in webs of significance he himself has spun'.[4] Our cultural values and experiences tell us who we are.

The emphasis for so many years in the historiography of social relations upon social class and the formation and expression of class consciousness meant that other forms of social identity tended to be overlooked. This engagement with social class owed much to the impact of Marxist historians, though it must not be overlooked that even such an influential Marxist historian as E. P. Thompson stressed that the cultural assumptions of those living in the past, as well as economic factors, influenced the formation of social consciousness. In the late 1980s and 1990s, however, the primacy accorded to class identities in the shaping of social relations began to be questioned with the rise of postmodernist and post-structuralist modes of social analysis and the associated 'linguistic turn' in the writing of social history.

One recent source of such thinking has been the work of Patrick Joyce, who has argued that class was not the dominant form of identity in Victorian England and that a confrontationist working-class consciousness scarcely existed. In *Visions of the People* he claims that working people possessed a spectrum of identities not only of class but also of neighbourhood, workplace, town, region, religion and nation, which in many cases involved shared values, loyalties and perspectives with people from other social groups.[5] Not all historians have accepted Joyce's interpretation of class relations in Victorian England,[6] whilst his methodology has been equally controversial and represents what he believes to be the import of postmodernist and post-structuralist thinking upon the role of language in constituting the 'self' and the 'social'. In *Visions of the People* and more particularly in his later book *Democratic Subjects*[7] he has argued for the 'pre-figurative' role of discourse, that language defined in its widest sense and narrative determine how individuals perceive the world and their place within it. 'Meanings make subjects', he urges 'and not subjects meanings.' The lesson of the 'linguistic turn' for Joyce is that 'language describes a human condition itself always marked by the making of meaning'.[8] It would seem that for him language and culture are inseparable, or even the same process, and that culture is the foundation of 'consciousness' [9] or what Thompson denoted as 'experience'. This methodology foregrounds *ideology* and harmonizes with the view of Roland Barthes, a key influence upon the 'linguistic turn', that what we know of the world and of the relationships that exist within it is derived from what is *represented*.[10]

Though alert to the ideological impacts of popular culture, Joyce has said nothing about sport, which is especially surprising as the relationship between sport and identity is so manifestly a close one. This omission might reflect more the development of historiography than Joyce's own process of selection. Sports history has been blossoming over the past decade or more and is now probably recognized by most historians as a legitimate sub-branch of the discipline. The capacity of sports historians to bring their subject matter into mainstream debates in social and economic history has ensured that the field is not now seen as a trivial pursuit, 'fans with typewriters' as Mason once aptly put it.[11] Like all relatively new areas of academic enquiry it developed a particular orientation in its early stages. This might be characterized briefly as: first, an *empiricist* methodology, showing a conventional concern for establishing general points on the basis of archival source material; and secondly a *reflectionist* approach which sees sport as something that affords an illustration of other (more important?) social processes – the growth of commercial football, for example, in the late nineteenth century providing a 'window' through which to study developments in population, transport, business, labour, popular recreation and so forth. In other words, there has been much written about the social and economic factors that have influenced the growth of sport. Little attention, though, has been directed to the effects of sport itself upon social consciousness. It is this latter approach which sports history, if it is to pursue its own version of the linguistic turn, now needs to be undertaking.

Three pioneering ventures in the study of sport and national identity have, however, undertaken such an approach and all have inspired the present volume. Each has a non-English focus and is concerned with areas where the links between sport and identity are perhaps more obvious than in England. *Fields of Praise* by Dai Smith and Gareth Williams, marking the centenary of the Welsh Rugby Union,[12] broke new ground in the writing of sports history by showing how rugby union had played a part in fashioning Welsh national identity and consequently helping in the consolidation of social cohesion during the late nineteenth and early twentieth centuries, a period that witnessed the massive expansion of the South Wales coalfield and its accompanying population explosion. More recently the forms of Irish and Scottish sentiment expressed through and modified by sport have been considered. Alan Bairner and John Sugden [13] have analysed the relationship between sport and the political affiliations of Protestantism and Catholicism in Ireland, while similar relationships are explored in the collection of essays edited by Grant Jarvie and Graham Walker, *Scottish Sport in the Making of the Nation: Ninety Minute Patriots?* [14] Among an excellent range of studies in this collection which illuminate several aspects of Scottish sport is Graham Walker's story of Nancy Riach and swimming in Motherwell. Just after the Second World War Motherwell enjoyed a meteoric rise to prominence in Britain largely because of the talents of Nancy Riach, a young sportswoman whose prodigious achievements were cut short by her early death in 1947. In telling Riach's story Walker weaves together a number of themes on the subject of identity: gender, locality, nation, and the role of the press in fulfilling the crucial role of representing the star to her public. It stands as a marvellous example of how to explore the relationship of sport and identity, emphasizing as it does both the effects of sport on other developments and the role played by sport in communicating ideas of the individual and the collectivity. Underpinning these important studies is the work of Bert Moorhouse, who has been arguing over several years in a series of case studies of Scottish football that the English obsession with class does not provide the key to unlocking the mysteries of Scottish sport. [15]

Only recently have cultural historians begun to consider the nature of English identities. What has emerged from their work is, among other things, a recognition of a number of competing versions of Englishness. Impressive evaluations of these have been produced in the separate collections of essays edited by Robert Colls and Philip Dodd, Roy Porter and Raphael Samuel. [16] Yet, as with Joyce, the role of sport in the construction of Englishness is overlooked, though the paperback edition of Porter's book significantly uses a picture of a cricket match on its cover. As John Bale has pointed out, cricket, and in particular a rural image of cricket, is a frequently used icon signifying Englishness, and especially a Southern and ruralized idea of England. [17] In seeking to investigate the the relationship between sport and identities in England the essays collected in this volume are focused on an area which, if not as distinctive as Scotland, nevertheless has powerful resonances in English cultural life: the North of England. It is based upon the belief that appraisals of the forms of regional and local identities associated with sport in different parts of England are a prerequisite for any study of sport and English national identities.

Understanding Englishness requires appreciation of what divides, as well as what unites, those who regard themselves as English.

As Richard Holt points out in his contribution to this volume, many European countries have a sense of distinctive regional differentiation within them. In England it is North and South. Not so long ago, it provided the basis of representative cricket matches. Even today, it is used in something as official and serious as road signing: on the Nottingham ring road at Clifton Bridge there is a sign indicating 'The South'. Whether this means anything to motorists other than a direction is difficult to say. Many might say not, that in England the concept of 'the South' is too vague, encompassing too many different cultures and ideas, to be meaningful, unless it were to be synonymous with London. Colls and Lancaster, however, in their study of Geordies, show that there is a deep-seated belief that the South has little understanding of, or sympathy for, the economic and consequent social difficulties of what were Northumberland and Durham,[18] and everyday experience shows that similar feelings are frequently expressed in other parts of the North. The notion of the North as a victim of Southern in-difference, or even worse, has a long provenance. Helen Jewell has found consciousness of a North–South divide as early as the eighth century in the writings of Bede.[19] The industrial revolution enhanced the importance of the North to the national economy, and perhaps encouraged many in the North to believe that Northern determination, resourcefulness, toil and sweat had become the basis of the nation's wealth, whilst the South was viewed as effete and a brake upon the economic and moral progress of the nation. As one Victorian apologist for the achievements of Northern industrialists remarked, it was north of the Trent where were found 'most of the backbone and manly virtues of the country'.[20] After the First World War much of the North's industrial heartland declined, and economic success gave way to dis-tressed areas, though by the 1950s, perhaps, ideas of embourgeoisement might have suggested that regional identity, linked as it clearly was to differences of social class, would soon become a thing of the past. But in the 1980s, as Jewell correctly perceives, the North–South divide was given a new lease of life as a result of economic conditions which lent credibility to the popular notion of an affluent South and a depressed North, with these varying economic fortunes becoming increasingly polarized at the general elections of 1979, 1983 and 1987.[21] Whatever the validity of these beliefs, they added to deep-rooted popular con-ceptions of regional diversity stretching back through J. B. Priestley's three Englands of the 1930s[22] to the Bounderby image of Northern businessmen of the nineteenth century, and back further to pre-industrial distinctions. In all this, what is significant is less the *objective* reality of the North and more the *idea* of it that exists in popular minds.

But as a recent review of Jewell's book asked, 'what precisely is northern consciousness?' [23]

Perhaps, like that other nebulous but much-used concept of 'Europe', the North of England is as much a state of mind as a place. Being a Northerner is a creation of the imagination, a product of cultural traditions, assumptions and memories. No doubt this is why notions of the North and of what constitutes Northernness have varied over time and between places. Geographically it has been a slippery entity. John Walton has pointed out that 'administrative boundaries do not always, usually or necessarily run congruent with economic, social, cultural or image-based ones, although the longer they last the more likely they are to exert an influence of their own on these other spheres.' [24] There is perhaps general agreement that the border with Scotland forms the northern boundary of the North, though the exact location of this on the ground has varied over time. Determining the southern boundary of the North has always been problematical. Many today might think that the rivers Mersey and Humber form the southern boundary of the North, but in nineteenth-century cricket discourse Nottinghamshire was usually regarded as part of the North. One person's awareness of being a Northerner is not necessarily the same as another's and, indeed, the same individual can subscribe to differing forms of Northern identity at different times. Sport offers one means of exploring these shifting states of mind. Although difficult to measure with scientific precision, interest in sport over at least the past century and a half does seem to have occupied a central space in Northern popular culture, especially among working-class males. How Northerners have seen themselves cannot be understood unless due stress is placed upon the meanings attached to sport.

This collection of essays sheds light upon how those living in the North have perceived themselves and the nature of their relationships with other parts of England and especially London. The extent to which sport has drawn upon and strengthened perceptions of the North as being different from, and a victim of, the South is examined in the essays of Mason, Holt and Hill. In his earlier, ground-breaking study of association football Tony Mason showed that this game was a creation of men from Southern public schools but was quickly taken up with enthusiasm in the North during the last third of the nineteenth century.[25] *Professional* football was very largely a product of the North of England (with the help of Scottish 'professors') and this was the crucial factor in the emergence of the Football League. In the present volume, Mason asks whether the belief that there was a distinctively Northern style of play, which rejected the Southern tradition of of amateur sportsmanship, was a myth: but a myth which helped to stimulate notions of the otherness of North and South. He further explores the nature of the partisanship connected with football before the First World War: did this express loyalty to town, or to the North, or to both?

The chapter by Holt discusses perceptions of sporting heroes in the North. He shows how it can be argued that the qualities admired in sporting heroes taught males, and especially those from the working class, what it was to be a man. Sporting heroes also, says Holt, privileged particular forms of masculinity which came to be associated with Northernness. Holt demonstrates that different sports in different parts of the North at different times have produced different notions of what constitutes a sporting hero. Some achieved a largely local celebrity and became forgotten, but are now being rediscovered by sports historians. Others have acquired a more lasting fame. Holt's work is highly pertinent to the issue of whether the characteristics of heroes from the North have differed from those found in other parts of the country. It also directs attention back to the important questions of *representation*: of how sporting heroes are created and the nature of the relationships they have with their admirers. Holt indicates that the qualities surrounding these heroes in the North have influenced how the South has imagined the North, and further shows how the production of sporting heroes has fostered rivalries between North and South.

Hill's chapter discusses the forms of celebration and festivity associated with cup finals, showing that these were rituals which expressed town-based identities and allegiances. He stresses in particular the mediating role of the provincial newspaper press in creating versions of community for its readership. An essential characteristic of such festivity in the North centred upon the fact that the FA Cup Final had almost always been held in London, and that in 1929 the Rugby League Challenge Cup Final began to be staged at Wembley. The visit to the metropolis for a cup final was not necessarily an occasion for the expression of North–South animosity, in contrast to the visits of Scottish football supporters for international matches which were often seen as an opportunity to express national feeling. But the rituals surrounding visits to cup finals indicated an awareness of London as a place apart, almost another world. As Mason shows, descriptions of Northern supporters arriving in London reveal a sense among Southerners of the otherness of those from the North.

Sport can be a rich source for learning about gender identity. The myths of male physicality discussed by Mason and Holt point to the relative absence of *female* sporting heroes and indicate the extent of popular assumptions that sport is primarily a male activity and one through which masculinity has been forged and expressed. As Jennifer Hargreaves has shown in her recent work,[26] much male involvement with sport is a register of male social power and reflects beliefs held for much of the nineteenth and twentieth centuries that the division of income and time within families should be budgeted in favour of male interests. The chapter by Williams reveals that far more males than females played for church and Sunday school sports organizations in the North during the first four decades of this century; the sporting activity associated with religious practice expressed and helped to strengthen assumptions that the playing of sport was an activity which harmonized with notions of what was accepted as respectable male behaviour. Metcalfe's discussion of how sport fostered community identities in the coal mining villages of eastern Northumberland before 1914 is very largely a discussion of male activity, but he also emphasizes how this was dependent upon the co-operation or, perhaps, exploitation of women, whilst at the same time showing that it was possible for women to identify with the forms of village allegiance which male sport, alongside other cultural practices as diverse as trade unionism and flower shows, stimulated. Hill's discussion of cup final festivities also suggests that the formation of community loyalties incorporated both sexes through the essentially male pastime of football supporting.

The capacity of sports to assist the emancipation of women, as well as to uphold male social power, has been a theme in a variety of writing, notably in the work of McCrone, Vertinsky and Hargreaves.[27] Catriona Parratt's contribution to this question analyses the interesting and previously neglected relationship between company provision of sports facilities and the position of women. In British sports history there has been a curious absence of attention upon the the role of companies in sporting provision, and to have this topic foregrounded, and linked to the theme of gender, represents a pioneering initiative in the discipline. The depth of detail permitted by Parratt's case study of Rowntrees in York, a firm with a reputation for its especially generous support for company welfare schemes, reveals that in the two decades before the First World War the sports and recreational facilities made available for its female employees were directed to training for motherhood and domesticity. In this instance company sport appears to have had little capacity to challenge conventional notions of female identity. The married mother in the home was exalted as the ideal role for women and did little to challenge the assumption that sports participation was primarily a cultural space dominated by men.

The depth of interest in sport in Northern communities provides an interesting perspective for considering not only feelings of shared interest and identity, but also the simultaneous creation of division and animosity. Metcalfe's discussion of East Northumberland, for example, shows that along with other forms of popular culture, inter-village sports could foster village identities that transcended occupational divisions whilst deepening rivalries between villages. Furthermore, village loyalties could co-exist alongside regional enthusiasms focused upon regional heroes who sometimes became national champions. Similarly, as Williams shows, the church presence within recreational sport provided opportunities for inter-denominational contact, though at the same time conflicting notions of respectability associated with religion added to divisions among working people.

Among such divisions those based upon ideas of racial community have probably been the most invidious. Racist attitudes can be interpreted as an expression of an imagined white identity which can be traced back to cultural assumptions of white supremacy which upheld imperialist expansion in the nineteenth century. There can be little doubt that racist beliefs and ethnic identities have been a potent cause of social antagonism especially during the past two or three decades. Indeed it can be argued that the intensity of ethnic divisions has been a powerful factor in undermining the credibility of social class as a conceptual tool for understanding the nature of social life in modern Britain. Apologists for sport have often asserted that games can create bonds which help to overcome the cultural assumptions that underpin racism. This argument was frequently employed against the sporting boycott of South Africa in the 1970s and 1980s. In certain historical situations it does seem that sport has the capacity to bring different racial groups together in harmony. Hill, for instance, in his study of the black cricketer Learie Constantine,[28] and Holt's comments in the present volume on the status of Billy Boston, the black player from South Wales who became one of the great icons of Wigan Rugby League Club in the 1950s and 1960s, provide examples of black sportsmen who became accepted as heroes among predominantly working-class whites in Northern towns. But these men were sports stars whose adopted communities were relatively free of the kind of racial animosities that prompted, for example, Enoch Powell's notorious remarks in his so-called 'Rivers of Blood' speech of 1968. Perhaps more typical of racist feeling in sport is the picture given in the studies by Searle and Williams,[29] and the evidence uncovered in the television programme 'The Race Game', which revealed much prejudice at both first-class and recreational levels of cricket in selected parts of the North.[30] The rise of Asian sports leagues, though by no means restricted to the North, might be seen as a determination to retain identities in the face of indifference or hostility on the part of white sportspersons. Moreover, although much more research needs to be undertaken into ethnicity and recreational sport there are suggestions that Asian sports teams have usually been recruited from distinctive religious or geographical groupings within the Asian population, which could be evidence of the persistence of traditional divisions between British Asians. Although Asian professional footballers are rare there is a considerable black presence within top-class football and rugby league, and black players have captained both the England football and Great Britain rugby league teams. There is, however, much evidence of racism within professional football and of racist attitudes among white football supporters. In the 1970s and 1980s it was noted that black footballers were rarely selected for the most responsible positions within professional teams,[31] though by the 1990s this was far less the case. Black players have achieved senior positions in football trade unionism but those who manage Premiership or Football League clubs can be counted on the fingers of one hand.

The essay by Holland, Jackson, Jarvie and Smith explores the nature of racist identities at one prominent Northern football club. They discuss how far racial feeling has become embedded in the football culture of Northern England. Much of what they have to say is, of course, not peculiar to the North. Parallels can readily be found in other big cities with black and Asian populations, and where long-established industries have collapsed or undergone massive structural change, developments which usually accompany or follow the dispersal of working-class communities through re-housing schemes. By being a case study of racial attitudes at one club, the chapter by Holland, Jackson, Jarvie and Smith is able to chart with precision the growth of racist identities surrounding a major sport. But it also shows how football fans have been able to organize themselves and so defuse aspects of racial animosities, by using language and imagery to construct counter-stereotypes of racial attitudes. Their essay thus provides an intriguing and valuable counterweight to the conventional tendency to see football culture and its activists as simply 'hooligans'.

The main conclusion to be drawn from this collection of essays is that different sports, in different localities, and at different times, have helped to construct, express and consolidate differing perceptions of Northern-ness. It is clear that in differing social settings individuals could subscribe to conflicting identities, yet without feeling any sense of paradox or contradiction. Town-based loyalties which were defined through antagonism to those from other towns could be expressed through support for a soccer or rugby league club, though such animosities could be forgotten when both groups of erstwhile rivals united to support the same county cricket team. These essays demonstrate that many of the supposedly distinctive characteristics of Northern sport are myths, though widely believed myths, and that these myths have influenced how individuals and groups have seen themselves. Sports and recreations in the North emphasize the fluidity and changing nature of identity. We envisage different roles for ourselves at different times and in different places. The examination of sport and identity undertaken in this volume show that the North and Northernness have had very many meanings. The North is an imagined territory with no fixed boundaries and the range of qualities which have been seen as characteristic of Northernness are so diverse as to defy neat definition. Some years ago Gwyn Williams asked 'When was Wales?'[32] These essays show that there can be many answers to the questions of 'When was the North?' and 'Who have been the Northerners?'

Notes

1. D. Storey, *This Sporting Life* (Penguin, Harmondsworth: 1962), p. 229.
2. T. Mason, *Sport in Britain* (Faber & Faber, London: 1988), p. 118.
3. A. D. Smith, *National Identity* (Penguin, Harmondsworth: 1991), p. 3.
4. C. Geertz, *The Interpretation of Cultures: Selected Essays* (Basic Books, New York: 1973), p. 5.
5. P. Joyce, *Visions of the People: Industrial England and the Question of Class 1848–1914* (Cambridge U.P., Cambridge: 1991).
6. M. Savage and A. Miles, *The Remaking of the British Working Class 1840–1940* (Routledge, London: 1994), for instance, argue that a working-class politicized consciousness had developed before 1914. See especially chapter 1.
7. P. Joyce, *Democratic Subjects: The Self and the Social in Nineteenth-Century England* (Cambridge U.P., Cambridge: 1994).
8. *Democratic Subjects*, p. 13.
9. *Democratic Subjects*, p. 12.
10. J. Culler, *Barthes* (Fontana, Glasgow: 1983), especially chapters 3 and 6.
11. T. Mason, 'Writing the history of sport', unpublished seminar paper delivered at the Centre for the Study of Social History, University of Warwick, October 1991.
12. D. Smith and G. Williams, *Fields of Praise: The Official History of the Welsh Rugby Union 1881–1981* (University of Wales Press, Cardiff: 1980).
13. J. Sugden and A. Bairner, *Sport, Sectarianism and Society in a Divided Ireland* (Leicester U.P., Leicester: 1993).
14. G. Jarvie and G. Walker (eds), *Scottish Sport in the Making of the Nation: Ninety Minute Patriots?* (Leicester U.P., Leicester: 1994).
15. H. F. Moorhouse, 'Repressed nationalism and professional football: Scotland versus England', in J. A. Mangan and R. B. Small (eds), *Sport, Culture, Society: International Historical and Sociological Perspectives* (Spon, London: 1986), pp. 52–9, and 'Shooting stars: footballers and working-class culture in twentieth-century Scotland', in R. Holt (ed.), *Sport and the Working Class in Modern Britain* (Manchester U.P., Manchester: 1990); C. Critcher, 'Football since the war', in C. Clarke, C. Critcher and R. Johnson (eds), *Working-Class Culture: Studies in History and Theory* (Hutchinson/Centre for Contemporary Cultural Studies; 1979), discusses class and football in England.

16. R. Colls and P. Dodd (eds), *Englishness: Politics and Culture 1880–1920* (Croom Helm, London: 1987); R. Porter (ed.), *Myths of the English* (Polity, Cambridge: 1992); R. Samuel, *Patriotism: The Making and Unmaking of British National Identity*, 3 vols (Routledge, 1989) – despite its title, most of the contributions to the three volumes of this work concentrate upon English patriotism.

17. J. Bale, *Landscapes of Modern Sport* (Leicester U.P., Leicester: 1994), pp. 153–65.

18. R. Colls and B. Lancaster (eds), *Geordies: Roots of Regionalism* (Edinburgh U.P., Edinburgh: 1992).

19. H. M. Jewell, *The North–South Divide: The Origins of Northern Consciousness in England* (Manchester U.P., Manchester: 1994), p. 4.

20. Talbot Baines writing in *The Times* 1897, quoted by C. Dellheim, 'Imagining England: Victorian views of the North', *Northern History* 22 (1986), p. 229. Dellheim's article provides fascinating insights into how the North was perceived by the Victorians, but its discussion of the North is restricted to Lancashire and Yorkshire.

21. Jewell, *The North–South Divide*, pp. 1–3.

22. J. B. Priestley, *English Journey* (Penguin, Harmondsworth: 1987 edn).

23. E. Lord, 'The road to Wigan's peers' (review of Jewell, *The North–South Divide*), *Times Higher Education Supplement*, 13 May 1994.

24. J. Walton, 'Professor Musgrove's North of England: a critique', *Journal of Regional and Local Studies* 12. 2 (1992), p. 24.

25. T. Mason, *Association Football and English Society, 1863–1915* (Harvester, Brighton: 1980), chapter 3.

26. J. Hargreaves, *Sporting Females: Critical Issues in the History and Sociology of Women's Sports* (Routledge, 1994), pp. 42–4 and chapter 8.

27. See in particular K. E. McCrone, *Sport and the Physical Emancipation of English Women* (Routledge, London: 1988); P. Vertinsky, *The Eternally Wounded Woman: Women, Doctors and Exercise in the Late Nineteenth Century* (Manchester U.P., Manchester: 1990); J. Hargreaves, '"Playing like gentlemen while behaving like ladies": contradictory features of the formative years of women's sport', *British Journal of Sports History* 2. 1 (1985), pp. 40–53, and *Sporting Females*.

28. J. Hill, 'Reading the stars: a post-modernist approach to sports history', *Sports Historian* 14 (1994), pp. 45–54.

29. C. Searle, 'Race before wicket: cricket, empire and the white rose', *Race and Class* 31. 3 (1990), pp. 43–8, and 'Cricket the mirror of racism', *Race and Class* 34. 3 (1993), pp. 45–54; J. Williams, 'South Asians and cricket in Bolton', *Sports Historian* 14 (1994), pp. 58–65.

30. 'Inside Story – The Race Game', BBC1, 2 May 1990.

31. E. Cashmore, *Black Sportsmen* (Routledge, London: 1982), p. 177; J. Maguire, 'Sport, racism and British society: a sociological study of England's elite male Afro/Caribbean soccer and rugby union players', in G. Jarvie (ed.), *Sport, Racism and Ethnicity* (Falmer, London: 1991).

32. G. A. Williams, *When was Wales? A History of the Welsh* (Penguin, Harmondsworth: 1985).

2. Sport and community: a case study of the mining villages of East Northumberland, 1800–1914

Alan Metcalfe

In 1872 and 1873 the *Newcastle Weekly Chronicle* published weekly articles on the living conditions in the mining villages of Northumberland and Durham. The view that emerged was a sobering one. Cramped living conditions and few amenities for social interaction made even the 'better' villages unappealing to the contemporary eye. Seghill was one of the worst:

> The ordinary houses in Seghill are easily described. You have one room on the ground floor, and the usual damp, stinking pantry, clinging as it were to the backside of the house and testifying by the state of its walls and floor to the inability of the badly-tiled roof to keep out the rain.
>
> From what I saw of the roofs of these houses I was quite convinced that it was no impossibility for any of the miners who might be astronomically inclined, to read the stars as they lay in bed through the chinks and crevices of the badly-pointed tiles.
>
> If decency or morality or health can exist in abodes such as I have described, it must be in spite of the surroundings of the place, for at present it is pregnant with every influence that can debase the physical, moral, and intellectual nature of man or woman. Privies are here almost unknown; the little patch of kitchen garden is absent from the front or back of the houses, and its place is supplied by the filthy ash heap.[1]

It is difficult to envisage life in these conditions, yet generations of miners and their families created, for themselves, meaningful lives. One of the few activities that transcended social and class barriers was sport. More closely related to the realities of daily life epitomizing strength, endurance, uncertainty and luck, sport is an ideal vehicle for exploring the nature of community and community values. It permeated the lives of the miners of East Northumberland throughout the nineteenth century. From cockfighting in the early years of the century to football at the turn of the century, sport was an essential element of mining life providing excitement, pride and status in conditions that can only be described as poor. However, sport was not just a momentary diversion from the harshness of life; it also served as a visible symbol of the community both within the mining villages and also in terms of their position relative to the outside world. Sport was one of the few activities that brought all segments of the community together; albeit in situations that served to reinforce the relationships which flowed from the mine. It is the object of this study to attempt to illustrate, in an embryonic fashion, the ways in which sport represented and reinforced the values of the mining communities.

Little attention has been paid to the ways in which the miners and their families created meaningful lives.[2] The few attempts that have been made tend to examine life through the eyes of middle-class observers and/or the articulate and literate segments of the community. Thus, the influence of Methodism on the mining villages has been well documented.[3] At the same time, while the influence of Methodists was great, a majority of mining families did not go to chapel on a regular basis. For this majority, meaning flowed from the reality of daily life in the pit and village – physically demanding work in difficult conditions, inadequate, substandard housing, ever present dirt from the mine, and limited social amenities.[4] These conditions promoted conditions and values at odds with those values preached by the Methodist preachers, the colliery officials and the Mechanics' Institutes. At the same time, there was one, overarching idea that tended to bring together these different ideologies – the word 'community'. The idea of community lay at the heart of life and was constructed, reinforced and promoted through a variety of activities and institutions – chapel life, the Mechanics' and Working Men's Institutes, public houses, annual celebrations, mass meetings, and, central to this study, sport. It is important to emphasize that community was not a static concept – the ingredients changed as the society changed and new elements were incorporated into this historically created view that the people had of themselves. Community comprises a vast array of elements of everyday life. Yet the establishment of a sense of community is a process of choice, choice that is an active process that never ends: some things disappear while other new ones are incorporated.

The question is: what does the word 'community' mean? As Raymond Williams stated, despite common use by both lay people and academics the word 'community' is characterized by its impreciseness.[5] At the same time it is possible to identify some basic characteristics that serve to provide a focus to our exploration of the concept of community. We may describe a community as 'a body of individuals organized into a unit usually with awareness of some unifying trait', and also as 'the people living in a particular place or region and usually linked by common interests'.[6] In other words, a community is identified with a particular location and is comprised of a group of people held together by unifying traits or common interests. Perhaps more important than this definition is the fact that 'unlike all other terms of social organization it seems never to be used unfavourably'.[7] 'Community' was always a positive term. As we shall see, in physical surroundings that could only be described as inadequate, sport was one of the few visible symbols that provided the miners with a positive view of themselves and with mechanisms for judging themselves against each other and the outside world.

It is important not to overemphasize the homogeneity of the mining villages; they were very much locations where interpersonal and intergroup differences served to attack the foundations of community life. There were, very clearly, differences between those individuals and groups whose social life focused around the chapel, the Mechanics' Institute and the educational initiatives, and those whose lives focused on drinking, gambling and the traditional sports. However, it is important to emphasize that the boundaries were often blurred and frequently good Methodists embraced some of the activities routinely condemned by the ministers.[8] Additionally, even though the mining villages were inhabited, for the most part, by miners they also included substantial numbers of non-miners. For example, 14 per cent of the male population of Seaton Delaval in 1891 were non-miners.[9] Even among those working at the mine there were distinct differences in hours of work, working conditions, earnings and status. From the early 1800s, the hewers, those who cut the coal at the coal face, worked shorter hours, earned more money, and had the highest status. During the 1830s and 1840s with the adoption of the two-shift system, the hewers worked eight hours while the rest worked between twelve and fourteen hours.[10] Additionally the putters, onsetters and drivers who worked underground earned more money and had a higher status than those working above ground. In other words there was a complex system of status, earnings and hours of work that translated to different lives outside the mine. Thus, in one sense the mining villages were never homogeneous and these powerful forces acted to divide the communities rather than integrate them. It should be apparent, therefore, that the forces emphasizing differences were always acting in a dialectical fashion with the forces drawing the community together. Thus, community was very much a contested domain.

It is important to recognize that the word 'community', in the mining districts, embraced a number of different meanings. To the outside world the miners were regarded as a group and not as individuals. Both within and outside the mining districts there were times when the word 'community' was used to denote miners as a collectivity. However, within the district itself the word 'community' was used to identify different villages. Each village was attached to a particular pit shaft; as Stephen Martin, a miner turned historian, stated: 'Amongst the mining fraternity a reference to a colliery means not only the mine itself with its essential surface buildings, but also the community attached to it.'[11] However, in the larger villages, such as Ashington, particular parts of the larger village were identified as communities within the village. Finally, there were a number of communities that transcended the boundaries of individual villages; in particular a number of ethnic groups comprised of migrants from Ireland, Wales, Cornwall and Devon. It is apparent, therefore, that an individual could, and in fact did, belong to several different communities at the same time. However, the development of a sense of community occurred only under certain conditions. In fact, there were four conditions that were fundamental, to a greater or lesser extent, to the development of a sense of community.

First, there had to be a stable, permanent settlement. The mining villages of East Northumberland were created during the nineteenth century. Prior to 1800 coal mining was restricted to the banks of the rivers Tyne and Blyth and the sea-sale collieries along the coast at Hartley.[12] The real development of coal mining coincided with the development of the permanent, deep and dangerous mines along the river Blyth at Cowpen. At the same time coal mining spread north from the river Tyne past the 90 fathom dyke. This resulted in the creation of what were to become the first permanent mining villages: West Moor (1802), Killingworth (1810), Backworth (1818) and Earsdon (1822). During the 1820s mining spread into the heart of the coalfield: Cramlington, Burradon, Wideopen (1825), Seghill, East Holywell and West Holywell (1828), Seaton Burn and Seaton Delaval (1838). In the late 1830s mining in Bedlingtonshire, long associated with coal mining, expanded with the sinking of pits at Barrington, Bedlington A Pit (1837), Doctor Pit (1854) and West Sleekburn (1859). Another group of colliery villages was spawned by the expansion of the coalfield between 1866 and 1874: Widdrington (1866), Cambois and Dinnington (1867), Longhirst (1868). By the late 1870s the physical configuration of the coalfield was set except for the creation of the largest mining village in Britain, Ashington-Hirst in the 1880s. By the beginning of the twentieth century there were 66 mining villages spread across the landscape of East Northumberland.

Secondly, the development of a sense of community was related to the stability and composition of the population.[13] Mining villages were notoriously unstable in terms of population – movement was a reality of mining life. Strikes, lockouts, closing of collieries and economic conditions made movement a way of life. The degree of movement can be gauged by one example: Richard Brown, a 48-year-old miner working at Seghill colliery in 1891, had lived and worked in eleven different colliery villages in 25 years; he was not atypical.[14] In the early years of the century the miners' terms of employment, a monthly or yearly bond, ensured massive instability. It was not until the abolition of the bond in 1872 that some of the villages acquired a more stable population. This is illustrated in the case of Seaton Delaval where, by 1891, 63 per cent of those under twenty had been born in Seaton Delaval. Additionally there was a difference in the composition of the village between the relatively small villages and the larger communities such as Ashington, Blyth and Bedlington. The smaller villages were comprised nearly exclusively of miners while the larger villages had a substantial professional and commercial class who tended to dominate local government, the churches and other institutions.[15] Finally it was people who created the communities. Thus the sense of community developed in Seaton Delaval was different from that developed in Ashington. Thus, the question of who the people were is important. Between 1851 and 1911 the population of the district increased from 20,552 to 111,098. The period prior to 1874 witnessed successive waves of miners and their families coming from other parts of Britain. The 1840s witnessed a substantial influx of Irish people, the 1850s people from adjacent districts and the late 1860s people from Cornwall and Devon. These groups gave to certain villages a distinctive flavour. For example, as a consequence of the Cramlington strike in 1868, the owners evicted all the local miners and brought in nearly 600 miners and their families from Cornwall and Devon. As late as 1891 the Cramlington district had a large number of miners from the South West. In the 1870s the influx of miners from outside Northumberland diminished, thus increasing the numbers of miners born and raised in the Northumberland coalfield. While this was true of the district as a whole there were significant differences between villages. For example, in 1891, in nine villages within a two-mile radius of Seaton Delaval the percentage of miners born outside of Northumberland varied between 18.2 per cent in Bates Cottage to 44.5 per cent in Cramlington.[16] This in conjunction with the miners' penchant for moving made for a relatively unstable population.

Thirdly, the physical layout of the villages and the location of the churches, schools, Mechanics' Institutes, sporting grounds and public houses determined the nature of the daily social interactions that were fundamental to a sense of community. The mining villages were, in every sense, 'constructed communities', constructed by the mine owners with no reference to the inhabitants.[17] One of the most important decisions which impacted on the development of a sense of community was the actual physical layout of the village. Certain forms of layout promoted different patterns of social interaction and different senses of community. Both the squares of Seghill and the rows of Ashington were conducive to developing a sense of community while the strip development of Bomarsund with its lack of a clear focus to the village retarded its development.[18] Additionally, the development and location of the main institutions determined the patterns of interaction underlying daily life. Nearly without exception the first social institution to be built was a public house or inn. For example, the Astley Arms Inn at Seaton Delaval was constructed in 1838, the same year that the coal company embarked upon digging the shaft. Additionally, the Hastings Arms Inn was built, by the colliery owners, early in the 1840s. With respect to schools, in the 1840s there were very few buildings 'exclusively devoted to the purposes of schools'. Most of the 'schools' were housed in colliery cottages adapted for the purpose or in colliery houses rented by the 'teachers'. The building of permanent school buildings occurred in the 1850s and 1860s. Just as important was the hiring of professionally trained teachers – these arrived in the 1860s and 1870s. A similar pattern can be seen in the building of permanent churches or chapels. Prior to 1860 the area was served by eleven churches. By 1886 there were 58 churches and chapels serving the expanding population.[19] The foundations for the development of community were being laid. However, it was not just the creation of these facilities that was important but their location. These varied from village to village. For example, in Seaton Delaval they were all located around the junction of the road to the colliery and the Bedlington road and thus provided a logical focus to daily life in Seaton Delaval. In many ways each mining village was unique.

Finally, there was one factor that was uniform across the coalfield – the power of the colliery owners and officials to determine the conditions under which the miners lived and worked. The coal companies and the landowners were the critical determining influences on the physical and to some extent the ideological boundaries within which the idea of community developed. They determined the physical layout of the villages, the conditions under which the inhabitants lived and worked, controlled the development of public houses, schools, churches, chapels and institutes and, in some instances, the availability of food and medical help.[20] In other words, they created the conditions within which the miners and their families lived their lives.

It would appear that there were as many different communities as there were mining villages. However, this is not quite true. There was one thing that transcended local differences and gave a real unity to the villages – the coal mine. It is impossible to understand mining communities without recognizing the all-pervasive influence of the pit shaft – it symbolized the community. It dominated the landscape, daily life and the way in which people thought about life. Representing both the certainty and uncertainty of life, it was the foundation upon which all communities were based. In a very real sense the colliery whistle controlled the ebb and flow of life – it called men to work, it signalled when the mine was closed and when there was a disaster. The colliery and the social relationships flowing from it are foundational to an understanding of these communities.

What should be evident from the above brief outline of the development of the mining villages in East Northumberland is that the development was uneven and historically created – the villages changed over time. Prior to the 1870s conditions militated against the development of a strong sense of community – transient population, a massive influx of miners from outside Northumberland, the lack of permanent schools and chapels and other institutions. There were other factors that point to the period after 1860 as one that was conducive to the development of a sense of community – the creation of a railway system within the coalfield, the inauguration of weekly and daily newspapers, and the emergence of compulsory elementary education.

The miners regarded themselves as different from other groups. The question is, did they consciously recognize the collective bonds and if so how was this made manifest? It was in their battle to improve working conditions that the miners of the different villages met to consider collective action. Although there were many individual strikes prior to the nineteenth century it was not until 1810 that the miners of Northumberland and Durham met to undertake joint action.[21] This was followed by the great strikes of 1831 and 1844, when the miners of the two counties met to consider the actions to be taken. The need for closer ties of a more permanent nature was made concrete in 1863 with the development of the Northumberland Miners' Union. This ushered in a new era, one in which the Northumberland miners met once a year to celebrate their unity. In September 1864, the miners of Northumberland descended on Blyth Links to hold the first Annual Miners' Picnic. Thus began one of the most important traditions of the Northumberland miners. While the focal point of the day's festivities was the platform where leaders spoke on relevant issues, games and sports were an integral part in that first and subsequent picnics. After the speeches some 'Played at quoits, others joined in festive games, and a large party danced on the green sward'.[22] Thenceforth, the games and festivities around the periphery of the picnic were an important adjunct to the more serious endeavours. Held either at Blyth Links or on Morpeth Common the picnic became a centrepiece of the whole year, when up to 20,000 miners and their families met to celebrate their unity. Paradoxically, however, the miners were more renowned for their individuality than for collective action. Thus, we must turn to the role of individual sportsmen in the community.

Certainly the most visible and easily identifiable were a very small group of sportsmen who represented the mining community in national and international competition. It was the development of rowing as the first major spectator sport on the river Tyne in the 1840s that precipitated Harry Clasper into the role of hero.[23] After a brief time working in the pit at Jarrow, Clasper turned to sculling in 1837. During the next twenty years he was recognized as one of the best in the world. His greatest triumph occurred in 1845 when he and his brothers won the World Championship on the river Thames. On his death in 1870, his funeral, held on a Sunday to allow working men to attend, attracted over 100,000 mourners, a sure testimony to his standing in the community. He was followed in the 1870s by William Elliott, a miner from Pegswood. He, too, rowed against the world's best on the rivers Tyne and Thames, culminating in his defeat in 1879 by the great Canadian, Ned Hanlan. His status within the community was demonstrated by various gifts and receptions. On 16 March 1878 he was presented with a gold watch at a special ceremony at the Theatre Royal, Blyth. Later in the same year he was greeted at Blyth station and carried in procession led by Cowpen Colliery Brass Band. On 22 March 1879 a reception was held at the Theatre Royal, Blyth to present Elliott with a handsome mounted gold Spanish coin.[24] The rowing heroes disappeared in the 1880s with the decline in professional rowing and were replaced by new heroes: football players.

Until the emergence of football heroes in the early years of the twentieth century there were few miners who achieved the international recognition of Harry Clasper and William Elliott. However, in a more local sense a number of miners brought recognition to their communities in the pedestrian and quoit competitions held regularly in Newcastle and Gateshead from the mid-century. Miners were regular participants in sprint races and quoit matches at Victoria Grounds (1858–63), Fenham Running Grounds (1862–75) and Grapes Running Grounds (1860–5) in Newcastle and Gateshead Borough Gardens (1868–75). After a brief hiatus in the mid-1870s when the authorities closed all the grounds in Northumberland and Durham, new grounds opened in the late 1880s: Eslington Park, Gateshead and Victoria Grounds, Newcastle. They, along with Borough Gardens, Gateshead (c. 1900) hosted regular competitions until the outbreak of the war, competitions at which miners were regular participants. Some of these miners, such as Will Summers of Shiremoor, became recognized throughout the coalfield for their athletic prowess.

A clearer indication of the importance of sportsmen in developing a sense of community is evidenced in potshare bowling, a game unique to the miners and the most popular sport in the nineteenth century.[25] As early as the 1820s, Davy Bell, a potshare bowler from Benton, was recognized as the champion of Northumberland and Durham. This was, in part, a result of the emergence of the Town Moor at Newcastle as the site of championship competition. Bell was followed by Harry Brown (1830s and 1840s), Tommy Saint (1850s and 1860s), Robert Gledson (1870s), John Gibson (1870s), James Nicholson (1890s) and Tommy Thompson (1900s). Their importance to the community is reflected in the fact that in the early 1900s, Tommy Thompson was frequently compared with Bell, Brown, Saint, Gledson and Gibson. These men were part of the orally transmitted heritage of the mining communities. It is important to emphasize their importance to the community as a whole. They were not simply sportsmen but representatives of the community. Potshare bowling was unique because it was the only sport played solely by miners. It reflected more than any other sport the basic elements of mining life. Success in potshare bowling and quoits while dependent on strength and skill depended just as much on luck. Unlike the amateur sports of the middle class which were predicated on skill, success in bowling always had an element of luck. These characteristics reflected, vividly, the realities of daily life – continuing confrontation with death, the uncertainty of work, the primacy of strength and endurance, and ever-present uncertainty. The status of these champions can be gauged from presentations made to them by their communities. On 3 December 1873 a massive gold watch valued at 20 guineas was awarded to Robert Gledson at the Clayton Arms, Dudley.[26] Two years later John Gibson of Pegswood was presented with 'a handsome gold stop lever watch with gold Albert and appendages' by the Mayor of Morpeth at the Earl Grey Inn, Morpeth.[27] Twenty years later the world champion, James Nicholson of Choppington, was presented with a gold Albert, and his wife with a gold brooch at the Lord Byron Inn, Choppington. The celebration was chaired by William Johnson, undermanager of Choppington Colliery.[28] These examples illustrate the degree to which potshare bowling penetrated the community. It was not just the preserve of a small athletic fraternity but recognized by the community as a whole.

The degree to which sport penetrated the lives of the miners and the point at which it was consciously recognized throughout the community are demonstrated vividly in the writings of a group of pitmen poets.[29] It was not until the 1850s and 1860s that poets emerged who celebrated the sporting prowess of the miners. The first, and arguably the most important, was Ned Corvan, a non-miner, whose 'Wor Tyneside Champions' celebrated the exploits of the local champion rowers, runners, potshare bowlers and quoiters. At the same time, his celebration of 'Tyneside' champions demonstrated the link with the larger region, one that was to grow more important as the century progressed.[30] It was followed by Joseph Skipsey's 'The Collier Lad' in 1886 and Matthew Tate's 'Pit Life in 1893–94'.[31] However, it was in Thomas Dawson's 1913 poem to Bill Summers, champion quoit player, that the real importance of these men was revealed. These sporting heroes were seen to epitomize the core values of mining life. The first verse of the poem celebrates Bill Summers' prowess as a quoit player:

> They call me Bill Summers, aw work at the Bell,
> Thor isn't a better man than mesel
> Ov awl ma hobbies, quoit playin's the pet,
> Aw'm stanned defying the univers yet,
> Ye'll not find maw equal between here and well
> Aw'm Champion Bill Summers that works at the Bell.

Not only was Summers a quoit champion, he was a worker who epitomized the values of mining life, as is reflected in the second and third verses:

> Aw can dee any work, and inspect the hyel pit,
> For bargains and styen work aw'm never unfit,
> Wi plenty explosives, and plenty strang drills
> Aw wad shift the foundations ov Simonside Hill.

> Aw care nowt for nee yen, Aw stand on me awn,
> Aw say what aw think, and Aw'm allus a man,
> Aw help up the fallen, Aw fight for the weak,
> Aw like the courageous, Aw pity the mek,
> If ye heor ov a man that thinks much of himsel,
> Send him on to the Champion that works at the Bell.

Sport and work were not separate entities but part of a whole way of life.

Of course, the miners who brought recognition to the mining community as a whole also brought recognition to the individual mining villages in which they lived. Thus we must turn to the role sport played in developing a sense of community within the individual villages. Throughout history the towns and villages of England have had annual celebrations that brought different segments of the community together to celebrate their communal association. In fact, traditional festivities soon developed in the new mining villages. In every instance sporting activities were the focal point of the day. However, these celebrations were not immune to the changes that took place during the second half of the century. In the smaller villages the traditional forms tended to persist. However, in the larger villages such as Ashington, which had a significant professional and commercial class, there were changes in the form of these celebrations. By 1914, the traditional celebrations of 1850 had been replaced by new forms of community celebrations.

On 14 July 1855 the inhabitants of Woodhorn held their annual village celebrations.[32] In the early afternoon the villagers congregated at the Plough Inn before processing, with banners flying, through the village to the community ground where they participated in traditional rustic sports: climbing the greasy pole, dancing on the green, gorning,[33] foot races, and jumping. The prizes were awarded later in the evening during the course of the ball that was held at the Plough Inn. Sports were the focal point of the day's activities. Fifty years later on 4 July 1904 the workmen of North Seaton Colliery celebrated their annual gala.[34] At 1 pm the children assembled at the Mechanics' Institute and, led by the Linton Miners Silver Model Band, marched in procession through the village to the athletics field which had been placed at the disposal of the committee by the owners of Cowpen Colliery Coal Company. There they participated in a varied programme of sports. However, the rustic sports of the past had disappeared to be replaced by the prestigious 120-yard handicap. The children danced round the Maypole. Arrangements were made to provide a free tea for the 500 school children, 40 widows, 18 aged miners and their wives, 16 lame and 16 sick people. It truly was a communal celebration that symbolized the cohesiveness of the community.

Between 1855 and 1904 galas such as those held at Woodhorn and North Seaton were celebrated throughout the smaller mining villages of Northumberland. Cambois, Widdrington, Shiremoor, Burradon, West Sleekburn and many others hosted annual galas. However, this type of village celebration had become the exception rather than the rule. Traditional events such as climbing the greasy pole, dancing on the green, and gorning had all but disappeared. The changes paralleled the development of a variety of institutions which provided a more varied social life. In the 1850s Methodist chapels started promoting annual picnics for their members and their children. They were followed in the 1860s by temperance groups, who in 1860 attracted over 10,000 to a picnic held in Seaton Delaval.[35] In the 1870s, Mechanics' Institutes, Oddfellows and Foresters added to the list of institutions sponsoring annual events. By the 1880s, the summer months were punctuated by a series of picnics sponsored by various institutions; brass bands, cycling clubs, Liberal clubs and a host of others. However, most of these events were characterized by their transient nature; few became institutions in the villages. In each case the day's festivities focused on a series of athletic events and it is at this juncture that it is possible to discern different responses flowing out of different relationships within the community. Over the years there was a gradual shift towards a stand-ardized programme of athletic events. The rustic traditions disappeared and were replaced by the prestigious 120-yard handicap, the quoit handicap, high jump, pole leap and jumping. Nearly without exception, these events by the 1890s were the focal point of the day. They had become athletic events attracting competitors from all over Northum-berland and the adjacent counties. It was only in some of the smaller villages that the traditions were maintained. Even in these instances pride of place was given to the 120-yard handicap. However, the competitors were drawn from the immediate vicinity and the pro-gramme included races for women, old men, putters and drivers. They often included three-legged races, pick-up-the-stones, skipping contests and the like. These incorporated, in an active sense, all segments of the community. In the larger centres the focus of community had changed to providing athletic spectacles where the objective was com-petition. The ways in which community was celebrated had expanded.

While the celebration of community had become more complex, there were a number of events that became annual celebrations and were recognized as vehicles for promoting the community. These events became permanent fixtures in the yearly calendar of a number of mining villages. The history of these events illustrates how, at the outset, they focused the different elements of the social life of the community in one central celebration of community. The growing of flowers and vegetables, baking, handicrafts and sports comprised the basic elements of social life. Although the showing of flowers and vegetables had been held in the villages throughout the century the commencement, in 1856, of Seaton Burn Floral and Horticultural Society Show inaugur-ated the first to achieve any degree of stability.[36] At first, these events were simply flower shows. However, within a few years, athletic sports became an essential component in the festivities. By the 1860s pro-grammes at Choppington, Seaton Burn and Cramlington held athletic sports, cricket matches, band contests and baking contests in conjunc-tion with the flower shows. At first, these events drew their support from the local community but by the 1870s they began to expand their horizons. For example, until 1873 Choppington Floral and Horicultural Show was limited to workmen in the vicinity.[37] In that year they encouraged entries from beyond the immediate vicinity. This reflected a shift from a focus within the community to a focus external to the village. This was a critical change in that it was no longer simply a community celebration. An unintended consequence of this change was the increasing importance of financial viability. By the 1890s, the focus of the day had shifted from flowers to athletic sports, offering substantial sums of prize money. In fact a recognized circuit of prestigious athletic sports developed focusing on the flower shows. This shift towards athletic sports served to place the smaller flower shows in jeopardy. In the first decade of the new century the flower shows became the focal point of community dissension rather than cohesion. For example, the Ashington Flower Show became a contest between the horticulturalists and the sportsmen on the meaning of the show. The sportsmen won and the athletic aspects of the celebration took precedence.[38] At the same time, other flower shows were forced to disband because they could not compete for athletes with the high profile sports in Ashington, Seaton Delaval, Burradon and Blyth. Thus the flower shows originally created to show flowers had become dependent upon financial resources raised through athletics for their own society. In 1913, New Delaval, Cambois, North Seaton, Newbiggin and Netherton discontinued their flower shows for this very reason.[39] The death of the flower shows in the smaller communities removed a central symbol of community. The world had changed.

This does not mean that the idea of communal celebrations had died but rather that the focus had changed. As the flower shows became focused on athletics, community attention shifted to a different group: the schoolchildren. From as early as the 1860s provision had been made for children. However, the provision was rarely on a community basis but rather was provided by particular segments of the community or as parts of larger celebrations. For example, in 1863 Choppington Sunday School held its annual picnic and sports.[40] Sunday schools, Mechanics' Institutes and Workmen's Institutes continued to provide sports and entertainment for children. Changes began in three villages, all belonging to the Seaton Delaval Coal Company: New Hartley, Seaton Delaval and New Delaval.[41] In 1887, the owners, officials and inhabitants of New Delaval inaugurated an annual treat for the school-children in the district. Seaton Delaval and New Hartley followed suit, as did Ashington and Cambois later in the century. During the first decade of the twentieth century the idea of children's galas spread throughout the coalfield and by 1913 over 16 school districts held annual galas and sports for the children. These truly were community celebrations and not just athletic sports. This is graphically illustrated by Children's Day at Ashington in 1913.[42] The Ashington Hirst Children's Sports Committee, comprised of representatives from the social clubs and various societies, went out of its way to provide a day to remember. The day started with the schoolchildren meeting at their own schools. In Hirst the pupils and teachers assembled at the six schools before marching in procession to People's Park where the sports were held. The procession was headed by the Seaton Hirst and Silver Model Bands. Each school was led by the headmaster and teachers. The Ashington schools procession was led by the Harmonic Band and the Linton and Ellington Schools by the Salvation Army

Band. One can imagine the excitement in the village as the various processions wended their ways to the Park. Each child received 1*d*., a bun and some sweets. The Committee had raised £130 to provide the 7,200 children with the treats. The parents turned out in full force for this gala celebration. There were races for all, Murphy's roundabouts and other sideshows, and even a baby show judged by Doctors Spence and Thompson. Ashington was not atypical. In Dudley in the same year the council schools processed through the village headed by their teachers and Dudley Excelsior Silver Model Band. Since it was Empire Day the children all carried flags, thus visibly reinforcing ideas of empire.[43] These two examples were typical. Thus by the outbreak of the war communities throughout the coalfield honoured and celebrated the youth of the community.

At the same time each celebration was in some respects unique, and reflected particular local conditions. The earliest initiative at New Delaval lay within the total community with the owners, officials and inhabitants each playing an important role. At Cambois in 1899 the leadership came from the miners and the £50 required to run the event was raised by subscription from the 'Workmen who allow 6*d*. per man to be kept off at the colliery'.[44] Thus, while the stimulus came from the miners it required active support from the colliery officials. Later, in 1908, at Cowpen Square the children's treat was the brainchild of Robert Henderson of the Golden Fleece Hotel.[45] He also provided the funding for the whole affair. The difficulty of identifying any overall pattern is illustrated in the history of the Children's Day in Ashington, where different groups assumed the leadership at different points in time. In the late 1890s the day was a small celebration. This eventually disappeared in 1903. The next year the local council took the lead and sponsored a Children's Day. By 1909 a new Children's Sports Committee had been formed. It had representatives from the thirteen social clubs that had only been formed during the 1900s.[46] Thus if Ashington was typical the stimulus to these events shifted with the changing nature of the community.

The complex nature of these annual festivals and the ways in which people adapted to the changes of the second half of the nineteenth century is illustrated in the history of Bedlington Hoppings, which were held for three days every Whitsuntide from sometime in the seventeenth century.[47] It is important to recognize that they were the culmination of many weeks of preparation. They celebrated the beginning of the year. In the weeks leading up to Whit weekend the miners' wives springcleaned their houses, laid new rugs that had been made during the winter, polished the silver, bought new clothes for the children, and painted and polished their houses. The focal point of the three days of festivities was Front Street and the side streets running off it.

The Hoppings brought in commercial attractions from outside Bedlington. Front Street and the adjacent streets contained 'numerous swing boats, galloping horses, shooting galleries, cocoa-nut sallys, ice screamers, hoky-pokites, Jaffa orange vendors, ginger bread stalls'.[48] Additionally, over the years they were visited by menageries, circuses, theatres, boxing booths and a variety of other entertainments. While, as we shall see, the athletic sports were the focal point of the festivities over the years a variety of groups used the occasion to celebrate their own identity – temperance groups, churches, the Salvation Army, the Mechanics' Institute and other groups, at times, promoted festivities. For a brief time, 1865 to 1881, one of the highlights of the week was the Poultry and Dog Show. In fact, the future of the Hoppings was threatened on several occasions – the opening of Bedlington West End Running Grounds in 1873 and East End Running Grounds in 1874 threatened to attract many of the competitors. Their closure in 1876 prevented any further damage.[49] The promotion of amateur athletics in the 1890s was a deliberate attempt to force the closure of the traditional Hoppings: it failed. And finally in 1899, the police tried, unsuccessfully, to remove the races from their traditional location – the main street of Bedlington. The focal point of the Hoppings were the races held on the main street of the town. In the 1850s the programme consisted of a variety of foot races, three-legged races, old men's races, tilting the bucket, and climbing the greasy pole for a leg of mutton. Over the next fifty years they witnessed standardization and the expansion of the basic elements. The horse races, which were an integral part of the celebrations, disappeared in 1865. Stability began to appear in 1866 with the inauguration of the quoit handicap. This became a staple of the events down to 1914. In 1874, the 120-yard handicap was introduced and became the most prestigious of the events. Bicycle races followed in 1880 and a football competition in 1884. The basic set of events remained constant until 1914. However, the traditional events did not entirely disappear; climbing the greasy pole was still a part of the activities in 1913. Additionally new events for boys and girls were intoduced in the 1890s, in particular skipping and ball bouncing for girls and top whipping for boys. Thus, the Hoppings did change and were responsive to what was happening in the society. However, there were some things that did not change: the central role of the inns and innkeepers and the tradesmen in organizing and sponsoring the events. They were from the outset a commercial enterprise. However, what is most significant is the real lack of change in the format and location. Despite efforts of the police in the 1890s to remove racing from Front Street and the various attempts to introduce alternative sports, the basic form of the Hoppings remained unchanged. Tradition was immensely powerful.

The above has focused on the ways in which various communities celebrated their collective spirit. Just as important to day-to-day life were the individual sportsmen who brought fame to their villages. Pride of place was given to the potshare bowlers and quoiters – these were the true heroes of the communities. The role of sport in the community can be seen through the visit of a reporter from the *Newcastle Weekly Chronicle* to the village of Dudley, population 1,000, in July 1873:

> Not only is Dudley famous for its coal, its poultry, and its kitchen garden, but it also claims to be great in the world of sport, sending out noted pedestrians to do battle for the honour of the village at Fenham Park or Gateshead Borough Gardens, and defying all competitors to a match across the mile at Newcastle, or Newbiggin with heavy weight bowls. For Gledson, the champion bowler, resides at Dudley, and on the day of my visit he was to be seen moving about the village towering head and shoulders above a small knot of admirers, who followed him about. Next to Gledson in bowling circles is Arthur Temple, also a Dudley man, so that Dudley is really the champion bowling village of the North.[50]

Throughout his career Robert Gledson brought status and fame to Dudley. His history demonstrates the important role sportsmen played in the community.[51] Born in 1846, Gledson burst onto the sporting scene in 1867. Between 1867 and 1873, he competed in pedestrian matches at Fenham Park Grounds in Newcastle and Gateshead Borough Gardens. However, it was in potshare bowling that he gained his greatest fame. From 1868 until 1879 he competed in 75 matches and handicaps. Robert Gledson dominated the potshare bowling scene during the 1870s and was recognized as the champion for much of the time. His career in championship level competition started in 1871 with contests against Tommy Saint, the reigning champion. Gaining the championship in 1872, he dominated the bowling scene until 1878. The period was highlighted by a series of fourteen matches with John Gibson of Pegswood. What characterized all Gledson's contests was that they were for money prizes. In fact, during his career he competed for over £3000 in stake money. His matches on the Town Moor, Newcastle and Newbiggin Moor were watched by up to 6,000 spectators. He also participated in handball and sparrow shooting contests. It is important to recognize that Gledson was basically a professional athlete. For example, prior to his match with George Laws of Choppington on Newbiggin Moor in November 1871, Gledson spent a few weeks in Newbiggin training for the event. His importance to the community was enhanced by the fact that extensive wagering accompanied all his matches. Thus, not only was the pride of the community at stake but also the financial welfare of some inhabitants of Dudley. The role of Robert Gledson in Dudley can be seen replicated throughout the villages of East Northumberland in the nineteenth century. The names of a host of potshare bowlers and quoiters resound down through the century. From the first champion, Davy Bell of Benton in the 1820s, to Harry Brown of Gateshead who competed from 1835 to 1868, to Robert Ward of Bebside who in 1876 competed for over £600, to Will Summers of Shiremoor, the quoit champion in the early twentieth century, a succession of champions brought fame to their villages. It is important to emphasize that these were not just the heroes of a small athletic fraternity but of the whole community. For example, in 1899 a presentation was made to M. Wardle, at the Collier Lad Inn, Burradon for his services to quoiting and the mining community.[52] Similarly on 27 April 1909 Thomas Wood, a hewer, celebrated his 70th birthday.[53] He was recognized by the Seghill Quoit Club for his contributions to quoiting. In each of these cases the celebrations were attended by leaders from within the community, in particular the Trades Union leaders. On the deaths of these sportsmen the community frequently turned out in large numbers to the funeral and then took up public subscriptions to erect headstones in the cemetery. For example, in 1875, donations were collected in various public houses to erect a headstone for Tommy Saint, the champion bowler, in the graveyard at Killingworth.[54] Contrary to the beliefs of contemporary middle-class observers sport was not divorced from the mainstream of life; instead it served as a vehicle for interaction between different groups within the community – it was, like mining itself, common ground for the miners.

Potshare bowling and quoiting provided a means for the various villages to judge themselves against each other – they were the exclusive preserve of the miners and did nothing for them in relation to other groups. Very simply, they perpetuated the isolation of the mining villages. However, this began to change in the 1880s. In October 1882 a team of tradesmen played a team of miners at a game of football in Bedlington.[55] This was the beginning of a new era in the history of sport and society.[56] Within a period of six years football had spread to all corners of the coalfield. As the *Blyth Weekly News* stated in 1888, 'Why every little colliery village in the county with a few hundred souls can boast of a football team.'[57] The game became increasingly important as the century progressed, penetrating to all levels of society. As the *Morpeth Herald* complained in 1899:

We are beginning to think now ... that football is exercising a great influence over the young people of our villages, and not a few who take up their newspapers read little or anything else. Take for instance

matches that are played weekly between village clubs. Strong feelings
are exhibited against each other, and it is no uncommon thing to see
spectators in open conflict in support of their respective teams.[58]

By 1914 football dominated the lives of males, young and old. It
permeated the workplace where it formed the topic of conversation at
'bait' times. Pubs, schools, churches and Temperance groups were all
subject to football mania. This was a far cry from the 1880s, when it
first appeared on the scene. How, then, did football relate to the total
life of the community?

Perhaps the single most important change lay in their relationship
with the outside world. Football helped them perceive themselves as
Northeasterners rather than as members of isolated mining villages.
This changing view of themselves was related to the emergence of
Newcastle United as the standard bearer of the pride of Tyneside. In
the early 1890s, Newcastle East End and Newcastle West End, who
eventually amalgamated in 1892 to form Newcastle United, were local
clubs playing in local competitions. Within ten years Newcastle United
moved from local competition to the First Division of the Football
League. Their position as representative of Tyneside was established
in the first decade of the new century when they were the most
successful team in England, winning three league championships and
appearing in five Cup Finals. They built up immense reservoirs of
support in the area. Miners were amongst their most ardent and
loyal supporters. Thus for the first time the miners did not look on
Newcastle as the arch enemy but rather as carrying the pride and hopes
of the Northeast.

After 1890 for a limited number of clubs and communities football
allowed them to judge themselves against communities outside the
district. Shankhouse Black Watch, joining the Northern Alliance in
1890, was the first of several teams to enter leagues based outside the
coalfield. During the next twenty years fourteen other communities
were represented in this type of competition. Perhaps even more
important for establishing the reputation of the district in outside
competition was the development of football in the schools. It was not
until 1898 that schools within the district entered into the Northumberland and Durham Schools Cup. In that year Shankhouse British
School entered the competition. Thenceforth increasing numbers of
school teams competed against teams outside the district, bringing
recognition to their local communities. In a broader sense the selection
of a representative East Northumberland team in 1903 brought
recognition to the district as a whole. This team played against teams
from Newcastle, Gateshead and Durham. In 1906 the East Northumberland team was replaced by six separate teams representing different

School Districts. On the inauguration of the English Schools Cup in 1906, East Northumberland Schools became regular participants in the competition, thus bringing the name of East Northumberland to the rest of the country. And for the young their view of the world expanded beyond the coalfield, thus bringing subtle but important changes.

Increased interaction with the outside world was not an unmitigated blessing. Although the miners were always recognized as different, these differences now became more open and visible and were given concrete form in the recognition by the Newcastle-dominated Northumberland Football Association that the teams in the mining districts played the game differently, they were more violent, more independent and prone to use inappropriate language.[59] Thus football helped to reinforce the view that the miners were, indeed, different and so in a sense turned the focus inward.

While teams such as Shankhouse, in the early years, then Ashington, Blyth and Bedlington brought honour and fame to East North-umberland, football, at the local level, served to exacerbate and intensify local rivalries. By the early 1890s a number of intense traditional rivalries had developed; Ashington versus Blyth, Seaton Delaval versus New Hartley, Seghill versus Burradon and a host of others emerged as the high points of the football season. At the same time these teams were not necessarily comprised of players from the village. Players were imported to play in village teams even at the minor and junior level where clubs, for the most part, competed within the district. Thus, the teams were symbols of the community rather than places where individuals from the community comprised the team. In fact, it was the club and not the players that carried the pride of the community. The intense rivalry in football was a result of subconscious forces rooted in historically based inter-community rivalries. These annual events frequently disintegrated into violent confrontations between rival supporters. Thus football served a twofold purpose, promotion of community solidarity on the one hand and the intensification of inter-village rivalry on the other.

In many of the smaller communities the football teams were organ-ized and run by the miners. However, in the case of the larger villages the teams were used by the colliery offficials to promote their own view of the community. This was the case in the three larger towns/ villages of Ashington, Blyth and Bedlington. In 1895, in Ashington, the colliery officials intervened to save the floundering Ashington Football Club. From that time the club was controlled by the colliery officials who embarked upon a programme to get Ashington into the highest levels of football. In 1908 they built Portland Park, the first football stadium in the coalfield, and in 1914 gained entry to the professional Northeastern League. The same process was followed in Blyth and

Bedlington. Football was an ideal vehicle for cementing relationships between different segments of the community. It was, in the eyes of the colliery officials, unimportant and ideologically neutral, one of the few areas in life in which the different groups could interact without threatening the basic social relationships.

The foregoing has focused upon the ways in which sport was related to the idea of community. None, however, has given any insights into the dynamics by which the community expressed itself.[60] It is in the creation of recreational facilities that some insights can be gained into the community in action. Prior to the mid-1880s there is little evidence that the miners were able to effect the construction of their social environment. For the most part colliery villages were run by the coal companies, as is evidenced in the support given to the construction of churches, chapels and Mechanics' Institutes by the colliery owners. Nearly without exception Mechanics' Institutes were built by the owners. From the foundation of Institutes at Bedlington Colliery (1857), Cramlington Colliery (1857) and Killingworth (1858) to the building of a new Institute at Seaton Delaval at a cost of £1,000, the owners played a pivotal role in the construction, outfitting and running of the Institutes. Thus the colliery owners did, indeed, define the structures within which communities developed. However, while the owners and colliery officials remained important in the decision making with respect to community institutions there is evidence of a shift in the final decision making to the miners themselves. Between 1887 and 1900 ten community recreation grounds were opened. In two cases, Ashington and Pegswood, the initiative came from the colliery officials. In the other eight cases the initiative came from the miners, albeit a particular group of miners. The Bedlington Station Recreation Ground (1892) was developed and run by miners at Bedlington YMCA.[61] Holywell Recreation Ground (1895) emerged out of Holywell Mechanics' Institute. Seghill ground was organized by the workmen at Seghill Workmen's Institute. These were all led by men who were heavily involved in the Mechanics' Institutes, Miners' Institutes or the YMCAs. Additionally they were all, except for Ashington, in medium-sized villages comprised nearly exclusively of miners. By the turn of the century recreation grounds for sporting activities were recognized as important ingredients within the community. This stands in contrast to the efforts of local councils after the enactment of the Local Government Act of 1894 transferred decision-making power within the communities. Without exception the councils were dominated by colliery officials, farmers and businessmen.[62] Even though miners had increasing representation on councils they never had, prior to 1914, a majority on any council. Thus it was the views of the middle classes that determined the nature of the facilities deemed to be necessary for a good life. In the two largest towns/villages, Ashington/Hirst and Blyth/Cowpen, public parks were opened. In each case they were conceived as ornamental parks with walks, gardens, lakes and perhaps lawn bowling. It was not until 1909 that any provision was made for facilities within the working-class areas. Between 1909 and 1914 eight recreation grounds were opened in Blyth/Cowpen, Earsdon, Bedlington and Seaton Delaval. In each instance they were intended not for sport but as children's playgrounds. Thus, the middle classes of the area did not see sport as warranting grounds at public expense. What these two views of community in action provide is a view of two different ideas as to what were the essential ingredients of a community. For the miners provision for sport and recreation was an essential component of community life. The colliery officials on the other hand did not see sport and recreation as central to the life of the community.

It is important not to overemphasize the homogeneity of the mining communities. There were always different groups with different views of the community, and sports and games were used to promote the differences as well as the commonalities. This was particularly the case in the Cramlington area, where Cornish and Devon wrestling was promoted into the late 1880s and served to maintain the culture of the miners brought into the district in 1868, a culture separate from that of the other miners. Additionally, temperance groups, churches and chapels used sport and galas to promote their own views. Not only did the different groups use sport to promote their own views but different sports attracted different segments of the community. The traditional games of potshare bowling, quoits, rabbit coursing and handball attracted a particular clientele. Cricket, and to a lesser extent cycling appealed to other groups. It was football that crossed the boundaries and was acceptable to all the different groups. By the second decade of the twentieth century even the churches and chapels had succumbed to the lure of football. Sport, perhaps better than any other single activity, reflected the reality of community life in the villages.

What then does this study suggest about the relationship between sport and community? To what extent and in what ways did sport provide the inhabitants of Ashington with a sense of being Ashingtonians? To what degree did sport promote mining solidarity? These are not easy questions to answer. Before attempting to answer them it is important to emphasize that in some respects it is impossible to generalize about the mining communities as a totality. The forces working against any ideas of community were formidable. As Stephen Martin suggested, the idea of community only developed under certain conditions. Many of the smaller mining villages never exemplified these conditions. The development of a sense of community was very much related to local conditions in the 66 towns/villages. Every town/village was different and in particular the population composition, the stability of the population, its past history, size, physical layout, and especially the role of the coal company in the total life of the community determined the nature of the particular town/village. It was within some of the villages totally dominated by coal companies that little sense of community developed. For example, as late as 1904, the village of Cowpen Isabella Colliery had no clubs, no public house, no church or chapel and not even a Mechanics' Institute – it was devoid of the basic infrastructure necessary for the creation of a sense of community. It is within this context that the development of an idea of community must be placed.

It is virtually impossible to determine whether the mining villages of pre-1850 Northumberland had any sense of community. The working and living conditions of the miners would suggest not. The fact that in most villages occupancy of a house was related to employment in the mine and the yearly bond would suggest an extremely unstable population. At the same time, from early in the century there was evidence that the miners were beginning to think of themselves as a collectivity. This was first recognized in 1810 when the miners first met as a group to consider joint action against the employers. In sport this identity was evident in the existence of recognized champions in potshare bowling from the 1820s, which indicates that the miners had a clear recognition of themselves as a group. However, the development of a sense of belonging to a particular village emerged in the second half of the century and was related to changes in the position of the miners and the development of the infrastructure of villages in the period 1820–60. By 1851 the physical environment, which remained essentially unchanged until the 1890s, was already in place and it was within this stable context that successive generations of miners and their families lived. While not overemphasizing the positive aspects, certain changes did take place that affected a miner's life. In particular the creation of the Northumberland Miners' Union in 1863 and the abolition of the bond in 1872 materially affected miners' lives. The abolition of the bond and the consequent freedom came at the high point of prosperity in the nineteenth century, a high point not to be reached again until after the First World War.[63] These changes took place in the context of expanding horizons, the creation of the railway network in the 1850s and the inception of the daily newspaper in 1858. Basically these changes gave the miners a greater, although still limited, say in the conditions affecting their lives and also brought them into greater contact with the outside world. It is within this context that the changing concept of community must be viewed.

This study of sport illustrates clearly that the mining communities were conscious of themselves. The traditional galas of the 1850s reflect the power of tradition. Additionally the existence of recognized pot-share bowling champions from the 1820s suggests that the miners had a strong sense of belonging. This was to change during the second half of the century. During the 1870s and 1880s significant changes took place in the ways in which the miners celebrated community. Although annual galas continued until the 1900s they witnessed a decline during this period with the development of a wide range of celebrations organized by particular segments of the community. Even in the cases where these days continued there was evidence of increasing standardization of events and increasing specialization. Additionally, it was during the 1880s that the first evidence of miners' being involved in creating their own recreational environment was observed. It was at this time that football moved to centre stage and became the major vehicle for promoting the status of a particular village. Thus it is during the last two decades of the century that we observe sport being used to promote a sense of communal solidarity and community identity.

While sport served to promote the image of the community it also served to exacerbate tensions both within the community and between communities. Within the community football and bowling were rarely regarded as positive attributes by certain groups. Thus, the growing importance of football brought with it significant intra-village dissension. At the same time sport served to intensify local rivalries and thus worked against the idea of a mining community. In terms of the community as a whole attention shifted to the larger towns/villages of Ashington, Blyth and Bedlington whose football clubs were a source of unity. More importantly, Newcastle United became the vehicle of intense pride and support.

Perhaps the most important change lay in the gradual shift in focus to the importance of children in the continuation of the community. The whole concept of a child changed during the nineteenth century. In fact, the changes can be measured, in a rough sense, by the gradual increase in the number of years of schooling, and it was the shift to the promotion of children's gala days that was the most important single change in the concept of the community. It reflected a clear recognition of the importance of children to the future of the society.

Of course, it is important to recognize that not all the towns/villages were the same. In some the dominant force in determining the structures within which the idea of community was constructed was the coal company. Ashington is a classic exemplification of the domination of the coal company.[64] Officials from the company were involved in the life of the community at all levels. It was not until 1899 and the development of independent social clubs that the miners gained a real say in creating their own social lives. Ashington classically illustrates how the

idea of community was, in itself, a contested domain. The ongoing
battle over the Ashington Flower Show and Sports illustrates the limitations on the power of the coal company to exert its will over significant
opposition from within the community. The officials of the company
attempted to ban gambling at the sports – they never succeeded.[65] In
the smaller mining villages the miners gained considerable decision-
making power and it is here that we see the immense strength of
community action. This is reflected most graphically in the development of community recreation grounds in the 1890s, far sooner than
the local authorities acted to provide recreational space in the larger
towns/villages. Thus it is important to emphasize the differences between the communities.

What this study suggests is that sport was used consciously and
unconsciously to promote the idea of community. At the same time
it is important to emphasize that sport must be examined within the
context of the society as a whole, in particular the groups that determined the structures within which people lived their lives. However,
it is also important to emphasize that the miners did not simply accept
the structures which were imposed upon them but attempted to create
communities of which they could be proud. In the final analysis the
idea of community was very much a contested domain. However,
perhaps the most important insight to come out of this study is the
symbolic nature of community. What made Ashington different from
Seaton Delaval? In many respects they used the same symbols but
attached to them different meanings. Providing the mining communities as a collectivity with common symbols were the potshare
bowlers who had no meaning outside the mining villages. As the
century progressed they increasingly shared athletic heroes with a
larger population located outside the mining villages. From Harry
Clasper in the 1860s to Newcastle United in the Edwardian years, the
miners shared these heroes. However, they attached their distinctive
meanings to them. The way football was played and watched by the
miners was different from the way it was played by other groups and
represented different concepts of masculinity. And masculine sport
certainly was. This whole study has illustrated the basic reality of
mining life: the villages were male domains. The women have been
absent from this account because they rarely strayed onto the sporting
fields. Their role in the society was clearly recognized; they were
important as home-makers and family sustainers but removed from
the formal decision-making positions within the community. They
played the same role in sport as they did in the society, supporting
the male activities. Although there were infrequent references to
women participating in rowing, athletics, quoits and shooting, there
is little evidence that women's role changed significantly throughout

the century. While the mining villages were increasingly exposed to the outside world, they maintained their independence by attaching different meanings to common symbols. Sport was an important vehicle for promoting a sense of community.

Notes

1. *Newcastle Weekly Chronicle*, 6 October 1872.
2. Limited consideration has been given to the social lives of the miners. Much that has been written focuses on work, religion, and to some extent the home. The only relatively full exploration is contained in J. Benson, *British Coalminers in the Nineteenth Century* (Gill and Macmillan, Dublin: 1980), pp. 142–213; M. Pollard, *The Hardest Work under Heaven: The Life and Death of the British Coalminer* (Hutchinson, London: 1984). These books are based on the assumption that all miners are the same and thus take their examples from all over Britain. A more in-depth examination of one community is contained in B. Williamson, *Class, Culture and Community: A Biographical Study of Social Change in Mining* (Routledge, London: 1982).
3. The influence of Methodism in the Northeast coalfield has been well documented in R. Moore, *Pitmen, Preachers and Politics: The Effects of Methodism in a Durham Mining Community* (Cambridge U.P., Cambridge: 1974), and R. Colls, *The Pitmen of the Northern Coalfield: Work, Culture and Protest, 1790–1850* (Manchester U.P., Manchester: 1987).
4. An excellent overview of conditions in the mining villages of Northumberland is contained in weekly articles which appeared in the *Newcastle Weekly Chronicle* from October 1872 until 1874. For an analysis of these articles see J. Y. E. Seeley, 'Coal mining villages of Northumberland and Durham: a study of sanitary conditions and social facilities, 1870–1880' (Newcastle University MA thesis, 1973). The view of life in the villages that emerges from these articles is sobering indeed and makes it extremely difficult to conceptualize what life would be like. The gap between what we are familiar with and this unfamiliar world is immense.
5. For a definition of the origin of the community see R. Williams, *Keywords* (Flamingo, Glasgow: 1979), pp. 65–6.
6. *Webster's Dictionary* (Springfield: 1969), p. 460.
7. Williams, *Keywords*, p. 66.
8. These insights were drawn from the author's unpublished research into the social life of the mining village of Seaton Delaval in 1891. There were several instances when potshare bowlers and quoiters were also active members of the Methodist Chapel.
9. 1891 Census.
10. B. R. Mitchell, *Economic Development of the British Coal Industry, 1800–1914* (Cambridge U.P., Cambridge: 1984).
11. S. Martin, *Bomarsund and Stakeford* (Bedlington: 1987), p. 21. This is one of a series of small booklets written by Stephen Martin, an ex-miner,

which contain a 'mine' of information on several mining communities in East Northumberland: Sleekburn (The Station), Netherton, Choppington and Bedlington.

12. Interestingly, there is no one source which provides an overview of the development of mining in East Northumberland. The following has been derived from Seeley, 'Coal mining villages', Martin, *Bomarsund and Stakeford*, and R. Fynes, *The Miners of Northumberland and Durham* (Davis Books, Newcastle: 1986 reprint of 1873 edn).

13. This analysis is derived from the 1841, 1851, 1861, 1871, 1881 and 1891 Census of Seaton Delaval.

14. 1891 Census, Seghill.

15. The control by the land- and mine-owners of the decision-making government bodies is discussed in J. M. Taylor, *England's Border Country: A History of Northumberland County Council, 1889–1989* (Northumberland County Council, Morpeth: 1989), pp. 6–47.

16. Derived from 1891 Census.

17. Williamson, *Class, Culture and Community*, p. 6.

18. Martin, *Bomarsund and Stakeford*.

19. The database was compiled from the *Newcastle Daily Chronicle*, 1858–1914; *Morpeth Herald*, 1853–1900; *Blyth News and Weekly Transcript*, 1870–1914, and *Kelly's Directories of Northumberland and Durham* for 1858, 1873, 1887, 1890, 1894, 1902, 1910 and 1914.

20. The landowners, in particular Sir Matthew White Ridley, Lord Hastings and the Duke of Portland, played an active role in the development of the area. Very little could be done without their express permission. Additionally the colliery owners played an increasingly important role as the century progressed, in some cases having total control of the physical development of the villages.

21. Fynes, *Miners of Northumberland and Durham*, p. 13.

22. *Morpeth Herald*, 10 September 1864.

23. D. Clasper, *Harry Clasper: Hero of the North* (Gateshead Books, Gateshead: 1990).

24. *Blyth News and Weekly Transcript*, 16 March 1878, 28 September 1878, 22 March 1879.

25. Potshare bowling was basically a simple game that pitted two men with potshare bowls weighing between five and fifty ounces against each other over a predetermined course usually called the 'mile'. The miner that reached the end first was the winner. For a history of potshare bowling see A. Metcalfe, 'Resistance to change: potshare bowling in the mining communities of East Northumberland, 1800–1914', in R. Holt (ed.), *Sport and The Working Class in Modern Britain* (Manchester U.P., Manchester: 1990), pp. 29–44.

26. *Newcastle Daily Chronicle*, 20 December 1873.

27. *Morpeth Herald*, 16 October 1875.

28. *Newcastle Daily Chronicle*, 26 October 1891.

29. For an insightful discussion on the relationship between poetry and community see R. Colls, *The Colliers Rant: Song and Culture in the Industrial Village* (Croom Helm, London: 1977).

30. E. Corvan, *Random Rhymes, Being a Collection of Local Songs and Ballads* (Newcastle: 1850).
31. J. Skipsey, *Carols From the Coalfields* (London: 1886); M. Tate, *Poems, Songs and Ballads* (Blyth: 1898).
32. *Morpeth Herald*, 14 July 1855.
33. Gorning entailed making a grotesque face in the opening of the bridle of a horse. The most grotesque face won.
34. *Newcastle Daily Chronicle*, 4 July 1904.
35. *Morpeth Herald*, 25 August 1860.
36. The first reference to the Flower Show was in the *Morpeth Herald*, 6 September 1862. It refered to the 6th Annual Seaton Burn Flower Show.
37. *Morpeth Herald*, 6 September 1873.
38. *Newcastle Daily Chronicle*, 4 June 1913.
39. *Morpeth Herald*, 13 October 1913.
40. *Morpeth Herald*, 22 August 1863.
41. *Newcastle Daily Chronicle*, 4 June 1913.
42. *Newcastle Daily Chronicle*, 4 June 1913. For a more complete view of the social life in Ashington see M. Kirkup, *The Biggest Mining Village in the World: A Social History of Ashington* (Sandhill, Newcastle: 1993).
43. *Newcastle Daily Chronicle*, 18 August 1913.
44. *Morpeth Herald*, 1 July 1899.
45. *Blyth News and Weekly Transcript*, 21 April 1908.
46. *Morpeth Herald*, 24 June 1899; 25 June 1910; *Blyth News and Weekly Transcript*, 1 July 1904.
47. The following history of the Bedlington Hoppings is derived from the *Newcastle Daily Chronicle, Morpeth Herald* and *Blyth News and Weekly Transcript* and from S. Martin, *Bedlington* (Bedlington: 1987), p. 22.
48. *Morpeth Herald*, 23 May 1891.
49. The closure of these grounds was part of a county-wide effort by the authorities to close all the commercial running grounds. They were successful in closing all the grounds in Northumberland.
50. *Newcastle Weekly Chronicle*, 19 July 1873.
51. The data for the history of Robert Gledson (Gledston) were derived from the newspapers mentioned previously.
52. *Newcastle Daily Chronicle*, 10 November 1899.
53. *Newcastle Daily Chronicle*, 27 April 1909.
54. *Morpeth Herald*, 10 November 1899.
55. *Newcastle Daily Chronicle*, 16 October 1882.
56. For a more extensive account of football in the district see A. Metcalfe, 'Football in the mining communities of East Northumberland, 1882–1914', *The International Journal of the History of Sport* 5.3 (December 1988), pp. 269–91.
57. *Blyth News and Weekly Transcript*, 6 October 1888.
58. *Morpeth Herald*, 10 November 1899.
59. Data taken from the Annual Reports of the Northumberland Football Association, 1890–1914.
60. The following discussion is based on A. Metcalfe, 'Sport and space: a case study of the growth of recreational facilities in East Northumberland,

1850–1914', *The International Journal of the History of Sport* 3 (1990), pp. 348–64.

61. S. Martin, *Sleekburn (The Station)* (Bedlington: 1987), pp. 19–23.

62. Metcalfe, 'Recreational space', p. 352. For the county council see Taylor, *Northumberland County Council, 1889–1989*, pp. 6–47.

63. Data on economic conditions derived from Mitchell, *Economic Development*.

64. For a more complete analysis see Kirkup, *A Social History of Ashington*.

65. This is classically illustrated in their failure to control pitch and toss, which was still popular in 1914 despite concerted efforts by the authorities to eradicate it.

3. Football, sport of the North?

Tony Mason

Charles Clegg did not enjoy his first game for England in 1872 because 'the great majority of players were snobs from the South who had no use for a lawyer from Sheffield. The ball was never passed to him and nobody spoke to him ... They did not understand him and he resented their superiority.'[1] Five years later, Billy Mosforth, another Sheffielder, also found playing for England a less satisfying experience than he had hoped. He was provoked into complaining to the Old Etonian the Hon. Alfred Lyttleton for not passing the ball to him, to which the young gentleman gave the well nigh immortal reply, 'I am playing purely for my own pleasure, Sir!'[2] Clearly he had a different conception of football to Mosforth and part of that gap between them was probably due to the fact that Mosforth was the only Northerner in a team mainly comprised of young men who had been educated at the public schools and ancient universities of the South. Mosforth had attended the elementary school and kept pubs, putting a wider social space between him and his ten 'teammates'. Clegg had been educated in Sheffield and at a private school in Darlington. He was the son of a local solicitor but still felt that he did not fit into the subculture of Southern football in the 1870s. He spoke with a Northern accent, was Nonconformist not to say Puritan in religion, a supporter of temperance and a professional Liberal, all identities unlikely to recommend him to the other members of that England team which drew with Scotland in the first football international between the two countries.[3] What follows is a short exploration of the connection between the development of football as an organized recreation and the notion of Northern consciousness. In particular, this essay will examine how football as a spectator sport might have contributed to an awareness of being from somewhere called the North as against somewhere called the South in late Victorian and Edwardian England.

Football certainly did not cause North–South rivalries which, as several historians have pointed out, already had a long history by the late nineteenth century.[4] People were aware of and regularly expressed the idea that North and South were two different worlds, with the South clearly dominant before the industrial revolution. The South was stronger economically and politically and in London it had one of the urban wonders of the world. The climate was more temperate and the land in the South flat or gently rolling compared with the bleak moors and mountains of the North. Lowland farming differed from that on the higher Northern pastures and the arable/pastoral distinction was thought to produce different types of Englishmen. The Northern male was more outspoken and independent, uncouth and obstinate, his critics said, and also more hardy and resilient than the conforming, conventional and effete Southerner. These images and stereotypes were doubtless reinforced by the thousands of casual encounters between those from North and South. Helen Jewell reminds us that these exchanges were not between equals. When Southerners travelled North, for example, they went from the more confident, dominant culture and nearly always found the North inferior. Northerners who journeyed South may have gone more cautiously, anxiously cultivating their inferiority. But for a hundred years after about 1780 all this changed. The North became the stronger as the development of manufacturing brought political influence in its train. This was the classic age of the rural South against the industrial North about which Mrs Gaskell so memorably wrote in *North and South*, first published during 1854 and 1855. It was out of this expansion of industry and in particular the growth of towns which went with it that football emerged, first as a recreation and later as a proto-business selling escape and excitement to the better-off section of a working class whose choice of such things was cruelly restricted by lack of education, income and time.

It is a well known fact that modern football was first organized by a group of young men who had played the game at their public schools or the Universities of Oxford and Cambridge. Most of them were engaged in one or other of the professions either in London or elsewhere in the South East. They formed the Football Association in 1863, inaugurated the FA Cup in 1871 and organized the first England–Scotland international in 1872. By 1882, after several meetings and many arguments, the FA presided over a game with a uniform set of rules and played in most corners of the kingdom. But there were already signs that there were more players and stronger teams in the North than in the South. On the eve of the football season of 1876–77, for example, a Northern paper could say that the metropolitan and university clubs 'naturally occupy the first rank' but no longer monopolized the interest.[5] By the end of that season it was claimed that out of 12,000 active footballers 9,000 were in the North of England and Scotland.[6] This growth in interest was reflected by the publication of the *Northern*

Football Annual in 1877 and the emergence of the *Athletic News* itself, based in Manchester and offering coverage of all amateur sport, in that 'wide district between the Trent and the Tweed'. It was soon running a series of articles entitled 'Football in the North'.[7] The Sheffield FA had been formed in 1867 and by October 1878 when about thirty clubs set up the Lancashire FA there were clear indications that on the field, if not off it, the balance of power between South and North was shifting in favour of the latter.

An early sign of this was Darwen's run in the FA Cup in 1879. A trip to London to defeat Remnants was followed by three matches against the eventual winners, the Old Etonians. In the first, Darwen fought back from 5–0 down to 5–5. The second was also drawn 2–2 but in the third Darwen were finally beaten 6–2. All the matches were played in London, the Old Etonians allegedly having refused an offer of £40 to play the third game in Darwen.[8] The Lancashire club's expenses were largely met from the proceeds of collections in local mills and workshops despite something of a recession in the local cotton industry at that time. This was one of the first matches between a team of gentlemen and an eleven made up of ordinary workers. One or two of the Darwen team wore long cloth trousers with braces over a dark shirt and most of those who wore shorts had made them from cut-down pairs of old trousers.[9] In February 1880 a representative team from Lancashire beat a similar combination from London 8–3. A year later Blackburn Rovers embarked on a Southern tour which saw them chalk up big wins against Notts County and, more significantly, over the cup holders, Clapham Rovers, in London. At the end of 1881, the biggest crowd ever to see a football match up to that point gathered at Blackburn to see the local Rovers draw with Queen's Park from Glasgow. North–South rivalries were also stimulated in the 1880s by regular matches between teams chosen to represent the two districts. The first was played at the Oval in 1880 and a large crowd of over 10,000 turned up at Bramall Lane in Sheffield in 1881 to see the South win 2–1. Sometimes these games were used as international trials, like the one in 1883, and there was clearly some feeling in the North that it was harder to win selection for the England team if you played your football north of Birmingham than if you were part of the magic circle of metropolitan sport. After Blackburn Olympic's FA Cup win in 1883 one Lancashire newspaper suggested that Northern and Midland players might now have a better chance to play for England and criticized the FA as a metropolitan clique which always held its meetings in London.[10] It might have been some recognition of Northern resentment which led the FA to move the England–Scotland match from the Oval to Sheffield in 1883 and 1903, Blackburn in 1887 and 1891, Everton in 1895 and 1911, Birmingham in 1899 and 1902 and even Newcastle in 1907. The Northern tours of the largely Southern-based amateurs, the Corinthians, also focused attention on football's geographical divide, especially in the 1880s.

But the real test of the respective strengths of Northern and Southern teams was their increasingly frequent meetings in the FA Cup. This was a knockout competition which, after a slow start, rapidly captured the imagination of the sporting public. Of 54 entries in 1879–80 only eleven came from the North. By 1883–4, 70 of the 101 entries were from Northern and Midland clubs. What these cup ties increasingly demonstrated was that the best teams were now in the North. Blackburn Rovers were the first Northern club to reach the Cup Final in 1882, losing a very close game to the Old Etonians at the Oval by one goal. This was Blackburn's first defeat in its 36th match of that season. In 1883 a record attendance for a Cup Final saw another team from Blackburn, the Olympic, finally lift the trophy following an extra-time win over an injury-hit Old Etonians. Before the final the Olympic's players had never been further South than Birmingham where they had defeated the Old Carthusians in the semi-final. Blackburn Rovers won the Cup in each of the next three years, 1884, 1885 and 1886, and only twice was it captured by a Southern club between then and 1930. By the time of that third successive Blackburn victory the Rovers were able to acknowledge publicly that their players were professionals who not only trained and practised football on a regular basis but were paid a weekly wage to do so.

The struggle to legalize professionalism is well known. It was not solely a matter between the North and the South but it was often couched in that sort of language and it was a group of Northern clubs who threatened to break away from the FA if the professional player was banned. The turning point in the conflict came at the beginning of 1884 after Preston North End had entertained a team of Southern amateur players, Upton Park, in the fourth round of the FA Cup. After a drawn match at Preston, Upton Park objected that Preston had included professionals. The charge was not proved but the club was found guilty of illegally importing players from other districts and finding them well-paid jobs. It was disqualified from the competition. The FA introduced a residence qualification for 'imports' of whom it was calculated in 1884 that 55 were Scots playing for eleven Lancashire clubs. These events caused an outcry especially among the football fraternity in Lancashire. Even if the players were professionals, what had that to do with anyone else? 'Is the Lancashire Association going to stand quietly by while Lancashire clubs are interfered with – many think unlawfully – by a caucus of South Country footballers?'[11] The *Preston Herald* suggested the formation of a Northern Football Association for the area from Warwickshire northwards, 'where football is no doubt best understood and enthusiastically followed'.[12] In the autumn of 1884 representatives of over 40 Northern clubs met in Manchester to discuss the formation of a British Football Association and fighting talk based on the idea of Northern independence was in the newspapers as well as in the bracing Northern air. The 24-year-old John Bentley wrote in the *Football Field* that Northern clubs were quite able to look after their own affairs and 'as they have received no support from Southerners in the past, they can well afford to live without it in the future'.[13] Early in 1885, at a special meeting of the FA, Northern representatives sat on the right of the President and Southern representatives on the left.[14] There were rumours of attempted takeover by Northern members with the headquarters moved to Manchester.[15] But the arguments about professionalism could not be reduced to geography any more than they could be reduced to class, though both were important. What was clear was that if the FA wished to remain in control of all football then some compromise with the largely Northern professional element would have to be reached. Charles Alcock and the small subcommittee of the FA saw that and eventually persuaded enough members of the wider committee to see it too so that professionalism could be legalized but restrained and controlled, which it was from the beginning of the 1885–6 season.

Football as a game was not invented in the North but football as a spectator sport was. It developed fastest in a number of Northern and Midland locations: Sheffield, Nottingham and Derby, the Potteries, Birmingham, but particularly Lancashire, in the cotton towns of Accrington, Bolton, Blackburn, Burnley and Darwen, all within fourteen miles of each other.[16] Nearby Preston was soon added to a list of local derbies which built on old local rivalries. It was in Lancashire that football first demonstrated its ability to seduce people into paying money to watch young men play it. Gate-money football was another Northern innovation which might have produced a permanent division within the ruling organization of the sport largely, though not totally, along geographical lines.

If football had been rationalized, regulated and reformed in the South whence it had spread to the North, professional football was to make the journey in the opposite direction. Its grip on the elite end of the game was assured in 1888 by the organization of twelve clubs – six each from the Midlands and the North – into the Football League. These clubs played a regular schedule of home and away matches with each other at the end of which the club with the best record was the champion. Regular training and practice for the best players and the more intense competition of the matches improved playing standards and underlined the dominance of the North. The Football League was a Northern organization, its offices being pointedly and appropriately located in Preston after 1902. Preston North End had also been the first champions, which had prompted Mr G. B. Browne, the chairman of the Clarence Music Hall in Grimshaw Street, to write a song about the North End football team which began:

> The noble game of football is all the rage you'll own,
> And lately in that kind of sport, Proud Preston she has shown,
> That in her town, she does possess, the men I'm proud to say,
> Who now can play and beat some of the crack teams of the day.[17]

In the 1890s Northern First Division teams were attractive visitors to Southern counties where they gave exhibitions of their prowess. When Bolton Wanderers visited Hampshire in 1893, for example, one local paper called it 'a red-letter day in the history of local football'.[18] In 1876, London was still the centre of the football world. In 1896, the *Manchester Guardian* was not contradicted when it announced, a touch smugly, that 'London is the capital of the kingdom certainly, but who in the football world regards London as a centre of any interest, either at Association or Rugby?'[19]

Professional football then was a Northern innovation at which Northerners were top dogs. Not only did they play it better than Southerners, they also watched it with more knowledge and intensity. Public comments on the expanding numbers prepared to pay to watch the new spectacle were regularly couched in terms designed to fuel North–South consciousness and prejudices. The *Sporting Times* hinted, in 1881, without offering any evidence, that the reason why two giants of the Southern game, the Wanderers and the Royal Engineers, had withdrawn from the FA Cup was their disgust at the rowdiness of gangs of Northern operatives who turned up at their matches. In fact, the Wanderers gave up as the Old Boys teams took all their best players while the soldiers played on in the Cup until 1883–4, by which time Northern competition on the field and other duties probably had more influence on their decision not to enter.[20] It was the behaviour of supporters of Blackburn Rovers who had travelled down to London to see their favourites in the Cup Final of 1884 which provoked the *Pall Mall Gazette* to label them a 'northern horde of uncouth garb and strange oaths' who were likened to a tribe of Sudanese Arabs let loose. The *Athletic News*, on the other hand, found their conduct wholly admirable, surprising and astonishing the Londoners when, at the end of the match, 'the northcountrymen hit one another in a playful yet vigorous manner and almost hugged one another in their excesses of joy'.[21] The self-restraint of spectators at matches in the South was commonly compared with the excited crowds at big matches in the

North and the middle-class composition of Oval Cup Final crowds with the largely working-class spectators of the North.[22] The Cup Final became a Northern day out but especially after its location was moved to the Crystal Palace in 1895. Working men in the North saved up for the trip. Holiday savings clubs were already a common feature in Lancashire and Cup Final clubs were set up in many Northern towns right up to 1914.[23] One local firm in Barnsley changed the date of their annual trip to London from July to Cup Final day and many Barnsley mine-owners followed suit. They were rewarded when their local Second Division club actually got there in 1910. Many citizens of Barnsley who travelled to London that day had never been there before. Some dressed up in the club's red and white and took with them bells, rattles and trumpets to help them get behind the team. In the Crystal Palace grounds before the game the visitors from Barnsley and Newcastle – United were the other finalists – played 'hoopla' for sweets and bowls for drinks, guessed the weight of friends and provided some business for the small army of tipsters, street musicians and red-nosed comedians including a gentleman in football gear who lifted chairs with his teeth. The three-card trick was worked in many corners and for those who wanted amazement there was a menagerie too. This might not have been rational recreation, but as a day out it would have been recognized by the residents of many places besides Barnsley for the best part of the century recently ended. Back home, the locals who were left behind stood outside shops whose keepers put up the score every fifteen minutes.[24]

Such adventures reminded people on both sides of the North–South divide that the other existed. The man from the *Times* found himself in a crush at the nearest railway station with 'small cast-iron northerners [working] their way relentlessly, lifting vast policemen off their feet, and seeing to it that their lady-loves were not crushed'. He eventually got into a carriage with some 'Barnsley folk', 'tough, stout-hearted colliers and factory hands who wore no collars' whom he surveyed with almost anthropological interest. Their humour was observed when the train stopped at Balham: 'Ba – laam! Why I thought it were i' Egypt'. He was amused by the comments aimed at the people waiting on suburban platforms. 'One man who turned his back disdainfully' was commended because 'all tha' good looks are on the back o' tha' yed'.

The visitors had a low opinion of Londoners, both of their looks and their manner. 'They don't know English i'London an' stare at us like we was pole-cats … and there's not a happy face in the streets. Why can't they be neighbourly?' 'Nobody's neighbours i Loondon. Tha's coom to wrong shop for that lass.' They would be glad to get back home to their own town in the 'Middle North', clutching toys for the children and memories of all the sights seen and things done.

The *Times* man thought Londoners should be more congenial to these spring-tide visitors.[25]

Football was part of the Northern way of life well before 1914. But was there a specific Northern style of play? A match card of a game between the Wanderers from London and Queen's Park in Glasgow in the autumn of 1875 set out the Scottish team in the more modern looking formation, with a goalkeeper, two full backs, two half backs and three back-up players behind the three 'front' men. The Wanderers had only one back, two half backs, two midfield 'wings' and five players apparently in the attack, two 'wings' and three 'centres'.[26] The game played in the South was still a very individual one in the 1870s. One player would obtain the ball and dribble or run forward with it until he lost it. The pioneers of a more collective, co-operative game were largely located in the North. The Scots developed the passing game, with players in more fixed positions and the amount of dribbling curtailed. The forward pass became a crucial skill and the wing evolved as a specialist player who could 'centre' the ball in front of the goal for the other forwards. By 1883–4 the third half back had replaced one of the three centres. It was the leading Northern clubs who adopted the new style most enthusiastically and developed teamwork in what contemporaries often called a scientific fashion. Darwen played a passing game against the Old Etonians in 1879.[27] The point was not that the gentlemen did not pass but that they looked upon giving the ball to a colleague as a kind of last resort. Their passing was not unselfish enough and by the early 1880s they were coming up against opponents who played a more varied game, including dribbling, short and long passes, crossing into the centre and heading, which one representative of the Southern elite, Montague Shearman, thought savoured 'more of clowning than manly play'. When this more modern and scientific style was allied to superior fitness and practice then Southern teams would have to follow suit or resign themselves to a perpetual second best.

After Blackburn Olympic had outlasted the Old Etonians in the Cup Final of 1883 there were suggestions of rough play. Were Northern teams rougher than those from the South East? Gibson and Pickford alleged that in 1879–80 it was the 'somewhat vigorous methods of the northern clubs' which had led to an addition to the laws forbidding any player from charging his opponent by leaping on him.[28] The sporting press is littered with accusations from both sides of the geographical boundary. When Preston North End played the Corinthians in 1889, for example, it was the over-vigorous play of the visitors from the South which dissatisfied the home crowd. They particularly disliked the heavy charging of the amateurs which 'knocked the North End team about like ninepins'. A Bolton newspaper sympathetic to the Northern and professional cause wrote that if any professional team had played like that they would have been reported to the FA.[29] Professionals played a more civilized and scientific game and were subjected to constraints which amateurs would have found irksome. Swindon Town from the Southern League accused Barnsley of kicking them to defeat in the FA Cup semi-final of 1912. According to the local paper Barnsley's 'obvious aim was to deplete the ranks of their opponents' – first by 'laming and incapacitating' their best players. These tactics succeeded so well that Swindon finished the game with only nine men.[30] Harold Fleming, Swindon's best player, was quoted by the *Daily Chronicle* lamenting the unfairness, 'that players should be tripped and hacked and kicked ... whilst the opposition escape scot free'. Two years before Barnsley had been on the receiving end of similar treatment from Newcastle United in their FA Cup Final replay but there is no sense that any of this had much to do with Northernness.[31] Rough play was not an uncommon occurrence in professional football. Such charges could have been levelled at Woolwich Arsenal, Chelsea, Clapton Orient, Fulham or Tottenham, all London clubs who had joined the Football League by 1910. By the end of Victoria's reign there was no Northern style but professional football was largely a slice of Northern popular culture.

'Northerners' and 'Southerners' were terms regularly used to describe football teams who represented more or less Northern and Southern towns. After 1895 rugby football became polarized on regional lines. The Northern Union, later to become the Rugby League, broke away from the Rugby Football Union over the issue of whether clubs should compensate players for time lost from work. In England the Northern Union/Rugby League remained embedded in Lancashire and Yorkshire from which counties it has scarcely been able to break out. There was nothing like this in football, although there might have been. The consciousness of North and South was well developed long before the invention of modern football but such a popular sport with its growing coverage in the local, national and specialist press was bound to reinforce prevailing images and stereotypes. But the idea of North and South remained very imprecise. Newcastle and Sheffield might both be labelled as Northern but their peoples spoke with very different accents and to Novocastrians Sheffielders might not seem Northern at all. There were at least four separate regions in the North; Lancashire, Yorkshire, the North East and Cumbria. Such diversity within as well as between regions should make people wary about talk of two nations. It has often been said that England is more an example of variations on a single culture. So far as the subculture of professional football was concerned, it would soon become less Northern-dominated as London clubs in particular began to make an impact on league and Cup, often with teams packed with players born and football-bred in the North.

Arsenal's triumphs in the 1930s suggested that football's regional balance of power had shifted again. But before 1914 professional football was largely a Northern phenomenon, a matter for pride or disappointment depending on one's angle of vision. The behaviour of football crowds there astonished contemporaries. Such scenes had 'no counterpart among the Southerners, who can hardly comprehend the joyous thrill of enthusiasm that passes through a whole community ... football in the North is more than a game. It excites more emotion than art, politics and the drama, and it awakes local patriotism to the highest pitch.'[32]

Only a Northern lover of football could have written so proud an encomium. Much of Northern England was industrial England where many people worked in mine, mill or factory and lived in neighbourhoods of terraced streets in urban communities. But Northern consciousness is a slippery identity. It was encouraged by the growth and expansion in circulation of local newspapers, party political organizations, dialect literature, a distinct musical tradition based on brass bands and choirs and a growing interest in the history of the North. Professional football could be added to this list.[33] But the local football team contributed more to the strong loyalties which grew up around individual towns rather than to the idea of a shared Northern regional identity. The FA Cup in particular gave relatively small Northern towns the chance to strut on a national stage and reminded both North and South of the former's place in the nation.

In 1884–5 professional football could have become as Northern as fish and chips and black slate roofs. But it did not. Its legalization prevented a Northern breakaway and in spite of the opposition to its further expansion by influential Southern groups like the London FA, by the 1890s, the first professional clubs were appearing in the South. As for Charles Clegg, he had opposed the legalization of professionals, but later, as Sir Charles, he was national president of the FA from 1923–37. The consciousness of a geographical divide which he identified in 1872 lives on. The classic Cup Final is thought to be when teams from North and South meet. People define themselves in different ways at different times. But in the complex world of individual loyalties to wider groups, family, street, town and nation will usually come before region. And football is the national game.

Notes

1. Sir Frederick Wall, *Fifty Years of Football* (Cassell, London: 1935), p. 31.
2. Quoted by Tony Mason, *Association Football and English Society 1863–1915* (Harvester Press, Brighton: 1980), p. 213.

3. Nicholas Fishwick, *From Clegg to Clegg House: The Official Centenary History of the Sheffield and Hallamshire County Football Association 1886–1986* (Sheffield and Hallamshire County FA, Sheffield: 1986) pp. 4–6.

4. See especially Helen M. Jewell, *The North–South Divide: The Origins of Northern Consciousness in England* (Manchester U.P., Manchester: 1994); and Keith Robbins, 'North and South, then and now', *History Today* 38 (April 1988), pp. 23–8.

5. *Athletic News*, 30 September 1876.

6. *Athletic News*, 10 March 1877. The Scottish Football Association was formed in 1873 and the first Scottish Cup competition was won by Queen's Park in 1874.

7. *Athletic News*, 30 June, 24 November 1877. It had first appeared in 1875.

8. *Darwen News*, 8 March 1879, 3 January 1880. This may have been prudent because when they did journey North to play a friendly on the New Year's Day holiday in 1880, they lost 3–1.

9. N. L. Jackson, *Association Football* (George Newnes, London: 2nd edn, 1900), p. 56.

10. *Accrington Times*, 7 April 1883.

11. Robert W. Lewis, 'The development of professional football in Lancashire 1870–1914' (unpublished PhD thesis, University of Lancaster, 1993), p. 152.

12. For more details see Mason, *Association Football*, pp. 72–81.

13. *Football Field*, 1 November 1884.

14. Lewis, 'Professional football', p. 56.

15. Jackson, *Association Football*, p. 113.

16. On the spatial spread of football see John Bale, *Sport and Place: A Geography of Sport in England, Scotland and Wales* (Hurst, London: 1982).

17. See the poster reproduced in Jeffrey Richards, *Stars in Our Eyes: Lancashire Stars of Stage, Screen and Radio* (Lancashire County Books, Preston: 1994), p. 7.

18. Quoted in Alfred Gibson and William Pickford, *Association Football and the Men who Made It* (Caxton Publishing Co., London: 1906), I, p. 106.

19. *Manchester Guardian*, 23 November 1896.

20. *Athletic News*, 28 September 1881.

21. *Athletic News*, 2 April 1884.

22. For example, *Licensed Victuallers' Sportsman*, 8 December 1888; *Athletic News*, 13 April 1886.

23. Gibson and Pickford, *Association Football*, IV, pp. 41–2.

24. See the *Barnsley Independent*, 16, 23, 30 April 1910.

25. *The Times*, 25 April 1910.

26. John Hutchinson, *The Football Industry* (Richard Drew, Glasgow: 1982), p. 35.

27. *Darwen News*, 8 November 1879.

28. See the match reports in the *The Times* and the *Manchester Guardian*. The main complaint of the Eton College *Chronicle* was that the working-class players of Blackburn Olympic had spent three weeks in special training for the match paid for by local businessmen. See Gibson and Pickford, *Association Football*, I, p. 62.

29. *Football Field*, 28 December 1889.
30. *Swindon Advertiser*, 1 April 1912. *Daily Mirror*, 22 April 1912.
31. *Daily Mirror*, 29 April 1910.
32. *Tinsley's Magazine* 46 (1889–90), p. 65.
33. Richards, *Stars in Our Eyes*, pp. 1–6.

4. 'The making of the healthy and the happy home': recreation, education, and the production of working-class womanhood at the Rowntree Cocoa Works, York, c. 1898–1914

Catriona M. Parratt

'It was felt that ... girls who leave school for the factory, and leave the factory to marry have little chance to become proficient in the domestic arts by helping at home.'[1] Benjamin Seebohm Rowntree's reflections on the motivations underlying the establishment of classes in domesticity at the Rowntree Cocoa Works in York in 1905 said a great deal about dominant understandings of what it meant to be a working-class woman in late nineteenth- and early twentieth-century England. This chapter explores how a particular ideal of working-class femininity influenced not only the educational provisions made for Rowntree workers, but also the recreational and social clubs which the firm's directors encouraged and sponsored. Educational programmes at the Cocoa Works were intended to provide the girls and young women employed there with a training in the necessary skills for being competent wives and mothers, while recreational clubs and classes underscored the formal lessons in domesticity at both an ideological and practical level. Together these programmes represented a conscious attempt to intervene in the lives of young working women and mould their social and personal identities along lines laid down over the previous century by gender ideologues of both the working and middle classes.

During the nineteenth century, diverse and often dichotomous models of masculinity and femininity were crafted by individuals and social groups attempting to come to terms with their changing world. After mid-century, the prescriptive ideal of working-class womanhood as defined by upper- and middle-class reformers, employers, clergymen, male working-class radicals and trade unionists, and numbers of working-class women themselves, emphasized domesticity and dependence. 'Good wives' and 'little mothers' were the working-class counterparts of the 'perfect lady' of bourgeois culture. Implicit in this conception of femininity was a particular view of working-class masculinity: that of the respectable, responsible, wage-earning husband and

father. The antecedents of these models of femininity and masculinity
can be traced back to eighteenth-century artisan culture and while they
did not exhaust in any sense the range of possible working-class gender
identities, they came to be widely accepted during the second half of
the nineteenth century.[2] The picture that historians have painted of
eighteenth-century life and popular culture indicates that the dis-
semination of these gender ideals represented a narrowing of the limits
to what was considered acceptable for women in terms of familial and
social responsibilities, duties, personal behaviour, and public presentation of self.[3]

The circumscription of women's social roles and identities was in-
timately connected to changes in customary practices and relationships
in the workplace and the family. Women had long been characterized
as cheap labour and employers' attempts to substitute them for more
highly paid male workers were vigorously resisted in many trades and
industries from the early decades of the nineteenth century. By the late
1870s, the trade union movement had established the exclusion and
marginalization of women workers as a central plank of its agenda.
'Wives should be in their proper sphere at home, seeing after their
house and family, instead of being dragged into the competition for
livelihood against the great and strong men of the world,' asserted
Henry Broadhurst at the Trades' Union Congress of 1877. Cheap
female labour posed a dual threat to skilled working men. In the artisan
and domestic work cultures of the eighteenth century, there had been
an intimate connection between a working man's skill and his status as
the head of the family; for the nineteenth-century heirs to this idea,
displacement by unskilled women represented an assault not only on
their identity as skilled, independent workers, but also as men. Changing
attitudes to marriage reinforced the tendency to cast men as workers
and breadwinners, and women as domestic dependants. The economic
and social climate of the early decades of the nineteenth century was
harsh and unforgiving, and women faced powerful material and moral
pressures to enter into formal marriages which increasingly came to
represent economic security and respectability. By mid-century, what
John Gillis terms an era of 'mandatory marriage' had begun and the
ideologies of separate spheres, domesticity and female dependency had
become dominant elements in much working-class thought on gender.[4]

These developments had significant implications for working-class
recreation. The identification of men with wage-earning, and women
with domesticity and dependence was paralleled and reinforced by a
sexual division of leisure. Early nineteenth-century commentaries on
the duties and rights of wives and husbands indicated that men's
responsibility for wage-earning earned them an unequivocal right to
leisure:

If a working man should make thirty shillings a week he may drink ten pints if he pleases; go to a coffee-house every night, and read the papers, and bring in fifteen shillings a week to keep home and pay the rent withal. *He has a right to do this* [original emphasis], for he makes the money.[5]

As domestic workers, or as marginalized wage workers, women could not lay as strong a claim to leisure as men. Rather, women were expected to labour in their homes to provide men with leisure services. Both working- and middle-class domestic ideologues characterized the ideal home for the working man as a refuge in which at the end of the working day he would find comfort and rest in the solicitous care of his womenfolk. John Watkins, the Chartist, described the sexual division of labour and leisure in his 1841 'Address to the Women of England':

> Man goeth forth to work and returneth for that rest and refreshment which his labour at once needeth and provideth. Woman, in the mean time, fitteth and prepareth the good things provided by his toil, and she cheereth his worn spirit by words and looks and deeds of love.[6]

In an 1866 essay entitled 'Domestic Economy', John Broadhead, a Birmingham compositor, idealized this arrangement of productive and social relations: 'Home is that hallowed spot where, after the toils, troubles, and difficulties of the day, we can rest our weary limbs ... Home is almost the only place in which we can fully enjoy the peace and comfort which are the just reward of our labours.' For Thomas Wright, 'the journeyman engineer', the end of the working day meant returning home to find 'a bright, cosy room, a nice warm tea, and a smiling wife, mother, or landlady'. In Wright's opinion the most critical factor determining the comfort of the working man's home was his wife's housekeeping skill: 'Among the working classes the *wife* [original emphasis] makes the home.'[7]

The broader social ramifications of women fulfilling their responsibility for creating homes conducive to men's comfort and leisure were significant. In their campaigns against women's waged work, middle-class and working-class commentators ascribed many of the problems facing labouring people to female employment outside the home. 'It is not the daily toil in the sweat of his brow which threatens the workman's domestic peace,' ran one essay on the topic, 'it is that we have taken the key-stone from his arch by tempting his wife away from her proper and natural sphere of domestic labour.'[8] According to critics of the practice, infant mortality, poor nutrition, dirt, disease and immorality could all be laid at the door of the woman who neglected her home in order to work for wages outside it. Women's waged work was identified as a major factor in the general degradation of the working classes and their failure to advance socially and morally, and as dominant social views of leisure changed throughout the course of the nineteenth century, and popular recreation came increasingly to be seen as offering potential for 'improving' the working classes, women's role in shaping a wholesome, home-centred leisure culture became critical.

There were two major concerns, the first being that girls and women who engaged in waged work either did not receive a proper training in the necessary housewifely skills or did not have the time and energy to service their husband's leisure. 'If our employers of labour desire to inculcate those habits of modesty, morality, docility, and domestic usefulness, which are essential to the duties and comforts of married life,' noted one commentator in the mid-1860s, 'they will do well to limit their employment of youthful labour to the male sex.' [9] The second matter of concern was that women's experiences in the culture of waged work were liable to give them such a taste for amusement themselves that they would be reluctant to settle for the quieter, self-denying role of providing for someone else's pleasure. Along with this argument ran the related one that waged work encouraged personal habits and forms of leisure which compromised the femininity and morals of working-class girls and women. This is apparent in the debates on protective legislation for female workers, especially those employed in trades and occupations like mining which came to be strongly associated with masculine strength and coarseness. Where female agricultural labour came under attack, for example, there was often a consensus that it encouraged a troubling lack of restraint on women's behaviour. The 1867 Royal Commission noted that employers and working people in the county of Northamptonshire were convinced that girls and women employed in field labour learned 'loose and disorderly habits'. Mr Portman's report on Cambridgeshire and the East, West and North Ridings of Yorkshire echoes this sentiment. Commenting on one of several industrial schools established in the latter county to train the daughters of agricultural labourers in domestic skills, the commissioner wrote: 'It is the only instance of the kind I met with, and it is quite worthy of imitation by those who have the opportunity with the view of drawing the tastes of girls away from the license of field labour, and fitting them for domestic service and their future duties in life.' [10] If working-class women were to be willing and able to perform their domestic duty of providing for men's comfort and leisure, care had to be taken that their own appetites for leisure were not piqued:

> The true comfort of man depends upon his home; men are capable of going through almost any labour when they have a comfortable

home waiting to welcome them; but the wild tone of reckless liberty acquired by a rude taste for the labours of the field in girlhood unfits the tastes and destroys the domestic habits in woman which alone can make home happy and comfortable to her husband.[11]

It was not simply the nature of the occupation which troubled opponents of women's employment in these fields, but also the workplace culture, which seemed certain to compromise a woman's gender identity and ascribed social role. Reformers subjected the personal habits and leisure practices of female workers to close and critical scrutiny. The Dudley nailmakers presented one of the starkest pictures of working-class womanhood apparently gone awry: 'The women seem to have lost all traces of the modesty of their sex, and from childhood are addicted to swearing, smoking – resembling as far as possible the other sex in their habits and deportment, even to the wearing of their coarse flannel jackets.' The behaviour of girls and young women in the Staffordshire brickfields seemed equally 'grotesque' and subversive: 'As they run from place to place, they sing snatches of coarse songs or crack obscene jokes for mutual encouragement ... The foreman's account of these girls was that they were "very bold and cheeky".' [12] In agrarian occupations, long-established leisure customs were enmeshed with work practices and the involvement of women in the one was as disturbing as their participation in the other. Feasts, frolics and largesses were a popular climax to the busy harvest season in agricultural districts in East Anglia, Essex and Hertfordshire, despite efforts to repress or reform them. These traditional bacchanalia persisted into the 1860s and beyond, and women's presence at gatherings 'at which the language, the drunkenness and riot, surpass ... more than we can conceive to be possible amongst a society calling themselves Christians', was a great concern to reform-minded individuals.[13] Even forms of employment which did not compromise women's femininity might be considered inappropriate because they encouraged frivolousness and shallowness, qualities unsuitable in the wife of a working man. Millinery, dressmaking and shop work were all characterized in this way. 'Dressy and vain', contemptuous of housework, a woman of the 'young-lady class' was likely to prove to be a sloven on marriage, incapable of making her home comfortable and attractive. In Thomas Wright's opinion, a woman such as this contrasted 'very unfavourably with ... the really clever housewife, who goes actively about her work, and in her clean, cotton working-gown looks to the full as comely and attractive as she does ... after her work is done.' [14]

Protective legislation, short hours movements and exclusionary trade unionism were all measures which, by restricting women's employment, might serve the purpose of ensuring that the 'representative artisan's' wife would indeed be Wright's clever, comely and attractive housewife. But only the most highly paid workers could afford the luxury of supporting wives and daughters who did not at some time or another contribute a wage to the family economy. Consequently, those concerned with shaping and restoring the key-stone to the arch of the working man's home and family had to find some means of reaching girls and women who were engaged in waged labour and of counteracting the dangerous independence and freedom that their employment seemed to give them.[15]

In the final quarter of the nineteenth century, rational recreation – girls' clubs, friendly societies, girls' brigades, travelling libraries, lantern-shows, socials, teas, entertainments and outings, all with a pronounced didactic and moralistic tone – became a favourite vehicle for the conveyance of the ideologies and skills of domesticity to working-class girls and women. Reformers had a clear sense of their purpose: to arouse young women's 'social conscience by teaching them ... the possibilities of mutual helpfulness and the joys of service'; to displace dissolute and degrading forms of leisure with the 'pure joy' and 'real pleasures' of nature, art, music and good literature; to urge young women 'to try to make their homes and workshops places of righteousness'; and, above all, to persuade them that 'wifehood and motherhood [are] women's best estate'.[16]

One of the first voluntary associations established to cater to working women was the Girls' Friendly Society. Founded in 1874, the GFS was an Anglican religious organization which attempted to facilitate cross-class relations: 'upper-class Lady Associates were to adopt a protective, motherly role towards unmarried, working-girl members'.[17] The organization's mission was to preserve the chastity and purity of working-class girls and women and also to promote domestic service as the form of employment most suitable for them. The main constituency for the GFS was the rural South, where domestic service was usually the only work available; 'Snowdrop Bands', on the other hand, were a similar enterprise popular with factory girls in Northern industrial areas in the early 1890s. Members of Snowdrop Bands promised to try to uplift themselves and those with whom they were associated: 'we will, with God's help, earnestly try, both by our example and influence, to discourage all wrong conversation, light and immodest conduct and the reading of bad and foolish books'. As Carol Dyhouse notes, the impetus for these organizations came from the upper and middle classes who feared that there were insufficient mechanisms for ensuring that young working women would recognize that innocence, modesty and docility were virtues and that wifehood and motherhood were truly 'women's best estate'. Reformers' own accounts of their efforts to achieve these ends are illuminating, not least because they speak to some of the difficulties they were likely to encounter in their social missionary work.[18]

The Reverend Robert Dolling conducted several different social groups for his parishioners in a slum district of Portsmouth in the 1880s and 1890s, including a girls' club, 'The Social'. Dolling believed that, with its games and sermons, carefully chaperoned dancing classes, and above all, the refining influence of his sister, 'The Social' served as an effective counter to the corrupting influences of Portsmouth's street and factory culture.[19] The thought may have been somewhat self-delusive, but it was one shared by others who advocated or took similar initiatives elsewhere. For example, in Nottingham, which by the mid-1890s had become a town 'thickly populated with women and girls employed in factories, "the devil's mission of amusement" forces its way with special temptations fostered by the public-house system'. To counteract this evil, reformers set up a system of 'Girls' Evening Homes' in which 'educated girls meet factory girls on common ground, and, by kindly intercourse and unselfish service, do much to raise the tone'.[20] Rural districts and villages were another field for reforming recreation. Itinerant potato and hop pickers were seen as 'a class of women and girls ... sorely open to the temptations of intemperance', but even they could be reached through outdoor lantern exhibitions and uplifting talks. Middle-class girls who had left school and were 'looking longingly around for something to do' were urged to use their talents by 'looking out for dull people and making them cheerful'.[21] Kathleen Townend attested to the happy results such efforts might achieve.

> A number of girls joined together in a country village and started a Girls' Club, which they invited the tradesmen's daughters and the working girls to join ... Amongst other things promoted has been a healthy tone of friendship, unselfishness, and thought for others, and girls with a tendency to run wild have been kept in safe companionship.[22]

Not everyone was quite so amenable to the refining influences of their social superiors and reformers frequently found that they had to accommodate the inclinations of the girls and women who were the objects of their reforms. The Reverend Dolling soon discovered that older girls stopped attending club meetings once they began to 'walk out' with their young men. His solution was a social evening to which both young women and men were invited, but finding entertainments which Dolling considered appropriate presented another problem: 'we tried games, but they always ended in horrid romps. All games seemed to end in kissing, and forfeits brought forth witticisms which were not always conducive to propriety.'[23] Workers at an Anglican settlement house in Bethnal Green, London also found that reaching the wilder elements of young working-class womanhood could be difficult. The quieter girls of the district attended a club which devoted its time to 'games and dancing, musical drill, and the like. Part-singing and brush-drawing [were] also popular with the members and the preparation of a play for performance at Whitsuntide gave interesting occupation for winter months.' But this was very tame fare for many girls of the neighbourhood, and for them, settlement workers established a 'rough girls' club'. Favourite amusements in the early days of this enterprise 'were swinging from the gas-pipes, fighting, rolling on the floor, and singing songs of an order not suited for the drawing-room, or any other respectable place'. Evidently, but to what extent and by what means it is not clear, club members were persuaded that quiet, womanly pastimes such as needlework, reading and listening to educational lectures were a more attractive way of spending one's free time. 'What a triumph this was can only be known by those who have done similar work.'[24]

For some reformers, the substitution of rough and riotous play with rational and respectable forms of leisure was not necessarily an advance. Edward Cadbury was among several who felt that the greater leisure resources and opportunities enjoyed by some working women were dubious benefits. The better paid daughters of skilled workers enjoyed much greater spending power than most women workers who earned barely enough to subsist. 'If the girl's parents are in very comfortable circumstances,' asserted Clara Collet, 'she frequently pays nothing towards the home expenses, and spends all she earns on dress and amusement.'[25] Because of their higher standard of living, these young women had higher expectations: 'they have more resources in themselves, but on this account they feel more need for change and pleasure'.[26] Materially better off than their lower-paid counterparts, skilled women workers had more vitality which sought its release at the end of the work day in the pursuit of leisure. 'They are too restless to stay indoors,' Cadbury objected. Some paid occasional visits to theatres or music halls, or joined dancing classes: 'for others, the churches and chapels find the recreation, and choir practices, Bible-classes, and missions fill all available time'. The unhappy consequence was that these girls and young women were 'seldom or never at home, except on Friday ... the universal night for housecleaning'.[27]

Underlying these criticisms and attempts at reform were the same fears identified by early nineteenth-century commentators on working-class life: fears that working-class women lacked the time, skills, energy and inclination to care effectively for homes, husbands and families. This was a lament which, with variations, was sounded throughout the

Victorian period, but one which by the turn of the twentieth century had become even more highly charged because of the connections made between national efficiency, imperialism and maternity. The growing industrial and political power of the United States, Germany and Japan; the dismal performance of British troops and the poor physical condition of recruits in the Boer War; a falling birth rate and an evident rise in infant mortality combined to fuel fears of national and imperial deterioration in the period before the First World War. A variety of state and voluntary agencies responded to the crisis with initiatives intended to combat the numeric and qualitative decline of the population. Parliamentary measures included the compulsory training of midwives, the provision of school meals to needy children, medical inspection in schools, and the comprehensive Children Act of 1908. Municipal authorities set up classes in motherhood, health visiting, and schemes for providing pure milk for infants. Organizations of doctors, social workers, teachers and legions of lady volunteers devoted themselves to what had become a matter of supreme importance: the revitalization of the nation through its children, 'the next generation of soldiers and workers, the Imperial race'.[28]

Anna Davin and others have pointed out that social and environmental factors, despite their undoubted significance, were given much less emphasis in the debate on the state of the nation than was the role of the mother. Eugenists, the medical profession, state officials, and educational and social reformers of varying political hues used the gender ideologies of the nineteenth century – domesticity, separate spheres and the like – to craft what Davin identifies as an early twentieth-century 'ideology of motherhood'. With the elevation of the status and dignity of maternity as their mission, proponents of the ideology urged upper- and middle-class women to choose marriage and motherhood over the pursuit of higher education or a career. Prescriptions for the working classes focused upon education, for, in the opinion of many, working-class women were indolent and ignorant mothers who needed instruction in the most basic domestic skills. To this end, lessons in cookery, laundry and housewifery were added to the girls' elementary curriculum in some schools, and the Board of Education encouraged the establishment of classes in infant care. Strategies for educating mothers in their communities included leafleting, lectures, infant consultations, health visiting, schools for mothers, and infant welfare centres.[29]

It was in the context of this national obsession with the fitness of women as mothers that the Rowntree firm began to concern itself with not just the manufacture of cocoa and chocolate, but also with the production of an elect working-class womanhood.

The Rowntree firm was established in 1862 when Henry Isaac Rowntree, a respected member of York's Society of Friends, purchased a small cocoa manufactory on the banks of the River Ouse in the centre of the city. The business was a modest affair in its early years, employing only a dozen or so workers, but two major innovations helped turn around the firm's fortunes and ushered in an era of rapid expansion and growth. The first of these was the introduction of a line of crystallized gums and pastilles in 1881 which proved to be enormously successful. The second was the installation of equipment developed in the Dutch chocolate industry which produced both a superior form of drinking cocoa and, more significantly in the long term, cocoa butter which could be used to make eating chocolate. By 1880, there were 100 workers on the Rowntree payroll; by 1894, 864; by 1904, almost 3,000; and by the outbreak of the First World War, 5,641. Facilities at the original Tanner's Moat location became inadequate for the rapidly growing enterprise and in 1890 Joseph Rowntree, who had taken sole charge of the firm on the death of his younger brother Henry in 1883, purchased a large area of land a mile or so outside the city and began constructing a modern, state-of-the-art factory covering some 220 acres. In 1908 the company transferred all its operations to the new Haxby Road Site.[30]

Like other Quaker industrialists of the period (most notably the Cadburys), the Rowntree firm enjoyed the reputation of being unusually enlightened employers. Combining religious principles with a belief that business should be both efficiently and humanely organized, Rowntrees practised what, in a study of the Cadbury firm, Charles Dellheim terms 'benevolence without autocracy'.[31] Both attempted to fuse commercial success with social progress and not just at the level of the individual factory, as Joseph Rowntree's comments in the first issue of the *Cocoa Works' Magazine* in 1902 indicated:

> The benefits of well-conducted factories in which the manufacture is carried on in healthful rooms and amidst pleasant surroundings are not confined to those who work in them. The example of such factories tends to improve the general conditions of labour in the country.
>
> The Directors desire that the Cocoa Works may be one of the places which exercise an influence of this kind.[32]

Rowntrees' growth reflected the general expansion of light manufacturing at the turn of the century, and like other businesses in this sector of the economy, they employed a high percentage of female workers. Food manufacturers, especially, relied heavily upon a female labour force which, because of the historical development of the industry and widely held beliefs about women's proclivities, was low-paid, largely unskilled, non-unionized, and easily controlled. The workforce in cocoa and chocolate confectionery manufacturing also tended to be young, another factor which contributed to its malleability. The exact proportion of female to male employees at the Cocoa Works varied from year to year, and seasonally, but over half the Rowntree workforce in the period with which this study is concerned were girls or young women. In Joseph Rowntree's estimation, by 1913 his firm was employing one third of York's fourteen- to seventeen-year-olds and half the girls and young women in that age group. The company did not take lightly its responsibility for ensuring that the time its young employees spent at the Cocoa Works would contribute to their development as models of a respectable and responsible working class: 'will [the boys] be likely to grow up as good citizens, and will the girls be helped to be good daughters and sisters, and in future years to become good wives and mothers?'[33]

Rowntrees clearly intended that the answer to this question would be in the affirmative. Their provisions and policies for female employees meshed both with their general philosophy of industrial and social betterment, and with contemporary ideas about the crucial importance of domesticity and motherhood. Between 1898 and 1905, small clubs and classes held during lunch breaks or after working hours were established for girls and women employed at the Cocoa Works. In addition to a Girls' Gymnastic Club, Girls' Swimming Class, Girls' Temperance Society, Mandoline Band, Miss Skirrow's Class (in 1905, this was re-named the Wednesday Class), and dressmaking classes, there were informal work groups in crochet, knitting, and plain and fancy sewing. With the exception of Miss Skirrow's class, it is not clear whether the impetus for establishing these activities came from the workers themselves or from female staff in the firm's Social Department; it was certainly the latter who organized and provided instruction. Rowntrees gave material assistance to the girls' classes and societies in several ways: permitting them to meet in the Girls' Dining Room, for example, or releasing staff from the Social Department to give secretarial and administrative assistance. The firm did not assume financial responsibility for the recreational societies, though it did provide facilities such as playing fields and changing rooms; made occasional monetary contributions; hosted teas, picnics and socials; and provided prizes, facilities and moral support and encouragement. This policy was in keeping with the Rowntrees' belief that although workers deserved decent wages, benefits such as pensions, and good working conditions, they should not be encouraged to be overly dependent on their employers.[34]

Women's dependency on a male wage earner was another matter, however. As Quakers, the Rowntrees believed that women and men were spiritual equals, but their administration of the Cocoa Works was contoured by very conservative ideas about gender. In the factory there was a strict sexual division of labour which was characteristic of the food industry in general. Girls and women worked primarily in un-skilled, routinized, labour-intensive tasks while male workers were trained and employed as skilled tradesmen such as mechanics, joiners and bricklayers, or worked in capital-intensive areas of production. In the confectionery industry this technological segregation meant that women were concentrated in the 'dry' end of production – packaging, weighing and wrapping – while men were clustered in the 'wet' end – chocolate making, mixing, and manufacturing units for coating or enrobing. Employment and contract policies reinforced gender segre-gation and hierarchies in the industry generally, and also at the York Cocoa Works. From the late nineteenth century to the 1940s, Rown-trees were among many employers who enforced a marriage bar which effectively segmented the labour force into full-time, permanent, male workers and full-time female workers who were dismissed when they married. Chris Smith, John Child and Michael Rowlinson note that this practice meant that the majority of workers in the industry were young, single girls who were only minimally integrated into the com-pany and lacked any career prospects unless they remained unmarried. The female labour force within individual factories was characterized by another hierarchy based on age and marital status: older, unmarried women held supervisory, clerical and low-level administrative positions, and young, single females worked on the production line. Women's wages were lower than men's and benefits such as pensions assumed that the former were supplementary, temporary wage earners who would eventually marry and become dependent on a husband. Rituals such as giving wedding gifts (a tea service, household linen, and the like) to workers who left Rowntrees to marry, and publishing wedding and birth announcements in the factory magazine further inscribed the Cocoa Works' culture with well-entrenched ideas about gender, and revealed much about its sexual politics.[35]

The congruence between the sexual division of labour and the rhetoric and practices of recreation at the York Cocoa Works was apparent. Classes in dressmaking for girls, and metal and woodworking for boys spoke most obviously to the ideological imperatives that shaped the recreational fare on offer, but very few club meetings or social events passed without some commentary which assumed or endorsed a gendered social system of male citizens and workers, and good daughters, sisters, wives and mothers. The 1906 membership drive by the Bowling Club Committee illustrated this. After beginning with the encouraging claim that 'the members are anxious to welcome *any employee*' (emphasis added), the notice in the *Cocoa Works' Magazine* went on to reveal the limits of the club's inclusiveness: 'He may smoke while playing, and is not bound to dress in his best clothes. He may bring his wife or his sister to watch the game, and she can enjoy the fresh air with her sewing or knitting.'[36]

Most social clubs at Rowntrees were segregated according to gender, and classes in domestic crafts, and dinner-hour work groups in crochet, knitting and sewing were understood and represented by the company as providing female workers with a rare opportunity to acquire and practise skills invaluable to the homemaker. Classes tended to be kept small so as to facilitate instruction, and fees and the cost of materials were moderate: Miss Weatherill's dressmaking class in the winter of 1904, for example, had about fifteen members who paid one penny a week for a course of twelve weekly lessons. Patterns and materials could be ordered at the beginning of the course and paid for in small instalments. The firm used several inducements to encourage partici-pation in these activities: they rewarded those who successfully completed the full course of dressmaking classes by reimbursing the fee; displayed workers' crafts in the corridors and communal spaces of the factory; and published in the works' magazine the names of those whose work had earned particular praise.[37] In addition, formal exhibitions of work encouraged excellence in domestic crafts. The observations and criticisms passed on the work illuminate some of the characteristics which the Rowntrees, in common with others of their class, valued most highly in working-class women: thrift, neatness, economy, industry, plain and simple tastes. In the 1907 and 1908 Arts and Crafts Exhibitions, Emily Rowntree and Mrs D. S. Crichton judged the entries in the various categories of 'Girls' Work'. 'The plain sewing, skirts, and blouses showed very creditable work, and a decided tendency in the right direction towards usefulness and thrift,' they noted encouragingly.[38] But the lack of entries in the plain sewing section and the over-abundance of fancy work, lace and crochet was disturbing: 'The practical value of the ability to make a nightdress thoroughly well is undoubtedly far greater than the ability to embroider a case for it.'[39] Furthermore, the judges felt that a mending competition would be a most useful addition, as 'darning, patching, turning up of skirts round the hem, etc., [are] all so necessary if we wish to be tidy with little expense'. A final word of advice on 'finishing off' under-scored the deeper lessons to be learned: 'finish off the turnings of the seams, arm-holes, vents, etc., as neatly as you would on the right side. Not only is this taken into account in the judging, but it helps in the training for neat work of all kinds, and indeed, in the character of the worker.'[40]

No other society was devoted as singlemindedly to developing the character of the Cocoa Works' girls and women as were the Girls' Temperance Society and the Wednesday Class, though the for-mer was certainly more focused in its purpose. Formed in 1902, the

Temperance Society held monthly meetings and, more occasionally, socials and concerts with other associations in York. Members submitted their names to the society's secretary, paid a small subscription, and signed a printed card pledging temperance. Initially, the weekly meetings were held after work hours, but shortly after the society's establishment they were switched to the Friday dinner-hour. The primary theme of the talks given at these meetings, of course, was resisting the temptations of drink. However, the emphasis was not simply upon individual abstention, but rather helping others – friends, family members, and especially male acquaintances – to avoid temptation. Addresses to Temperance Society members resonated with contemporary, contradictory understandings of women's nature. Characterized in literature, art and scholarly works as both corrupters and guardians of morality, working-class women had to be encouraged to use their influence 'on the side of all that is best'.[41] The Christmas season was viewed as a time when the power of that influence was especially needed. In the final week before Christmas, the Girls' Temperance Society held a series of special dinner-hour meetings to fortify their members against the heightened temptations and dangers of the holiday. The December 1902 number of the *Cocoa Works' Magazine* carried a suitably inspirational, and typical, message from the society:

> Shall we, the women and girls in this factory, each one determine that we will do all we can, and use all our influence, which is often greater than we know, to resist this evil; so that in the hundreds of homes represented here, however humble they may be, this Christmas time may be a 'happy' one, with the real happiness which leaves no sting or shame behind.[42]

The purpose of the Wednesday Club was to inspire and elevate the moral character and social conduct of its members, too, as its first teacher Florence Skirrow made clear:

> Let us take [our Heavenly Friend] for our example day by day, and try to live our life as He lived His. It was just to help each other to do this that our class was ever started, and its purpose is the same now as it was then.[43]

The Wednesday Class was founded in 1898 and for four years met in Emily Rowntree's office at the old Tanner's Moat factory. First at these 'cosy little gatherings' and then later in greater numbers in the new Lecture Room at the Haxby Road works, Florence Skirrow and Emily Rowntree led Wednesday Class members in lessons in submission to

God's will, service to others and self-denial. Truth, courage, love, perseverance, and above all prayer, were the means; personal salvation and the welfare and moral regeneration of the larger community were the ends: 'as women and girls working in a large Factory [sic] in a city of old England that is very dear to us, we mean to use our influence, and *make our force felt* [original emphasis], on the side of all that is good and strong and noble and self-respecting.' [44]

Physical training was also enlisted in the cause of fitting Cocoa Works' girls and women for lives spent in the service of such ideals. The notion that the education of muscles and morals were one and the same thing had acquired wide currency by the beginning of the twentieth century and this, together with the national obsession with physical fitness, hygiene, health and maternity clearly influenced Rowntrees' thinking and policy. Beginning in 1902 with weekly evening lessons in swimming and gymnastics the firm made early, if not extensive, provisions for women's physical recreations. For a fee of 2*d.* a lesson, plus an additional penny for the hire of a costume and towel, enthusiasts could enjoy the health benefits and acquire proficiency in the 'useful art' of swimming on Wednesday evenings at the municipal baths. With the opening of the New Yearsley Baths in 1909, a gift from the Rowntree firm to the citizens of York, the opportunities for women's swimming significantly expanded, as on Tuesday and Friday evenings the new facility was reserved for their exclusive use. Admission to the open-air pool was free but towel and costume hire were a penny each, and the charge for the slipper baths was 3*d.*[45] The Girls' Gymnastics Club also earned the firm's approbation. The club met weekly in the evenings and was instructed primarily in the Swedish system which was designed to promote all-round development and muscular strength. 'What elasticity and suppleness of movement is secured,' enthused a member of the Social Department staff in reference to the physical benefits of the gymnastics class, 'what grace of movement; what increased stores of health, giving added resistance to any disease and especially to lung troubles.' [46] The training that Swedish drill gave in discipline, precision, thoroughness and efficiency – qualities which employers and educators often felt the working classes sorely lacked and which descriptions of the club's annual demonstrations highlighted – was an equally if not more valuable aspect of the system. 'In comparing the display [1904] with that of the two or three previous years,' ran one account in the *Cocoa Works' Magazine*, 'we may note a marked improvement in the discipline of the class. There was no whispering or fidgetting [sic] or self-consciousness'; 'precision and good-timekeeping (a quality more difficult to secure with girls than with boys), was the feature of the evening,' commented another of the 1902 spectacle.[47]

Rowntrees' sponsorship of these two physical activities, especially

Swedish gymnastics, underlined the hegemonic cast of the firm's recreational philosophies and provisions. Swimming recommended itself to middle-class reformers as an appropriate recreation for the working classes because it combined utility, health and hygiene. Swedish gymnastics served similarly pragmatic ends and in addition was imbued with a powerful ideology of racial betterment, social control, moral uplift and motherhood. Martina Bergman-Osterberg, the Swedish system's most eloquent propagandist, frequently spoke to these themes. She argued that Swedish gymnastics provided the best possible training for motherhood and that the progress of the Anglo-Saxon race had to begin with a healthy, strong and pure womanhood. Bergman-Osterberg's concern with invigorating England's womanhood did not extend to factory workers. Though she had first made a reputation for herself and the gymnastic system she espoused in working with board school children in London, by 1887 Bergman-Osterberg had decided that the working classes were not the best material for national and racial regeneration. However, through the medium of middle-class graduates of the 'tight little specialist empire' [48] of women's physical education colleges established between 1885 and the First World War (Bergman-Osterberg's college in Hampstead, which was later relocated to Dartford, was the first and arguably most influential of these), Swedish gymnastics were brought to the working classes. The instructor for the first women's class at Rowntrees was a Miss Procter who had trained for two years with Bergman-Osterberg, and in 1909 when the firm appointed the first full-time mistresses of gymnastics and hygiene to their staff, one was a graduate of the Anstey Physical Training College in Birmingham, and the other a graduate of Dunfermline Physical Training College. By this time gymnastics was no longer simply within the realm of Cocoa Works' recreation, but was a core element in the educational programme developed for female employees under the age of seventeen (this shift is discussed in more detail below). In fact, from 1909 gymnastics was the only subject at the works' Domestic School which girls studied in each of the three years they attended, something which testifies to the high regard in which it was held by the firm's directors. [49]

The arrival of the specialist trained physical education mistress facilitated the development of another facet of women's recreation at the Cocoa Works: team games. By the early years of the twentieth century sports such as hockey, cricket, lacrosse, netball and rounders had been popularized at Oxbridge women's colleges and at many elite girls' schools, and it was generally acknowledged that athletic games should be an integral part of the upper- and middle-class schoolgirl's curriculum. Despite criticism from some quarters that girls and women who played vigorous sports risked masculinization, or nervous and physical enervation and damage, progressive educators were able to represent team games as a valuable complement to the training provided by gymnastics. Games 'produced beauty, grace, mental lucidity, quickness, steady nerves and good health, and better than anything else, imparted self-control, endurance, patience, courage, resourcefulness, modesty, generosity, unselfishness and the ability to command and obey'. Furthermore, while Kathleen McCrone points out that the ethos of girls' and women's games lacked the jingoistic overtones found in male sports at this time, a eugenic strain was to be heard in the rhetoric of some proponents who appealed to the role games could play in preparing healthy and hearty wives and mothers of the imperial race.[50] There is little historical research on working-class women's sport of this type, but what there is suggests that industrial workers in the North of England were among the first to play organized team games, and that hockey was the game of choice. The Northwestern textile towns led the way organizationally with a hockey league by 1910, and it was around the same time that two of the Domestic School mistresses introduced the game at the Rowntree factory. By its second season, the Girls' Hockey Club had approximately thirty members who paid an annual subscription of two shillings. Practices and matches were held on Saturday afternoons on a pitch adjoining the works, and in its 1912–13 season the team's competitive schedule included both home and away games against ten other clubs in the York vicinity. A girls' cricket club was established in 1912, too, but its competition did not extend beyond the factory.[51]

Relative both to the more obviously utilitarian activities of swimming and gymnastics, however, and to boys' and men's sport at the Cocoa Works, the opportunity to play competitive sport came only latterly and to a limited extent to most of Rowntrees' female employees. Formally constituted clubs and facilities for association football, cricket, lawn tennis and croquet had been established by 1897, and for bowling, cycling, and boating and swimming by 1902. It was not until 1911 and 1912, respectively, that the girls' hockey and cricket clubs were founded. For the men's sports of cricket and association football, there was an elaborate and extensive structure of inter-departmental competition as well as several Cocoa Works' representative teams, but there was no parallel inter-works' competition in girls' hockey and cricket, and only one representative team in the former sport. In addition, while there were no formal barriers to any female employees joining the tennis and croquet or cycling clubs, the gender and occupational status hierarchies which structured work experiences and relationships in the factory operated as an informal mechanism of exclusion. Despite notices in the works' magazine encouraging any employee to join, the female membership of these clubs appears to have been limited to office staff

and members of the Social Department. This *de facto* exclusion of the
vast majority of Rowntrees' female workers reflected and reinforced
widely-accepted, 'commonsense' divisions of gender, class and occupation within the Cocoa Works' culture. There is little direct evidence
to support the notion that this might also explain the relatively low
numbers of female hockey and cricket players, but some source material
suggests that this might have been so. Ruth Slater's reflections on the
striking contrast between her fellow Social Department staff members
and the women who had worked for fifteen years or so on the production line certainly speak to this issue. Slater's office colleagues had
enjoyed the benefits of an extended education, and had the luxury of
choosing from a number of employment opportunities in professions
such as social work. She envied them the 'jolly time' that they had spent
in school and college, their buoyancy of spirits, their 'smooth and fair
and healthy' looks, and she felt keenly the toll that her own early work
experience as a clerical drudge had taken on her health. While she was
in a relatively privileged position in the female occupational hierarchy
of the Cocoa Works, Slater felt a close affinity with the tired, faded-
looking women on the factory floor who, like her, had been constrained
by economic necessity to start work on leaving school at the age of
fourteen. Neither Ruth Slater nor the majority of the girls and women
who worked for Rowntrees had the requisite cultural, material or
physical resources for membership in the firm's sports clubs, and their
under-representation in those organizations reflected this fact.[52]

In one case the exclusion of women was quite deliberate and extended
even to office and Social Department staff. The Boating and Swimming
Club refused to admit women members, and notwithstanding attempts
by opponents to have this policy changed, it remained in effect until
the inter-war period. The Boating and Swimming Club represented
the more extreme wing of male conservatism at the Cocoa Works, but
every aspect of the factory's recreational life was penetrated by gender
politics. In activities in which the body and physicality were central,
the dynamics of power and control were played out in a singularly
heightened way. Each practice, match, prize-giving, speech and account
of these social practices was an occasion for the representation and
reproduction of dominant cultural meanings about women and men.
Women's gymnastic displays were 'pretty entertainments' which demonstrated not only the skill but also the 'grace' of the performers, and
the 'taste and industry' of those who had made the 'becoming costumes
of dark blue and scarlet' the gymnasts wore. On the other hand,
photographs of 'the average Cocoa Works' lad' and details of the
girth of his chest, biceps, forearm, calves, and thighs before and after
a course of gymnastics affirmed that bulk, strength and power were
masculine attributes. Similarly, the girls' events at the annual Works'

Sports Day were characterized as a 'picturesque' interlude, a 'welcome touch of relief' in the 'strenuous', serious programme of competition between boys and men. Thus, while the swimming and gymnastics classes and competitive sports provided for Rowntrees' female workers certainly can be seen as advance of a kind, as Jennifer Hargreaves notes of working-class women's physical education and sport more generally in this period, it was a highly qualified advance.[53]

The didactic impulse behind Rowntrees' promotion of recreation at the Cocoa Works is unquestionable; whether or not it had the intended effect is another matter. This is not an issue explored fully here but one or two observations are appropriate. Frequent exhortations and encouragements to employees to participate in clubs and classes indicate that interest and demand were neither high nor sustained. Inducements such as prizes for regular attendance, reductions in subscription fees, and the promise of socials, concerts and outings reinforce this impression, as do attendance figures reported in the *Cocoa Works' Magazine*. The latter suggest that only a very small percentage of the female employees availed themselves of the recreational opportunities Rowntrees offered. Indeed, workers showed considerable particularity in their patronage of social activities. Lectures and classes, no matter how inspiring or utilitarian, were not guaranteed to attract or hold the interest of large numbers, even when leavened – as they usually were – with tea, music and songs, but picnics and outings invariably did. The shifting fortunes of the Girls' Temperance Society illuminate the fastidiousness of its members and of Rowntree workers more generally with respect to their recreation. The decision to hold meeetings in the dinner hour rather than the evening seems to have been an attempt to boost dwindling attendance, but even then, the society found it difficult to compete when alternative attractions were available:

The monthly meeting was held on Friday May 29th ... when Mrs. Thomson kindly came up and gave us a very helpful address ... The fine weather attracted many of the members into the garden, but those who stayed had an equally enjoyable quarter of an hour.[54]

As a number of historians have pointed out, the voluntary nature of this kind of rational recreation scheme significantly lessened any educational or ideological impact that it might have had. After all, middle- and upper-class employers and reformers brought very different agendas to such enterprises than the working classes who were supposed to benefit from them.[55] This was clearly a concern at the Rowntree Cocoa Works where, despite the best efforts and intentions of the directors, workers did not always appreciate or take advantage of the opportunities and facilities provided. The opening of the Cocoa Works'

Domestic School in September 1905 was a tacit acknowledgment by Rowntrees that if their female employees were to be moulded into exemplars of working-class womanhood, then education and compulsion had to be conjoined with recreation and choice:

> The contention that factory life unfits a girl for home duties, by allowing her neither the time nor opportunity for learning what is necessary for the management of a home has decided the Directors to provide the school and a staff of teachers, as a means by which to remedy this defect.[56]

Some of the language used in the works' magazine to describe the purpose and manner of operation of the school implies that attendance was voluntary, but this was not the case. For two hours a week all girls between the ages of fourteen and seventeen – approximately 650 in all in the school's first year – were required to attend classes in cookery, dressmaking, and health and hygiene. A cookery school, comprising a kitchen equipped with gas and oven ranges, and a lecture room were built to accommodate the classes, and two teachers trained in domestic science were employed. The Domestic School operated under the supervision of the Education Department and was therefore subject to its inspection.[57] Joseph Rowntree frequently expressed his personal interest in the school's success:

> I look upon these classes as exceedingly valuable ... A knowledge of cooking and the selection of economical foodstuffs and diets, of dressmaking, and of what perhaps is as important as anything, of the laws of health, including the management of young children, may be invaluable to those who in the future will be responsible for the management of homes.[58]

Over the next seven years, the firm expended more and more resources on the domestic education of its female workers. In 1909 the curriculum was expanded to include physical training and by 1911 some 1,100 girls received three hours of instruction a week in dressmaking, cookery, housewifery and gymnastics. Also in 1911, Rowntrees began constructing a large block of facilities opposite the main entrance to the factory on Haxby Road. Most of the ground floor of the New Block was taken up with classrooms, a lecture room, a concert room, clubrooms, gymnasia, changing rooms, showers and baths, and offices for the teaching staff. Dining facilities (segregated according to gender and occupational status) and a large kitchen occupied the first and second floors of the building. The Domestic School now boasted a staff of a headmistress and eleven assistant mistresses, all fully trained and qualified in the subjects they taught. Its accommodation consisted of two cookery classrooms, two dressmaking classrooms, a 48-foot square gymnasium, a large dressing room with 20 slipper baths, and two model cottages, designed and built for the purpose of teaching 'practical housewifery'.[59]

The new buildings were a powerful affirmation of Rowntrees' commitment to fitting the girls and women in their employment for their prescribed role in a society ordered by gender. The Cocoa Works themselves were viewed by civic, religious and educational leaders as a model community, a centre of family life, a place in which there was a common life and spirit. Within that community, everything that was done – the organization of the work, the creation of wealth, the earning of wages, the recreational and educational activities – was directed to reinforcing and reproducing a stable social organism in which every individual had her or his place and role to play.[60] Speaking on the occasion of the formal opening of the New Block in June 1913, the Archbishop of York confirmed the place allotted to women in this scheme and the role that Rowntrees played in moulding them for it:

> I will venture to say ... that whatever honour they may receive, or whatever positions of prominence they may gain in the Works here ... the greatest honour that can possibly await them is to become a wife, and that there is an even greater honour that may in God's providence await them, and that is to become a mother. There is ... nothing ... that is more well worth doing than giving our girls the best possible training in the greatest of all arts, housecraft, in the making of that one article upon which everything else in the community depends, the making of the healthy and the happy home.[61]

Hugh Cunningham has characterized the rational recreation movement of the mid-Victorian period as 'almost exclusively ... men dealing with men'.[62] By the late Victorian period this was clearly not the case. In the last quarter of the nineteenth century, upper- and middle-class reformers concerned with the impact that women's waged work seemed to be having on working-class homes and families made a conscious effort to intervene and provide working girls and women with some training in the practice and ideologies of domesticity. Rational recreation was a significant aspect of this intervention. For these reformers, the answer to the question of how the improvident and ineffective working-class wife and mother was produced was clear. To begin with, her employment in shops, factories and workshops provided her with no experience or training in domestic skills. Then, despite her lack of preparation for it, she rushed into an imprudent marriage, the demands and circumstances of which, after the hustle and bustle and companionship of her working days, seemed tame and monotonous in comparison. Uninterested and unschooled in the domestic duties which should have filled her days, the young working woman thus became the indolent, ignorant, working-class 'woman of leisure' who passed her time gossiping in doorways, drinking, gambling, and raising a future generation of similarly inept mothers and unemployable sons.[63] Clubs, socials, and the host of other recreational activities that upper- and middle-class reformers sponsored were meant to break this pattern, to provide a different, more worthy model of womanhood for the working classes to emulate.

The Rowntree recreational and educational programmes were conceived, offered and widely accepted as a valuable exercise in this kind of social intervention. They were not unique, as Kathleen McCrone's recent and important article on women's sport, class and gender in this period shows. At the Bournville model factory near Birmingham, the Cadbury firm instituted a very similar system of sports, clubs and classes. McCrone comments on the distinctly public-school rhetoric and ethos embedding the programmes at both the York Cocoa Works and Bournville. In theory and in poetry, at least, she writes, 'the ideal Bournville girl ... was very much like the ideal public school girl, although the twain were destined rarely to meet'.[64] The analogy holds to some extent for the ideal Rowntrees' girl, particularly after the establishment of hockey and cricket clubs in 1911 and 1912. Photographs of uniformed players and tunic-clad gymnasts; articles praising the keenness, energy, enthusiasm and spirit displayed in their matches, competitions and practices; colours, badges and cups awarded for success – the rhetoric, rituals and symbols were much more redolent of the public school than of a prosaic factory in the North of England. But what was most significant about the manner in which the *Cocoa Works' Magazine*, the Social Department and teaching staff, and the Rowntree directors represented the girls and women at the Cocoa Works was not that it cast them in the image of the public schoolgirl but that it effectively obliterated their identity as factory workers. This was crucial to the process of producing an exemplary working-class womanhood, of shaping a gender identity consonant with long and widely held beliefs about what was fitting, proper and necessary for the working-class woman; and what was fitting, proper and necessary for the working-class woman was that she should be able to cook her husband a decent dinner, wait upon him with a solicitous and charming manner, manage his home, and bear and nurture his children.[65]

Rowntrees worked hard at encouraging their female employees to assume characteristics which identified them primarily as wives and mothers, but they were not able fully to resolve the contradictions that the wage-earning working woman represented. The sources upon which this research is based only hint at these tensions, but they were there, as Benjamin Seebohm Rowntree acknowledged. Writing in the 1920s, Rowntree expressed his belief that a considerable number of the female workers enjoyed, appreciated and benefited from the domestic classes, but he admitted that 'a few take little interest and it hardly seems to affect them'. Furthermore, although the girls found the classes a pleasant change from work, 'the piece-workers cannot be persuaded that they do not lose money by attending, and some of these would absent themselves if attendance were not compulsory'.[66] The experiences of several women who worked at the Cocoa Works in the inter-war period suggest that Rowntree's reading of the equivocal impact of the classes, and certainly the recreational clubs, was on the mark. Ethel Thompson had no involvement with any of the recreational or sports clubs and knew no one among her workmates who did. Her only memory of the gymnastics classes was that there was not enough time to take the mandatory bath after the lesson, 'so we just pretended to splash around in it ... got back into our dresses and overalls and scampered ... back to the cardboard box mill'. Ethel's most indelible memory of the factory was its discipline – enforced by stern and unsympathetic chargehands ('they were all "company people"') – and the exhausting, unremitting work of the production line. Neither experience predisposed her to spend any more time or energy at the works than she had to: 'I was too whacked, poor little skinny thing, too whacked after my full day ... you didn't want anything more to do with Rowntrees, a lot of us.' Ruby Pearson also remembers the strict discipline and hard work but appreciated the firm's attempt to provide for recreation. She talks fondly of Greek dancing and music for the girls, and the large recreational room in which they gathered during their dinner hour for dancing or simply relaxing. The New Yearsley Baths were a real boon for Ruby who, like many working people in the period, had no bathing facilities in her home: 'it was super having that hot bath once a week, and a swim in hot weather'. Joan Sadler was appreciative of the weekly gymnastics classes for much the same reason, but also because she valued what she learned: 'We used to enjoy the keep-fit sessions [her term] because they provided baths as well and lots of us didn't have a bathroom in the home ... I remember what an extremely good keep-fit teacher we had ... she really was a fine person and told you things that I've certainly remembered for the rest of my days.' Like Ruby Pearson, Joan had nothing to do with any of the girls' sports clubs, in fact she has no memory of them at all, but she recalls that there were many sports teams and clubs for the male workers. For Joan, too, 'it was the discipline there that I remember more than anything ... [it was] a continual grind ... you were so pleased when it was half past five'.[67]

The Rowntree firm's identification of the girls and women in its employment as prospective wives and mothers first, and only secondarily as workers, was open to challenge because the female factory worker was a deeply contradictory figure; the firm's recreational and educational programmes can be read as an attempt at resolving the tensions she embodied. But if the explicit concern was fitting Rowntree workers to play the roles which late Victorian and Edwardian society demanded of them, it was not coincidental that these same programmes also enabled the firm to characterize their exploitation of a young, cheap and malleable labour force in a wholly positive light. Mediating characterization and concern was a web of historically produced, hierarchical social and economic relations between women and men which, while complex and variable, endured nonetheless. At the York Cocoa Works these relations took the form of a patriarchy in which recreation and education were understood as mechanisms for shaping the gender identities of the girls and women employed there. The impact that Rowntrees' training in womanhood had on those who experienced it is a topic for future research.

Notes

1. Benjamin Seebohm Rowntree, *The Human Factor in Business* (Longmans, Green & Co., London: 1921), p. 101.
2. There is a rich scholarship on the historical and cultural processes shaping gender ideologies and practices. Recent works include Anita Levy, *Other Women: The Writing of Class, Race and Gender, 1832–1898* (Princeton U.P., Princeton: 1991); Michael Roper and John Tosh (eds), *Manful Assertions: Masculinities in Britain since 1800* (Routledge, London: 1991); Desley Deacon, *Managing Gender: The State, the New Middle Class and Women Workers 1830–1930* (Oxford U.P., Oxford: 1989); Carol Smart (ed.), *Regulating Womanhood: Historical Essays on Marriage, Motherhood and Sexuality* (Routledge, London: 1992); Franca Iacovetta and Mariana Valverde (eds), *Gender Conflicts: New Essays in Women's History* (University of Toronto Press, Toronto: 1992).

   On the formation of gender ideologies in nineteenth-century England see Leonorre Davidoff and Catherine Hall, *Family Fortunes: Men and Women of the English Middle Classes 1780–1850* (Hutchinson, London: 1987); Catherine Hall, 'The early formation of Victorian domestic ideology', in Sandra Burnam (ed.), *Fit Work for Women* (St Martin's Press, London: 1979), pp. 21–31.

   For influences upon and gender ideologies among the working classes see Catherine Hall, 'The tale of Samuel and Jemima: gender and working-class culture in nineteenth-century England', in Harvey J. Kaye and

Keith McClelland (eds), *E. P. Thompson: Critical Perspectives* (Temple U.P., Philadelphia: 1990), pp. 86–99; Harold Benenson, 'Victorian sexual ideology and Marx's theory of the working class', *International Labor and Working Class History* 25 (1984), pp. 1–23; Wally Seccombe, 'Patriarchy stabilized: the construction of the male breadwinner wage norm in nine-teenth-century Britain', *Social History* 11 (1986), pp. 53–76; Keith McClelland, 'Some thoughts on masculinity and the "representative ar-tisan" in Britain, 1850–1880', *Gender & History* 1 (Summer 1989), pp. 166–8, 172–4; Robert Gray, 'Factory legislation and the gendering of jobs in the north of England, 1830–1860', *Gender & History* 5 (Spring 1993), pp. 63–7; Carol Dyhouse, *Girls Growing Up in Late Victorian and Edwardian England* (Routledge & Kegan Paul, London: 1981), pp. 79–114; June Purvis, *Hard Lessons: The Lives and Education of Working-class Women in Nineteenth-Century England* (Polity Press, Cambridge: 1989), pp. 63–70.

3. On work, see Harriet Bradley, *Men's Work, Women's Work: A Sociological History of the Sexual Division of Labour in Employment* (Polity Press, Cam-bridge: 1989), pp. 41–2; Louise A. Tilly and Joan W. Scott, *Women, Work, and Family* (Holt, Rhinehart & Winston, New York: 1978), pp. 12–24, 30–60, 64–77, 123–36; Ivy Pinchbeck, *Women Workers and the Industrial Revolution, 1750–1850* (Frank Cass & Co., London: 1930; reprint edn, 1969), pp. 7–19, 53–65, 111–21, 282–4.

    On politics, see Benenson, 'Victorian sexual ideology', pp. 6–7; Anna Clark, 'Queen Caroline and the sexual politics of popular culture in London, 1820', *Representations* 31 (Summer 1990), pp. 50–1, 62; Ruth L. Smith and Deborah M. Valenze, 'Mutuality and marginality: liberal moral theory and working-class women in nineteenth-century England', *Signs: Journal of Women in Culture and Society* 13 (Winter 1988), pp. 286–90; Edward P. Thompson, 'The moral economy of the English crowd in the eighteenth century', *Past and Present* 50 (February 1971), pp. 115–19; Iowerth Prothero, *Artisans and Politics in Early Nineteenth-Century London: John Gast and his Times* (Dawson, Folkestone: 1979), p. 160; Dorothy Thompson, 'Women and nineteenth-century radical politics', in Juliet Mitchell and Anne Oakley (eds), *The Rights and Wrongs of Women* (Penguin, Harmondsworth: 1976), pp. 136–8; Dorothy Thomp-son, *The Chartists* (Temple Smith, London: 1984), pp. 120–51; Barbara Taylor, *Eve and the New Jerusalem: Socialism and Feminism in the Nineteenth Century* (Virago, London: 1983), pp. 261–75; Jutta Schwarzkopf, *Women in the Chartist Movement* (St Martin's Press, New York: 1991); Hill, 'The tale of Samuel and Jemima', pp. 84–5.

    On recreation and sport, see Thompson, *The Chartists*, pp. 120–51; Taylor, *Eve and the New Jerusalem*, pp. 217–37; Shirley Maxwell Reekie, 'The history of sport and recreation for women in Britain, 1700–1850' (PhD dissertation, Ohio State University, 1982), pp. 33–152, 166–70.

4. Sonya A. Rose, 'Gender antagonism and class conflict: exclusionary strategies of male trade unionists in nineteenth-century Britain', *Social History* 13 (May 1988), pp. 196–8; Ivy Pinchbeck, *Women Workers and*

the Industrial Revolution (Cass, London: 1969), pp. 19, 59–60, 62, 66, 86, 100, 126, 275, 289, 307, 315; Neil Smelser, *Social Change in the Industrial Revolution: An Application of Theory to the British Cotton Industry* (University of Chicago Press, Chicago: 1959), p. 232; Taylor, *Eve and the New Jerusalem*, pp. 107, 205; Cynthia Cockburn, *Brothers: Male Dominance and Technological Change* (Pluto Press, London: 1983); Sally Alexander, 'Women, class and sexual difference: some reflections on the writing of a feminist history', *History Workshop Journal* 17 (Spring 1984), p. 137; John Gillis, *For Better, For Worse: British Marriages, 1600 to the Present* (Oxford U.P., Oxford: 1985), pp. 231–59. The quotation is from Barbara Drake, *Women in Trade Unions* (Virago, London: 1984), p. 16.

5. *The Pioneer*, 22 March 1834, quoted in Taylor, *Eve and the New Jerusalem*, p. 100.

6. John Watkins, 'Address to the Women of England', *The English Chartist Circular* 1. 13 (1841), p. 49.

7. *The Working Man: A Weekly Record of Social and Industrial Progress* NS 2. 24 (15 December 1866), p. 238; Thomas Wright, *The Great Unwashed* (Tinsley Bros., London: 1868; reprint edn, Augustus M. Kelley, New York: 1970), pp. 31, 190. See also Hugh Cunningham, *Leisure in the Industrial Revolution c. 1780–c. 1880* (St Martin's Press, New York: 1980), pp. 129–30.

8. *The Working Man* 1. 21 (26 May 1866), p. 327. For a discussion of the nineteenth-century debate on women's work see Judy Lown, *Women and Industrialization: Gender at Work in Nineteenth-Century England* (Polity Press, Cambridge: 1990), pp. 172–209.

9. *The Working Man* 1. 4 (27 January 1866), p. 57. See also *Parliamentary Papers (Commons), 1867–68*, vol. 17, C 6867, 'Report of the Commission on the Employment of Children, Young Persons, and Women in Agriculture', Appendix Part I, xviii, xxiii, xxvi; *Parliamentary Papers (Commons), 1893*, vol. 23, C 6894, 'Report of the Commission on Labour', p. 102.

10. 'Report of the Commission on Agriculture', 1867, xxiii, xxvi. Opinions on the suitability of agricultural work for girls and women, and its effect on their moral character and wifely and maternal abilities varied considerably according to region, among the middle and upper classes, and among working people themselves. See *ibid.*, x, xiii–xiv, xviii, xxiii–xxiv. For an account of a similar debate in coal mining see Angela V. John, *By the Sweat of their Brow: Women Workers at Victorian Coal Mines* (Croom Helm, London: 1980), pp. 36–65, 167–222.

11. *The Working Man* 1. 4 (27 January 1866), p. 57.

12. *The Working Man* 1. 23 (9 June 1866), p. 362.

13. The quotation is from 'Report of the Commission on Agriculture', 1867, p. 146. On the repression and reform of popular recreation, see Robert W. Malcolmson, *Popular Recreations in English Society 1700–1850* (Cambridge U.P., Cambridge: 1973); Peter Bailey, *Leisure and Class in Victorian England: Rational Recreation and the Contest for Control* (Routledge, London: 1978).

14. Wright, *The Great Unwashed*, pp. 37–41, 48.

15. On the importance of women's contribution to the family economy, see Elizabeth A. M. Roberts, 'Women's strategies, 1840–1940', in Jane Lewis (ed.), *Labour and Love: Women's Experiences of Home and Family, 1850–1940* (Basil Blackwell, Oxford: 1986), pp. 223–47; Diana Gittens, 'Marital status, work and kinship, 1850–1930', in Lewis (ed.), *Labour and Love*, pp. 249–67.

For contemporary accounts of the inadequacy of working-class wages see Benjamin Seebohm Rowntree, *Poverty: A Study of Town Life* (Longmans, Green & Co., London: 1901; 2nd edn, 1922); Margaret Llewellyn Davies (ed.), *Maternity: Letters from Working-Women* (G. Bell & Sons, London: 1915); Magdalen S. R. Reeves, *Round About a Pound a Week* (G. Bell & Sons, London: 1913).

For different interpretations of the family wage issue see Hilary Land, 'The family wage', *Feminist Review* 6 (Autumn 1980), pp. 55–77; Jane Humphries, 'Class struggle and the persistence of the working-class family', *Cambridge Journal of Economics* 1. 3 (1977), pp. 241–58; Harold Benenson, 'The "family wage" and working women's consciousness in Britain, 1880–1914', *Politics and Society* 19. 1 (March 1991), pp. 71–108.

16. Kathleen E. McCrone, 'Class, gender, and English women's sport, c. 1890–1914', *Journal of Sport History* 18 (Spring 1991), p. 165; Dyhouse, *Girls Growing Up*, pp. 104–14; Albinia Hobart-Hamden, 'The working girl of today', *The Nineteenth Century* 43 (May 1898), pp. 724–30. The quotations are from Lily H. Montagu, 'Popular amusements for working girls', *National Council of Women of Great Britain Handbook: The Official Report of the Central Conference of Women Workers*, 1902 (University Microfilm, Ann Arbor, MI: 1980), pp. 154–5 (hereafter cited as *NCWGB, Report of Central Conference*).

17. Dyhouse, *Girls Growing Up*, p. 108.

18. *Girls Growing Up*, pp. 109, 110.

19. Robert R. Dolling, *Ten Years in a Portsmouth Slum* (Swann & Sonnenschein, London: 1898), pp. 38–48.

20. Kathleen M. Townend, 'Methods of recreation as they affect the causes of intemperance amongst women', *NCWGB*, Report of Central Conference, 1894, p. 41.

21. Townend, 'Methods of recreation', p. 140.

22. 'Methods of recreation', pp. 140–1.

23. Dolling, *Ten Years in a Portsmouth Slum*, pp. 41–3.

24. *The Englishwoman's Review* (15 January 1900), pp. 67–8.

25. Edward Cadbury, M. Cecile Matheson and George Shann, *Women's Work and Wages: A Phase of Life in an Industrial City* (University of Chicago Press, Chicago: 1907), pp. 241–2; Clara E. Collet, 'Women's work', in Charles Booth (ed.), *Life and Labour of the People of London* (Macmillan, London: 1893), IV, pp. 319, 320–2.

26. Cadbury, Matheson and Shann, *Women's Work*, p. 241.

27. Cadbury, Matheson and Shann, *Women's Work*, p. 242.

28. For a detailed examination of the national efficiency, imperialism and maternity debate, see Anna Davin, 'Imperialism and motherhood', *History Workshop Journal* 5 (1978), pp. 9–65 (p. 12). See also Sheila Fletcher,

Women First: The Female Tradition in English Physical Education 1880–1980 (Athlone Press, London: 1984), pp. 22–4, 25–7.

29. On contemporary criticisms of working-class women's abilities as wives and mothers, see Dyhouse, *Girls Growing Up*, pp. 79–105; Jane Lewis, *The Politics of Motherhood: Child and Maternal Welfare in England, 1900–1939* (Croom Helm, London: 1908), pp. 61–88, 89–113; Davin, 'Imperialism and motherhood', pp. 24–8, 36–8.

30. Charles Feinstein *York, 1831–1981: 150 Years of Scientific and Social Change* (The Ebor Press, York: 1981), pp. 123–5; Gillian Wagner, *The Chocolate Conscience* (Chatto & Windus, London: 1987), pp. 24–30; *The Cocoa Works' Magazine* 24 (February 1904), pp. 147–8 (hereafter cited as *CWM*).

31. Asa Briggs, *Social Thought and Social Action: A Study of the Work of Seebohm Rowntree, 1871–1954* (Longmans, London: 1961), pp. 86 (quote), 87, 91; Charles Dellheim, 'The creation of a company culture: Cadburys, 1861–1931', *American Historical Review* 92 (February 1987), p. 14; McCrone, 'Class, gender, and English women's sport', pp. 172–9; Wagner, *The Chocolate Conscience*, pp. 72.

    Robert Fitzgerald argues that the kind of industrial welfare usually associated with Quaker families like the Rowntrees and Cadburys was not exceptional. See Robert Fitzgerald, *British Labour Management and Industrial Welfare 1846–1939* (Croom Helm, London: 1988), pp. 17, 19–20, 157, 180, 181, 186. For the development of industrial welfare, women's recreation and sport in the United States, see Monys Ann Hagen, 'Industrial harmony through sports: the industrial recreation movement and women's sports' (PhD dissertation, University of Wisconsin-Madison, 1990).

32. *CWM* 1 (March 1902), p. 2.

33. *CWM* 24 (February 1904), pp. 147–8; 136 (June 1913), p. 1500 (quote); Bradley, *Men's Work, Women's Work*, pp. 164–6; Chris Smith, John Child and Michael Rowlinson, *Reshaping Work: The Cadbury Experience* (Cambridge U.P., Cambridge: 1990), pp. 10–12, 16, 23, 42–8, 61.

34. Rowntree, *The Human Factor in Business*, pp. 121–6, 106–7, 109–10; Fitzgerald, *British Labour Management*, pp. 14, 15, 17, 181; *CWM* 1 (March 1902), p. 10; 4 (June 1902), p. 46; 17 (July 1903), p. 62; 29 (July 1904), p. 64; 35 (January 1905), p. 143; 42 (August 1905), p. 69.

35. McCrone, 'Class, gender, and English women's sport', pp. 173–4; *CWM* 24 (February 1904), pp. 147–8; 51 (May 1906), p. 179. 57 (November 1906), p. 253. On gender segregation in the confectionery industry see Bradley, *Men's Work, Women's Work*, pp. 164–6; Smith, Child and Rowlinson, *Reshaping Work*, pp. 40–8.

36. *CWM* 49 (March 1906), p. 157.

37. *CWM* 31 (September 1904), p. 79; 57 (November 1906), p. 259; 59 (January 1907), pp. 287, 288.

38. *CWM* 62 (April 1907), pp. 327–9.

39. *CWM* 78 (August 1908), p. 57.

40. *CWM* 62 (April 1907), p. 329.

41. *CWM* 4 (February 1902), p. 46; 12 (February 1903), p. 134; 15 (May 1903), p. 35; 24 (February 1904), p. 140; 59 (January 1907), p. 287.

42. *CWM* 10 (December 1902), p. 111.

43. *CWM* 35 (January 1905), p. 134.

44. *CWM* pp. 133–4; 33 (November 1904), pp. 104–6 (quote); 35 (January 1905), pp. 133–4.

45. W. David Smith, *Stretching their Bodies: The History of Physical Education* (David & Charles, Newton Abbot: 1974), pp. 79–80; Fletcher, *Women First*, pp. 33, 35, 39, 55; *CWM* 1 (March 1902), p. 12; 7 (September 1902), p. 84; 12 (February 1903), p. 144; 18 (August 1903), p. 76; 29 (July 1904), p. 64; 43 (September 1905), pp. 78–9; 52 (June 1906), p. 193; 63 (May 1907), p. 348; 75 (May 1908), p. 531; 87 (May 1909), p. 698; 88 (June 1909), p. 707; 116 (November, 1911), p. 1171.

On physical training and moral and social reform in the United States, see Dominick Cavallo, *Muscles and Morals: Organised Playgrounds and Urban Reform, 1880–1920* (University of Pennsylvania Press, Philadelphia: 1981).

46. *CWM* 10 (December 1902), p. 130.

47. *CWM* 1 (March 1902), pp. 10, 12; 2 (April 1902), p. 22; 4 (June 1902), p. 41; 8 (October 1902), p. 93; 10 (December 1902), p. 130 (second quote); 15 (May 1903), p. 33; 18 (August 1903), p. 76; 22 (December 1903), p. 122; 24 (February 1904), p. 145; 26 (April 1904), p. 21; 27 (May 1904), p. 33 (first quote); 46 (December 1905), p. 115; 57 (November 1906), p. 259; 60 (February 1907), p. 301; 85 (March 1909), p. 665; 94 (December 1909), pp. 803–4. See also McCrone, 'Class, gender, and English women's sport', p. 163; Jennifer Hargreaves, *Sporting Females: Critical Issues in the History and Sociology of Women's Sports* (Routledge, London: 1994), pp. 48–9, 58, 69–74, 82.

48. Fletcher, *Women First*, p. 4.

49. For the influence of Bergman-Osterberg on the professional development of women's physical education, see Fletcher, *Women First*, pp. 4–6, 17–55; Kathleen E. McCrone, *Playing the Game: Sport and the Physical Emancipation of English Women 1870–1914* (University of Kentucky Press, Lexington: 1988), pp. 73, 104–22, 223; Hargreaves, *Sporting Females*, pp. 49, 69–79, 80, 82, 83, 85–6.

For an account of the development of elementary physical education in England in general (and one in which Bergman-Osterberg's role is under-emphasized), see Smith, *Stretching their Bodies*, pp. 72–121. *CWM* 1 (March 1902), p. 10; 94 (December 1909), pp. 799, 803–4; 103 (September 1910), p. 933.

50. McCrone, *Playing the Game*, pp. 75 (quote), 21–99, 127–53.

51. McCrone, 'Class, gender, and English women's sport', p. 176; *The Hockey Field* (13 April 1911), p. 414; (19 October 1911), p. 9; (9 April 1914), p. 398. I am grateful to Dr McCrone for sharing this material with me.

While there are indications that working-class women were forming hockey clubs and establishing leagues, preliminary research on the Oldham Hockey Club, one of the founder members of the 1910 Ladies' Hockey League, shows that one player received a university education, and that another later became the secretary of a local ladies' golf club. *CWM* 116 (September 1911), p. 1156; 117 (November 1911), p. 1175;

118 (December 1911), p. 1186; 122 (April 1912), p. 1276; 123 (May 1912), p. 1295; 126 (August 1912), p. 1338; 128 (October 1912), p. 1374; 131 (January 1913), p. 1430.

52. *CWM* 1 (March 1902), pp. 7–9; 2 (April 1902), pp. 21–2, 29–30; 4 (June 1902), p. 37; 6 (August 1902), p. 68; 8 (October 1902), p. 86; 12 (February 1903), p. 142; 26 (April 1904), pp. 15, 23; 29 (July 1904), p. 63; 38 (May 1905), p. 31; 40 (June 1905), p. 46; 50 (April 1906), pp. 167, 168; 108 (February 1911), pp. 1028–30; 110 (April 1910), pp. 1063–5, 1071; 113 (July 1911), pp. 1111–14; 122 (April 1912), pp. 1266–8; 146 (April 1914), p. 1664; 147 (May 1914), pp. 1670–1.

Ruth Slater was employed by Rowntrees as a welfare worker in 1916. Conscious of the fact that the Cocoa Works were well planned and equipped, and that some pains had been taken to ensure that the factory was a pleasant place in which to work, she nonetheless found her duties and surroundings dreary, the noise and smell oppressive, and the long hours exhausting. See Tierl Thompson (ed.), *Dear Girl: The Diaries and Letters of Two Working Women 1897–1917* (The Women's Press, London: 1987), pp. 287, 289, 291, 296, 300.

53. *CWM* 2 (April 1902), p. 22; 4 (June 1902), p. 41; 15 (May 1903), p. 33; 27 (May 1904), p. 33; 63 (May 1907), p. 342; 81 (November 1908), p. 617; 85 (March 1909), pp. 663–4; 92 (October 1909), p. 768; 93 (November 1909), pp. 781–3; 148 (June 1914), p. 1684; Hargreaves, *Sporting Females*, p. 80.

54. *CWM* 16 (June 1903), p. 44.

55. Some indication of the conflicts surrounding recreational provisions at the Cocoa Works can be found in notices such as the following: 'In consequence of the serious damage that has been done to the hedges and fences surrounding the park and playing fields, the Directors wish it to be known that the use of the playing fields in the evenings is strictly forbidden, unless permission has been obtained, and anyone found trespassing in there, or in the other grass fields belonging to the firm, is liable to be prosecuted.' See *CWM* 4 (June 1902), p. 39. See also *CWM* 6 (August 1902), p. 68; 13 (March 1903), p. 17; 15 (May 1903), p. 31; 15 (May 1903), p. 48.

For the mixed results of rational recreation schemes and working-class resistance to them see Bailey, *Leisure and Class in Victorian England*, pp. 50–1, 101, 171, 175; Richard Holt, *Sport and the British: A Modern History* (Clarendon Press, Oxford: 1989), pp. 136–48; Stephen Jones, *Workers at Play: A Social and Economic History of Leisure 1918–1939* (Routledge & Kegan Paul, London: 1986), pp. 63, 70, 88, 177.

For a somewhat different interpretation of the extent to which middle- and upper-class advocates of rational recreation were able to influence working-class culture, see John Hargreaves, *Sport, Power and Culture: A Social and Historical Analysis of Popular Sports in Britain* (Polity Press, Cambridge: 1986), pp. 6, 27, 206–7, 210.

56. *CWM* 42 (August 1905), p. 74.

57. *CWM* 43 (September 1905), pp. 78–9; 58 (December 1906), p. 263; 82 (December 1908), p. 620.

58. *CWM* 58 (December 1906), p. 263.
59. *CWM* 94 (December 1909), pp. 799, 803–4; 103 (September 1910), p. 933; 108 (February 1911), pp. 1034–5; 113 (July 1911), pp. 1127; 114 (August 1911), p. 1133; 117 (November 1911), p. 1167; 118 (December 1911), p. 1194; 121 (March 1912), p. 1258; 130 (December 1912), p. 1382; 136 (June 1913), pp. 1508, 1510–11.
60. *CWM* 136 (June 1913), pp. 1501–7.
61. *CWM* 136 (June 1913), pp. 1505–6.
62. Cunningham, *Leisure in the Industrial Revolution*, p. 129.
63. Townend, 'Methods of recreation', p. 142; Collet, 'Women's work', p. 318; Cadbury, Matheson and Shann, *Women's Work*, p. 233; Helen Dendy, 'The children of working London', in Bernard Bosanquet (ed.), *Aspects of the Social Problem* (Macmillan, London: 1895), p. 36.
64. McCrone, 'Class, gender, and English women's sport', p. 176.
65. *CWM* 26 (April 1904), p. 15; 116 (September 1911), p. 1156; 117 (November 1911), p. 1175; 118 (December 1911), p. 1186; 122 (April 1912), p. 1276; 123 (May 1912), p. 1295; 126 (August 1912), p. 1338; 128 (October 1912), p. 1374; 131 (January 1913), p. 1430; 136 (June 1913), p. 1506; 139 (September 1913), p. 1547.
66. Rowntree, *The Human Factor*, p. 109.
67. Interviews with Ruby Pearson, Joan Sadler and Ethel Thompson, York, July 1990.

    For an interesting examination of some aspects of the leisure experiences of young working-class women in the inter-war period, see M. Judith Giles, '"Something that bit better": working-class women, domesticity and respectability 1919–39' (PhD dissertation, University of York, 1989), pp. 153–88.

5. Rite of spring: Cup Finals and community in the North of England

Jeff Hill

Ideology, Althusser once remarked, is something that takes place 'behind our backs'. In other words, the social construction of meaning through the signs and symbols that represent our world to us is a process of which we are largely unaware. It is the very 'taken-for-grantedness' of the cultural artefacts – whether films, television programmes, newspapers, sporting events or simply everyday speech – which structure our thoughts and give meaning to our lives that obscures their *ideological* significance.

For millions of (mostly male) followers of association or rugby football the Cup Final is just such a symbol. However measured, its appeal has been immense. Its hold on the male psyche is neatly summed up in the oft-quoted story of the former Prime Minister Harold Wilson who, it is said, carried in his wallet a photograph of the Huddersfield Town Cup-winning side of 1922. Moreover, at the slightest provocation, he would reel off their names. Wilson, of course (as the obituaries following his death in 1995 did not fail to point out) was a man of the people. His own social origins were sufficiently close to the working class for him to have assimilated a culture in which sport – and especially football – had a peculiarly strong place. The connection between working class, football and Cup is an intimate one. The historian Patrick Joyce has described the FA Cup Final, in fact, as 'that most distinctive of proletarian rituals'.[1]

It is this aspect of the Cup Final that makes its cultural *meaning* particularly difficult to penetrate. As with other facets of working-class life it was there to be enjoyed, or endured, not to be analysed. Although there has been a multitude of books and pamphlets commemorating the Cup Final none has attempted to lay bare the meaning of the event to those who held it dear.[2] It is extremely rare to encounter the kind of reflection offered by the writer and academic Fred Inglis, who looked back in his book *The Name of the Game* on a visit as a child to the Cup Final:

The occasion took on for me the shape of an unrepeatable rite – a long train journey, a night in a London hotel, the packed un-precedented ride to the stadium, and then the unbelievable numbers of people. After all this the football: the goals and the sacred cup were the operatic climax of two days of the most intense, purposeful living I had known.[3]

Such an attempt to record the *personal* experience and meaning of the event is so rare as to make the analysing of Cup Finals by means of such evidence impossible. There is, however, a more commonplace source, from which an idea of the *collective* meaning of the Cup Final might be gleaned.

Each year the newspaper press devoted ample space to reports of the event. The national press, for the most part, confined its attention to the match itself. But the local newspapers of the towns whose teams were competing in the Final offered a far less circumscribed coverage. Until well after the Second World War the local press celebrated its team's appearance in the Cup Final in numerous ways which reveal much about the ritual and impact of a Cup Final on a local community. Newspapers are, of course, extensively exploited sources for historians, who tend often to treat them simply as repositories of information. But one of the most intriguing features of newspaper coverage is its duality. That is to say, the press not only provides, through its routine reporting, a description of a community's activities; at the same time, in its choice of stories and 'angle' and through the very language used, there is an element of creativity about newspaper reporting. It creates legends about people and places. Approaching the newspaper text from this perspective there emerges from it a multiplicity of ideas about com-munity, bringing into play a sense of the interrelated loyalties and identities of locality, region and nation. As such, the press is not simply a passive reflector of local life and thought but an active source in the creation of local feeling. And in reading press accounts of themselves and their community the people who buy the newspapers become accomplices in the perpetuation of these legends. To paraphrase a famous observation by Clifford Geertz, the local press is one of the principal agencies for 'telling ourselves stories about ourselves'.[4] The Cup Final was one of many subjects to figure in this process of story-telling and the formation of identity.

Because of the preponderance of Northern teams in the FA Cup Final until at least the 1960s – and because by its very nature the Rugby League Challenge Cup was *always* a Northern affair – legends of the Cup have a particular resonance in Northern industrial communities. In fact, alongside the working-class connotations of the Cup there has been a strong association in the popular mind between the Cup and the North – never better illustrated than in the Southerner's image of the Northerner in London 'Oop for the Coop'. Donald Read has stressed the 'football mania' which took root in the North in the late nineteenth century. He further argues that it was one of the chief causes of an 'inward-looking spirit' which developed in the North and which replaced the more nationally-minded, political provincialism to be found in Chartist and early Labour movements.[5] But it should be remembered that, as the subject for a text in which a variety of identities were juxtaposed, the Cup Final was never an event of exclusively local significance. In the story of the Cup, people were being invited to identify themselves in a number of guises and with a variety of allegiances. Of these, membership of the nation was perhaps the most obvious.

I

For all its local significance, it is the Cup Final's status as a *national* event that first and foremost establishes its claim to our attention. Its national prominence dates from the emergence of football itself as a mass spectator sport in the late nineteenth century, and has much to do with the close association between the Cup Final and London. From its inception in 1872 the Final Tie of the Football Association Challenge Cup has been staged in London except for the three occasions in 1893, 1894 and 1915 when it moved to Manchester (1893 and 1915) and Liverpool.[6] When it settled at the Crystal Palace in 1895, where it was to remain until 1914, the first historians of football commented: 'It is good that the Cup Final is played in the great Metropolis again, for however much our cynical provincial friends may affect to despise Lunnun and Cockneyism, there is no denial that London is the place for a great sporting battle.'[7] The somewhat incongruous venue for the contest at this time was a Victorian pleasure-garden in the south London suburb of Sydenham, where a less than adequate pitch was overlooked by a variety of amusement attractions including the fearsome 'Switch-back' and the famous glass structure of the Crystal Palace itself. Nevertheless, in these surroundings a popular festival was quickly established with attendances exceeding 100,000 on occasions. The Final was frequently played in fine, dry weather, which added to the holiday atmosphere of the event.

When the Final moved across London to the Empire Stadium at Wembley in 1923 its national mystique was not only continued but instantly amplified as a result of the particular circumstances of the first Wembley Final. For one thing the new stadium's size – 'a monument to sport so vast as to be unrivalled' as the *Bolton Evening News* loftily and inaccurately alleged (ignoring the larger Hampden Park in Glasgow)[8] – and its link with the Great Empire Exhibition of 1924 assured it of immediate attention from a clientele wider than that of the football enthusiast. But its place in the public memory was most clearly guaranteed by the near-disaster that accompanied its inaugural match – the Final of 1923 between Bolton Wanderers and West Ham United. The Football Association and the stadium management had underestimated the attraction of this fixture (neither club had a big reputation and attendances in the immediately preceding Finals – played at Stamford Bridge – had not been excessive) and allowed tickets for some parts of the ground to be purchased at the turnstiles. This encouraged speculative attendance which, along with thousands of 'gate-crashers', resulted in an excess of at least 50,000 spectators over and above the official capacity of the ground. But instead of tragedy – though there were more casualties than the subsequent legend allowed for – the first Wembley Cup Final produced a national epic. The myth of the solitary mounted policeman on his white horse methodically clearing the playing area, where many of the excess spectators had congregated, survived in the folklore of 1923 until well into the post-Second World War era. Equally compelling was the image of the calming and obedient atmosphere instilled by the arrival at the stadium of King George V, whose presence ensured that the innate orderliness, deference and good humour of the English public prevailed. The crowning achievement was the fact that, though delayed by 45 minutes, the match itself went ahead. And in a masterpiece of understatement typical of the legend already being created, the victorious Bolton captain summed up: 'It was a good hard game, and I was delighted with the way our boys played.'[9] In this way the 1923 Final came to represent a certain kind of Englishness, a feeling which was no doubt responsible for T. S. Eliot's inclusion of the Cup Final – or, at least, 'a cup final' – in his constellation of rituals that defined the national culture.[10]

Apart from the myths of 1923, a number of other features accounted for the Cup Final's continuing place as an icon of nationality. For one thing, the event was the culmination of a long and complex competition of national proportions organized by the Football Association, the governing body for football in England. The FA has itself been one of the keenest promoters of the national symbolism of the Final, being especially anxious to ensure its preservation as a national occasion rather than one which foregrounds the partisanship of the two clubs involved. This is exemplified in the philosophy which underpins the distribution of tickets, a longstanding source of grievance among local supporters.[11] Following the introduction of 'all-ticket' Finals after the problems of 1923, the FA took over control of ticket distribution and allocated less than half of the available tickets to the two clubs competing in the Final. The majority have gone in a strictly proportionate way to the various sections of the Association itself. The justification for marginalizing local loyalties in this way has been that the Final is not simply a match between two professional clubs, but the conclusion of a competition in which several hundred clubs of varying abilities have participated during the course of the season and whose contributions, however brief, should be acknowledged, however nominally.[12] One consequence of this policy, of course, has been the FA's ability to control the composition of the Wembley crowd. Not only were the disorderly scenes of 1923 never repeated, but ticket allocation ensured a 'mixed' crowd at the Final. In spite of the tendency for the local press to emphasize the 'take-over' of London on Cup Final day by hordes of enthusiasts from the provinces, Wembley never was so dominated. Indeed, there was good reason to believe that the Cup Final crowd was a reasonable cross-section of the nation.

Moreover, the FA was always anxious to preserve the *metropolitan* location of the Final.[13] This has been reinforced by the increasing – and since the 1960s exclusive – use of Wembley as the venue for England's international football fixtures. In this way Wembley, though simply a privately-owned sport and entertainment centre, has come to be seen as the 'national' stadium. Though scarcely an architectural masterpiece its outward appearance, dominated by two squat towers symmetrically framing the main entrance, has a memorable simplicity and the 'twin towers' have passed into popular imagery as a visual signifier of England, similar to Big Ben and the Union Jack. This image has been reinforced in sporting literature, especially in the 'ghosted' autobiographies of leading footballers, where the twin towers are treated with totemistic reverence. 'Butterflies started at the beginning of Wembley Way', says the rugby player David Watkins, of his first visit to Wembley in a Rugby League Final. 'We had been scanning the horizon for the famous twin towers and suddenly there they were ... Even the few brave souls who had been trying to break the tension by singing, lapsed into silence.'[14] This mystique is understandable when it is considered that to play in a Wembley Final was the goal of many professional players' careers, though many careers concluded without the twin towers coming into sight. Getting to Wembley was a 'rocky road', as Harry Johnston – the captain of Blackpool in the famous 'Matthews Final' of 1953 – put it in the title of his autobiography.[15]

Gary Whannel has pointed out that the FA Cup Final combines several 'messages' simultaneously. It is, he says, 'an event that manages to be a popular celebration, with strong working class roots, a shared national ritual and a constitutional link between royalty and popular culture.'[16] It was this last element – the link between royalty and popular culture – that most conclusively assured the Cup Final of national status. The link, however, was always a restrained one. The Cup Final never became a 'royal' event in the same way as, for example, the Ascot race meeting,[17] nor was it ever made an occasion on which to stage a ritualized state pageant.[18] More so than most football grounds on match days, Wembley might be viewed as a symbolic representation of English society, with its hierarchically structured crowd, the singing of the national anthem before the kick-off and the prevailing presence of the monarchy in the Royal Box. But these were scarcely the predominant messages. For one thing, the Cup Final had established itself as a popular festival long before the monarchy became associated with it. In spite of the origins of the game in the public schools and the respectable social backgrounds of its legislators, football (and indeed ball games of all kinds) lay well outside the interests of the Royal Family. George V's sporting proclivities, for example, were essentially those of the aristocrat [19] and this distanced him socially from football which, by the time he came to the throne in 1910, had acquired a distinctly 'cloth cap' image. Neither Victoria nor Edward VII had attended football occasions, though the latter had accepted in 1892, as Prince of Wales, the role of Patron of the FA, having earlier declined the offer.[20]

The restrained nature of the royal involvement in the Cup Final was set by the very first visit made by a monarch when George V attended the Crystal Palace match of 1914. By this time there could be little doubt that the Final, which in its early years had been an event of limited social and geographical appeal, was now an occasion of country-wide significance which justified the King's presence. *The Times* celebrated this new departure with an eccentric piece of reporting which (perhaps for the first and last time) placed emphasis on the *royal* aspects of the event. The anonymous reporter devoted much space to describing the King's mode of travel (motorcar) and the route to be taken to Sydenham, the flora to be enjoyed in the vicinity of the Crystal Palace, the ground improvements recently made, the likelihood of hearing a cuckoo, and the precautions being made against possible suffragette demonstrations. All this came before attention was turned to the match itself, on which the reporter gave what proved to be a remarkably prescient analysis. The chosen emphasis served to confirm the social status of the match to the readers of the newpaper. Though, in keeping with the unostentatious royal presence, the King's entourage was wearing only workaday clothes – 'bowler hats and short coats' – *The Times* nevertheless felt compelled to mark the event as having sealed a new social acceptability for the game:

> professional football of the best kind is no longer regarded as a
> spectacle only suitable for the proletariat ... the fact that the King

himself has attended a Cup Tie [sic] and shown a keen interest in its vicissitudes ... will, let us hope, put an end to the old snobbish notion that true-blue sportsmen ought to ignore games played by those who cannot afford to play without being paid for their services.[21]

Association football's success in thus establishing a 'national' sport and a Final with strong resonances in popular consciousness is underlined when the contrasting experiences of rugby league are taken into account. This professional variant of the game of rugby, which had been developed in the North of England following the secession of several Northern clubs from the Rugby Union in the 1890s,[22] had played the final tie of its Challenge Cup competition at various Northern venues before the decision was made to stage it at Wembley in 1929. This decision is an interesting one in that it seems to reflect a conscious wish by the Rugby League authorities to take its game onto the same national stage as that of its arch-rival the Rugby Football Union.[23] It is very doubtful, however, whether the attempt to shed the game's regional character was successful. Although the attendance of 41,000 at Wembley for the 1929 Final exceeded that for previous Rugby League Finals, the stadium was less than half full and the match itself – Wigan v. Dewsbury – was one-sided and rather dull.[24] As the *Yorkshire Post*, not a strong supporter of the league code, commented, the match was unlikely to have impressed 'the habituees of Twickenham, Richmond and Blackheath'.[25] Whether the Wembley venue, which was retained for all subsequent Finals,[26] justified the cost of travelling to London for the relatively small contingents of Northern spectators who made the journey before the Second World War must be doubted. There was always a lobby of rugby league supporters who campaigned for using one of the larger Northern grounds for the Final, and the immense attendance at Odsal Stadium, Bradford, for the replayed Final of 1954 added fuel to their arguments. According to one influential critic of Wembley, the 1954 match 'demonstrated to the rulers of the Rugby Football League in a clear and unmistakable manner that [people] desired the final of the game's major trophy to be played in their midst'.[27] Although attendances at Wembley Finals soared after the Second World War – especially following the first Final to be attended by the monarch in 1948 [28] – it is interesting that the St Helens player Vince Karalius felt it worth observing in his autobiography that as late as 1953 the Wembley programme notes still included an explanation of the scoring system in Rugby League.[29] There must remain some doubt over the impact made by the game outside the North before the BBC began to promote it vigorously on television in the late 1950s.

Even in this respect, there was an obvious difference in the representation of the sport by contrast with association football. The latter found its national status enhanced by the embrace extended to it by the broadcasting authorities. In spite of recurring fears – largely on the part of the Football League rather than the FA – about the effect of broadcasting on match attendances, the FA Cup Final has long been regarded as (in the BBC's own language) 'a must': an event in the sporting calendar that cannot be overlooked.[30] Radio commentaries have been continuous since 1930, television coverage since 1936 (with the exception of 1952). There can be little doubt that the link between the monarch and the Cup Final caused the Reithian BBC to treat the event seriously. Rugby league, on the other hand, was viewed warily – 'a socially inferior, local sport', according to Briggs[31] – and even its biggest event was not regarded as a 'must' in the schedules. When attitudes changed in the 1950s and rugby league matches came to be televised nationally they were presented in a self-consciously 'Northern' style; the commentators – usually Alan Dixon or Eddie Waring – had Northern accents which distinguished them from the orthodox style set by the BBC's football commentators, from 'By Jove' Allison to Raymond Glendenning and Kenneth Wolstenholme.[32] Eddie Waring, through whom the BBC later sought to personify rugby league, became almost a caricature of Northernness, to the dismay of many of the game's followers.[33]

Until the image of the football crowd underwent a transformation in the 1970s with the onset of 'hooliganism', it had invariably been represented by press, radio and television in a comforting form, almost as a physical manifestation of a united English nation. This was particularly so of Cup Final crowds. The first Wembley Final, for example, was accounted by *The Times* an 'ugly day', retrieved by two things: the spirit of the people and the police, and the loyalty of the 'mixed congregation' to the King. Spectators responded enthusiastically to the arrival of the monarch, and sang 'God Save the King'. As to general behaviour, 'there seems to have been no hooliganism or wanton disorder'.[34] In the more structured space of Wembley (by comparison with the rather chaotic nature of the Crystal Palace), the Final acquired a more stage-managed appearance during the 1920s, with military bands, the presentation of teams to the royal party, and community singing. Perhaps the most striking feature of all this, and of almost ineffable significance in the meaning of Wembley, was the singing of the Victorian hymn 'Abide With Me'. It was introduced in 1927, apparently on the suggestion of the master of ceremonies (and possibly because it was a favourite hymn of the Queen). Despite (or, perhaps, because of) its dirge-like tones it provided, as one historian has put it, 'a moment of deep emotion that moved the great crowds'.[35] Only by the wildest stretch of the imagination could the words be thought have any connection with football and yet the hymn somehow aroused sentiments that could never have been provoked by the national anthem itself. The Scot Pat Crerand of Manchester United apparently found it a very calming experience just before his appearance in the Final of 1963, [36] and for many ordinary working-class spectators the singing of 'Abide With Me' was possibly the nearest they came to any formal spiritual experience. Its impact, both personal and collective, on a Wembley crowd almost defies analysis. No doubt in a general sense, because it was recognized as a hymn through its words and form, it was accorded respect, in the same way that clergymen are accorded respect even in a largely secular society. But the meaning of the song surely transcended religion. Patrick Joyce has suggested that it expressed feelings of home, fatherhood, rest and peace, which were deeply embedded in working-class culture.[37] Perhaps also, being sung in common in circumstances of extremely close physical contiguity, the song evoked memories of adversity and loss, striking chords in the minds of people in much the same way as Armistice Day did in the inter-war years.[38] If, as Simon Inglis has suggested, there is an 'almost indefinable, inherent Englishness' about Wembley[39] then the singing of 'Abide With Me' at the FA Cup Final has surely been one of the chief ingredients of that national feeling.

II

Previewing the 1962 Cup Final, the association football correspondent of *The Times* echoed an idea expressed some thirty years earlier by the long-serving secretary of the FA, Frederick Wall. Wall had described the FA Cup as a 'national football festival' and whiggishly noted its steady development as such from the 1880s onwards.[40] The correspondent of *The Times* took up this theme in positively lyrical mood:

> This is the national stage of football at home ... here is an occasion that lives on in the hearts of those who follow the game in these islands. Beyond the company compressed within the rim of Wembley itself will be another army. Countless and unseen, they will have the setting brought to front parlours north, south, east and west by the eye of television. This is more than a football match. This is a festive day in the sporting calendar; a day out, a day for celebration, no matter how good or how poor the game itself. And when north faces south, as it does this afternoon, a spice is added to the picnic.[41]

The writer here was highlighting something central to the Cup Final: 'a day out, a day for celebration'. But if Cup Final day was presented to us through various 'official' agencies – the FA, the Wembley stadium authorities, *The Times* newspaper – as a celebration in which we were invited to see ourselves as part of a nation at play, there were also other celebrations fusing with these national ones, coalescing the national with the local and inflecting the 'official' text of celebration with popular practices.

Although Frederick Wall was no doubt correct in seeing the Final as a national institution, the competition of which it formed the climax had, for much of its first fifty or so years, possessed strong regional characteristics. It had been dominated by Northern and Midlands clubs. As Keith Robbins has pointed out, early professional football introduced as much regional diversity into sporting competition as it did national integration.[42] The FA Challenge Cup perfectly exemplified the point, being virtually monopolized by the clubs of the Football League, a Midlands-North organization whose headquarters from 1902 until 1959 were in Preston and whose leading officials possessed a self-consciously 'Northern' identity.[43] Between 1882, when the first Northern club (Blackburn Rovers) appeared in a Cup Final, and the outbreak of the Second World War, there were only nine Finals in which a team from Lancashire, Yorkshire or the North East did not figure. Thirteen Finals during this period were exclusively Northern affairs.

This Northern presence in the Cup Final provoked, from an early stage in the competition, a remarkable display of local festivity which endured in a more or less unchanged form until well after the Second World War. The three main strands of this sustained celebration were: 1) the journey of spectators to London; 2) the enjoyment of the match itself, not only inside the stadium itself but vicariously by thousands of of followers at home; and 3) the welcoming home of the team, usually on the Monday after the Final, with or without the trophy. The scenes associated with these various activities produced possibly the clearest illustration that urban areas were able to produce in the twentieth century of the nebulous concept of 'community'. It was the reporting of these events by the local press that served to foster the sense of community.

The dominant image of the Cup Final is of masses on the move:

INVASION OF LONDON
Great Trek to Wembley from the North
By Rail Road and Air
Big Bolton Crowds to Cheer the
Wanderers

Thus was the first visit to Wembley from the North proclaimed by the *Bolton Evening News*.[44] 'Contingents of the Northern Army', it went on, 'armed with megaphones, bells, rattles and bedecked with favours arrived by crowded trains, more travelled in motor coaches and others descended from aeroplanes today.' [45] Thirty years later 17 special trains left Newcastle for the 1952 Final, though an indication of the increasing use of motor travel was provided when local papers started printing maps of the road approaches to Wembley.[46] For the most part, however, it was the availability of relatively cheap rail travel that made the journey to London possible. By the early years of the century a cheap day excursion was obtainable for approximately one quarter of a working man's average weekly wage. For the 1914 Final, for example, the Lancashire and Yorkshire Railway advertised such trips for 12s. (60p) starting between late Friday night and the early hours of Saturday. Weekend excursions of between two and three days were also offered and towards the end of April the advertisements of the railway companies in the local press were joined by those of London businesses offering overnight accommodation, refreshments and amusements, such as the Zoological Gardens and Madame Tussaud's. But most people no doubt minimized expenses by eliminating the overnight accommodation. For the 1914 Final the Burnley newspapers estimated that most travelling supporters would complete their excursion in one day, sleeping on the crowded trains or at the station on arrival, possibly having taken advantage of the packed meals of sandwiches and pies offered by local grocers for 'saloon parties'.[47]

The cost of all this for many working people could be steep, even in the so-called 'age of affluence' after the Second World War. In his autobiography Gus Risman, who was the player-manager of Workington Town at the time of their appearance in the Rugby League Final of 1952, tells a story (which had been current in the local press at the time) of Workington people mortgaging their radios and television sets to raise money for the journey.[48] The irony was that, as the *Workington Star* pointed out, 'only a fraction of the stadium crowd could have seen [the game] so well' as those who watched it on television.[49] In the early days there seems to have been recourse to mutualist efforts to meet the cost. Gibson and Pickford, in their comprehensive history of the early game, dwell at some length on what they term (in a subsequently much-overused phrase) 'cup fever'. In particular they explain the 'clubbing principle', which they date from the visit of the working-class team Blackburn Olympic, the first professional club to win the FA Cup, in 1883. These 'outing clubs' seem to have been especially well supported in the North. Supporters clubbed together their savings in order to make what was, for many, a unique visit to London, combining sporting enthusiasm with an atmosphere of holiday. 'Next to the annual holiday at Blackpool, there is no objective dearer to the provincial's heart than the "Coop" Final.' [50] The savings were not just for the price of ticket and travel, but also contributed to carnival. Eating and drinking were clearly important parts of the proceedings, though the experience of a Sheffield outing club, whose barrel of beer was too gargantuan to go through the railway carriage door, was perhaps exceptional. But excess was nevertheless expected. In spite of a tendency for some parties to be independently victualled – excursionists from Bury in 1903 laid up a stockpile of food and drink in two large parcel vans at Euston station for their return journey [51] – London business people generally welcomed spectators from the North and Midlands because (it was said), unlike Southerners they spent good money. 'The southern spectator', claimed the Crystal Palace company, 'only comes to see the football, and not to spend his money.' [52] Presumably they went straight home after the match.

Northern supporters stayed on, conspicuously. Over many years a fixed pattern of pleasures was indulged in. Prominent among them was sightseeing of national monuments: Buckingham Palace, St Paul's Cathedral, the Tower of London, Westminster Abbey and the Houses of Paliament were all on the itinerary. Visits to the Commons to meet the local MP were popular before the First World War. One man had written beforehand, accepting the invitation of Philip Morrell, MP for Burnley: 'I have reached the age of 77 years, and I am coming to London for the first time, bringing my five sons with me. Hoping we shall have a good time and win the Cup.' [53] After the Great War the Cenotaph was added to the list of places to visit, especially for official parties representing clubs, players and supporters' groups. 'Old Hand' of the *Dewsbury Reporter* noted the few moments of solemnity in 1929 when representatives of both teams playing in the first Rugby League Final at Wembley placed wreaths at the Cenotaph: 'it was at this period of the day that the fun and shouts of the partisans subsided, hats were removed, and except for the noise of the passing traffic, there were periods of impressive silence'. [54] After which, exuberance was restored. Club colours, favours, mascots, carnival costumes and chants were ostentatiously exhibited. Huddersfield Town supporters took their mascot donkey on the train for the 1922 Stamford Bridge Final, parading it down the Strand and stopping the traffic. [55] In 1947 Burnley's supporters, in a now well-rooted tradition, swept four-abreast through the West End, bedecked with streamers and wearing skull caps or three-foot-high top hats in claret and blue. [56] The bizarre was, for many, the order of the day and few scaled greater heights in the pursuit of the surreal than Blackpool's Atomic Boys, the pinnacle of whose exploits in the 1940s and 1950s was their delivery of Blackpool Rock to 10 Downing Street. [57] Alertness to style and respectability for those 'on show' in the metropolis was not forgotten, however. The Elton Ironworks excursion party from Bury no doubt felt that they had struck the right note for London fashion in 1900 when it was made a condition of joining that members wore 'new clogs and slouched hats' for any visit to London.[58] Behaviour was noisy and rowdy, but not usually violent. In 1923 some threats of physical violence seem to have been exchanged between groups of the respective supporters, but it was treated lightly by the press. In a portentous comment which nevertheless revealed deep local pride the *Bolton Evening News* noted:

> Cockney sportsmen found their first taste of a dish of 'Trotters' very unpalatable, and far from being the wholesome feast as suggested by we Boltonians. It is whispered that some of them angrily tried in vain to find the young collier who paraded the Strand early on Saturday morning, draped in the Wanderers' blue and white colours, with a string of trotters dangling round the front and back of him in very curious fashion.[59]

The main physical danger in 1923, however, seems to have been confined to the stadium itself, with around a thousand people treated for injuries, many at the local hospital.[60]

For those who stayed at home there was a different atmosphere to be experienced. Before the arrival of mass radio and television, it was not uncommon for crowds of people to congregate in the central parts of the town in the hope of picking up news of the match. Elaborate arrangements had been made to relay the news by local shops in Blackburn for the 1885 Cup Final, and conflicting reports caused confusion among the throng of people massed in the town centre.[61] In Bolton in 1923 there was 'great pandemonium' in the middle of the town, as people gathered to hear latest scores. Rumour abounded to the effect that the match had been called off, but when the news came through that David Jack had scored the opening goal 'people were shaking hands with one another, slapping backs, being as familiar and hail-fellow-well-met as most other folk would be if their team was winning the English Cup; and David Jack was the hero of the piece'. At the news that Bolton had scored a second goal, traders in the Market Hall went wild in a spontaneous display of rough music: 'crockery dealers rattled plates ... hardware merchants banged out their joyous feelings with the aid of pans, toy-sellers blew trumpets, twirled rattles and rang bells, whilst those who had no noise-producing instruments handy joined the general public in a glad shout which echoed and re-echoed through the great glass-roofed building'.[62] Clubs competing in Finals at this time often played reserve team fixtures on the same day, and if these matches were at home the crowds would be swollen dramatically from their usual numbers; not only would messages constantly be issued about the state of play in the Final, but the cameraderie of the crowd provided a substitute for being in London. At such a match in Huddersfield in 1922, when the news was announced that Town had taken the lead over Preston North End with a penalty, 'Hats, caps and sticks were hurled wildly in the air, and the scared carrier pigeons which were released to carry the glad tidings to many outlying districts were fortunate to escape injury.'[63] As radio developed, but before many homes possessed receivers of their own, people gathered outside the premises of retailers to hear the commentary, or bought seats at local cinemas where enterprising managers had made an arrangement with electrical dealers for sets to be installed to provide a 'listening-in' service.[64]

In a later age of electronic media these surrogate Wembley crowds disappeared. Those who did not journey to London watched or listened to the Final in the more privatized settings of family or neighbourhood groups. The legend of the 'ghost town' was thus created. So quiet was Workington in 1952 (in contrast to the 'pandemonium' of Bolton in 1923) that shopkeepers complained of loss of business.[65] In St Helens in 1956 complaints intensified. It was estimated that a fifth of the town's population would actually make the trip to Wembley and many of the remainder would stay indoors rather than go out shopping. One local paper, whose headline proclaimed 'Wembley Match will make St Helens a Ghost Town', quoted local tradespeople concerned about business losses; one greengrocer was worried about leftover lettuces, potatoes and fruit; publicans reckoned that their beer takings would be down by £500. The Chamber of Trade put overall losses at something like £150,000. More darkly, the comments of the business community were directed disapprovingly at working-class hedonism and irrationality; rents would fall into arrears and hire-purchase instalments would be missed – 'and they won't be made up, you know', warned one furniture shop manager.[66]

Such pessimism did not, however, prevent a general air of festivity from prevailing. There was, as in carnival, a sense of the normal conventions and routines being temporarily suspended. In the days when the working week continued into Saturday a visit to the Cup Final represented a welcome break from work. For those who stayed behind the peak of enthusiasm was reached when the local football team returned from London to be greeted rapturously by thousands of its followers, many of whom had taken at least the afternoon off. The ritual followed a well-established protocol whose origins were in the 1880s. The welcome given to the victorious St Helens team in 1956 provides a typical example. The players detrained at Liverpool where, though the city was not a rugby league stronghold, ethnic and religious ties ensured them of a large reception. A coach ride to St Helens in pouring rain, the players covering themselves in blankets to keep dry as they sat atop the coach, brought out (it was estimated)

100,000 people along the processional route. It climaxed in an enthusiastic reception in St Helens itself, with some 30,000 'packed like sardines' into Victoria Square. Speeches and cheering followed, and the players went on to visit local hospitals to display the Cup they had won for the first time in 59 years, accompanied by the local industrial magnate Sir Harry Pilkington.[67]

This kind of scene differed little whether the team had won or lost. When Preston North End returned in 1937 following a defeat by Sunderland there was a throng of 8,000–10,000 people in a Market Square appropriately bedecked with bunting for Coronation Day. 'The reception could not have been more spontaneous,' claimed the *Preston Guardian*, 'if the club had brought the Cup with them.'[68] They actually did the following year, when the *Guardian* reported 'the greatest crowd ever to assemble' in the main square.[69] Nine years later the Burnley team, who had narrowly lost in the Final to Charlton Athletic, were similarly received as heroes. 'Watchman' of the *Northern Daily Telegraph*, under the headline 'ALL BURNLEY OUT TO GREET CUP LOSERS', reported that from Bury onwards the team's coach was cheered, and as it entered Burnley itself the crowds were so enthusiastic that the last mile of the journey took twenty minutes. The club chairman, Tom Clegg, announced: 'I have lived in Burnley 75 years and I have never felt as proud of the town and its people as I do tonight.' The captain, Alan Brown, greatly moved by the display of affection shown to his team, told the thousands assembled outside the Town Hall: 'We lost the Cup, but you have given us something Charlton cannot win from us.'[70] The scenes in Burnley were virtually identical to those of 1914 when the club had returned with the Cup and the mills stopped on Monday to allow everyone to celebrate.[71]

Emotions such as these were a remarkably constant feature of Cup Final celebration. There was little, if any, variation, either over time or in relation to the size and sporting renown of the community involved. Thus, for example, it might be expected that Huddersfield, a medium-sized industrial town whose previous association football history was undistinguished, would go wild after the victory of its team in 1922. So overwhelming was the welcome for the returning players that the *Huddersfield Examiner* was moved to comment that it was 'probably the biggest demonstration ever known in Huddersfield'; its ecstatic nature was of a kind 'which could have been secured only by a monarch, or by the more famous kinema artists'.[72] Similar scenes were witnessed in the isolated West Cumbrian heavy industrial town of Workington in 1952. The professional Rugby League club, which had only been in existence since the end of the Second World War, quite suddenly shot into the limelight by winning the League Championship in 1951 and, in the following year, the Cup. 'What a return we had on the Monday', recalled Gus Risman, for whom the Cup victory was the fulfilment of a prediction he had made on becoming the club manager in 1946: 'We travelled North by train and then went across country by coach from Scotch Corner. And every village in Cumberland turned out to cheer us home. When we reached Workington you could hardly get near the Town Hall.'[73]

Very similar was the reception given to Newcastle United's FA Cup-winning team a week later. In Newcastle's case, however, it was a large regional centre with a long history of football success. 1952 was the club's ninth Cup Final appearance, and it had never lost at Wembley. But neither this tradition, nor the narrow margin of the victory over Arsenal – with an injury to one of their players resulting in much sympathy in the national and local press for the losers – prevented an estimated quarter of a million people coming into the centre of the city to give the players what the *Newcastle Journal* described as a 'delirious welcome'. When the team paraded around their stadium with the Cup, some 45,000 supporters 'nearly took the roof off the stands', to the extent that some players looked 'overwhelmed, even after Wembley'.[74] Clearly, mass enthusiasm was not confined to small town parvenu teams, and the more recent examples of civic celebration following the Liverpool–Everton Finals of 1986 and 1989 confirm the continuing ability of the Cup Final to influence big city consciousness.

However, beneath the surface of these seemingly changeless celebrations of local achievement were concealed interesting developments in civic relationships. In short, the reception of the Cup Final team was gradually transformed from being a spontaneous celebration of *club* into a semi-official glorification of *town*. The reception was appropriated into civic ideology. The spontaneity of the occasion was typified in the very first mass reception for a Cup team in the North. This occurred at Blackburn in 1883 after Blackburn Olympic had defeated Old Etonians in the Final at Kennington Oval and thus become the first provincial and professional team to win the Cup. Olympic's victory provoked a torrent of eulogies from press and public figures, none more redolent of class consciousness and local patriotism than the one offered by the *Blackburn Times*:

It is the meeting and vanquishing, in a most severe trial of athletic skill, of a club composed of the sons of some of the best families of the upper class of the Kingdom – of born and bred gentlemen who may be justly described as 'the glass of fashion and the mould of form' – as the Old Etonians club is, by a provincial Club composed entirely, we believe, of Lancashire Lads of the manual working class, sons of small tradesmen, artizans and operatives.[75]

It also provoked a demonstration of affection and enthusiasm from the people of Blackburn that far exceeded any expectations. As the train carrying the players approached the town it was cheered by supporters who had gathered along the line. In Blackburn the crowds were so large that the fifty or so policemen on duty were completely unable to enforce any kind of control. The procession of four wagonettes and three bands that headed off in the direction of the Cherry Tree Inn, the club's headquarters, was frequently dispersed and several times had to pause and reform. Celebrations and speeches were held at the Cherry Tree, and later in private houses, but there was no formal attempt to place a civic stamp upon the proceedings. Nor was there in the following year when the socially superior Blackburn Rovers won the Cup. This time the police were better prepared and at least cleared a space outside the station for the vehicles to assemble, but otherwise the scenes were identical, with the procession making for the White Bull on this occasion. In 1885, when the Rovers won again, there was no reception at all when the team returned on the Sunday morning. Celebrations took place at the Rovers' ground after a scheduled match on the Monday evening.[76]

By the turn of the century official attitudes towards Cup teams had noticeably changed. Whereas the Cup Final in the 1880s was a relatively small-scale affair – still regarded by some as less important than the Lancashire Cup – by the 1890s its success at the Crystal Palace ensured national prominence for those taking part. This no doubt explains the increased attention paid to it by local corporations. By the time Bury appeared in two Finals (1900 and 1903, winning both by record margins), an attempt was being made to elevate the reception onto a semi-official footing. The team's arrival on Monday evening was to be greeted with a carefully laid plan which foregrounded the Mayor and his entourage: 'arrangements were made for keeping the railway platforms clear of persons who had no business there, and a few minutes before the train arrived there was no one on the platform but a few privileged persons'. Nevertheless, 'unofficial' interlopers did break through on the first of these occasions, so that the Mayor's party was not alone when the train arrived. In 1903, however, the 'privileged' were kept apart from the masses. But thereafter the customary wagonette and band procession made off, accompanied by the Mayoral party, for the public house where the club normally met, rather than an official reception at the Town Hall.[77] The Town Hall, however, was certainly the focus of the proceedings at Huddersfield in 1922, when the event was virtually an official celebration. The team was met at the station by a Mayor's party and conveyed through the streets in two Corporation buses to the Town Hall, where a reception and speeches were held before the Cup was displayed to the crowds from the balcony.[78] This became the usual pattern for Cup celebrations by the 1920s. At Sunderland in 1937 a moral element was introduced when the arrival of the team, originally scheduled for 3.30 pm, was delayed until the evening to avoid the temptation for men to stay away from work.[79] The stage-managing of the event probably reached its most carefully rehearsed proportions at Newcastle in 1952. Here, the linking of civic authority to football culture was achieved by having the Lord Mayor and the Town Clerk, who had been at Wembley, leave the team's train at Durham in order to arrive slightly earlier in Newcastle. There they changed into their official robes and, equipped with sword and mace, were ready to greet the team formally when its train arrived at the station.[80]

III

In the reporting of the rituals which made the Cup Final a popular festival, the press often stepped into the realm of myth-making. By offering comment and opinion on the events, or simply by selecting certain aspects for attention, newspaper editors and reporters played upon notions of identity which drew on and at the same time reinforced a sense of local distictiveness.

Like Northern dialect literature, which which they have a close affinity, stories about the Cup Final hinged on ideas of the locality and its customs in the face of the 'otherness' of the rest of the country, particularly London.[81] Part of the attraction of the Cup Final was the opportunity it afforded for small, comparatively unknown places to enjoy a brief moment in the limelight and to parade their locality on a national stage. '[N]othing has been produced in this district nor has there been an event to attract to it a spotlight of such brilliance', commented the *Workington Star* on the town's Wembley success of 1952.[82] Sometimes this opportunity was seen as a chance to put the community on the map with a view to reviving its economic fortunes; Burnley's Wembley appearance in 1962, for example, came at a time of absolute decline in the cotton industry and it was felt that it might attract new industries.[83] But often the story was about less material issues. It was about local pride, an opportunity simply to assert the local identity. This was what Dewsbury seemed to extract from their Cup defeat by Wigan in the 1929 Rugby League Final. 'We are very proud', said their captain, Joe Lyman, 'that our men come from within six miles of Dewsbury. That means a great deal. It means that if we win it will be a real Dewsbury victory, and also there will be a far greater team spirit than ever one could find in a side made up of players from all parts of the country. We know one another well, and we shall all work together.'[84] 'Old Hand' of the *Dewsbury Reporter* analysed the team's qualities as 'grit, staying power, team spirit, all-round sound-ness':[85] the very stuff of Yorkshire. By contrast Wigan was a more cosmopolitan team which included Welsh, Scottish and New Zealand as well as English players, and ten of them were internationals.[86] The authentic Yorkshireness of Dewsbury consoled their supporters in de-feat – 'it's nobbut t'League o' Nations that bet us': as if Dewsbury had been the victim of international forces beyond its control.[87]

The linking of football to local traditions and customs was usually a marked feature of press coverage. Dialect was a convenient mark of distinctiveness and identity. '"WOR CUP" COMES BACK TO THE GALLOW-GATE ROAR' proclaimed the *Newcastle Journal* in 1952 and recorded the lusty singing of 'Blaydon Races' at the station, 'loud enough, it seemed, to reach Scotswood Road'. On this occasion there was a strong North East sentiment evident. Newcastle were seen to be carrying the pride of a distinctive region to London for their match against Arsenal, and local rivalries were suspended as the people of Sunderland, Hartlepool, Shields, 'the Northumberland farms and the Easington pits' all united behind Newcastle.[88] For the other North East club, Sunderland, the local paper made great play of the cries of 'Ha-way the lads' by their supporters in the Final of 1937.[89]

The dialect tradition also extended to features on local personalities. An interesting example was included in the *Northern Daily Telegraph*'s coverage of Burnley's appearance in the Final of 1947. 'Ma' Bray of Oswaldtwistle, the mother of one of Burnley's players, was interviewed. She was portrayed as the embodiment of locality and family. She stood stoically behind her two sons, both professional footballers, and kept firm to solid Northern values in the face of the 'magic' of Wembley and, one may suppose, the lure of the metropolis. She recalled how, when her elder son had returned home to Oswaldtwistle after taking part in Manchester City's Cup victory of 1934, the entire street had been decorated end-to-end. But such enthusiasm was for family and neighbourhood. The Final itself was put firmly in its place. 'I don't want to go … I don't think I could face it. I've never been to London, and I've no desire to go.' The reporter summed up: 'She'll be proud tomorrow as she sits by the wireless, win or lose. And if it's "win" she won't swank. She's not that kind.'[90]

'Ma' Bray's reluctance to leave Oswaldtwistle was not, of course, shared by the thousands who relished the opportunity to make a rare, possibly unique, visit to London. The mass excursion, and the various holiday activities associated with it, brought into play in press reporting a series of oppositions that would not have been present if the Final had been staged at a Northern venue. These essentially converged around the idea of London and the South as being not only different but also the seat of power, which was temporarily being 'occupied' by the North. 'Lancashire takes over as London is invaded – Atomic Boys at No. 10' declared the *Evening Gazette* on the day of the Blackpool–Bolton Final of 1953.

> The West End was Lancashire on the Thames today. They came in their thousands from Blackpool and Bolton. Hundreds were in town before a grey dawn which heralded a day of sunshine and gentle breezes. They went out on the streets, waking the sleeping city at four o' clock in the morning. Only the old and the weary huddled in Euston's waiting rooms till the early morning cafes opened. They made the traditional tour of the town. They went to Covent Garden, Buckingham Palace and a few made a pilgrimage to Whitehall, where they left posies of flowers tied with tangerine and white and black and white ribbons.[91]

This piece, utilizing the idea of the 'Northern invasion', could have been written at any time during the previous sixty years. The images, even the language, had changed little.[92] London, in the days before motorways and high-speed trains, was still distant enough from the North for there to be a sense of expedition about the journey. The *Workington Star* reported a 'trickle of cars leaving Workington for the South' as early as Wednesday evening in 1952.[93] Advanced columns of Burnley's invading army in 1947 were greeted 'where Middlesex meets London' by the exhortation of an emigré Lancashire greengrocer, whose shop-window sign urged: 'Wap it Whoam, Burnley'.[94] It was, of course, a friendly invasion. 'London loved it all', claimed the *Northern Daily Telegraph*; compared to the reception of the Scottish supporters who had visited earlier for an international match, the liaisons between Londoners and Lancastrians were all waves and greetings.[95] Nevertheless, there was a sense in which London was to be placed in true proportions. Northerners were determined not to be seduced by the sophistication of the city. Here the tone of the press reports was often that of the seaside postcard, where the Northerner abroad implants authentic Northern values in an alien soil, but at the same time indulges in gentle self-mockery. At the Crystal Palace in 1914, for example, spectators had to pay a shilling (5p) admission to the pleasure grounds before gaining access, at additional cost, to the football stadium. This was naturally frowned upon at first, but having seen the famous glass edifice visitors generally reckoned it to have been worth the money. The grandiose was nonetheless placed in realistic perspective. 'By gum,' remarked a Burnleyite, 'aw wouldn't like to go and mend a brokken pane up theer.' [96] This was local humour, presenting a reassuring image of the Northerner to readers back home. But there was also a feeling that Londoners themselves could not fail to be amused by the jokes, songs and accents of this invading force. Boltonians arrived for their visit of 1923 apparently armed to the teeth with all kinds of street maps and directories. Their confused antics in the vicinity of the railway station became the scenario for much humour, some of it inevitably pitched at the mythical 'gormless' Northerner at large in the big city – asking directions to the pub called the 'Old Lady of Threadneedle Street', or declining the theatre after the match in favour of a visit to the circus at Piccadilly.[97] Boltonians could recognize and laugh at this, but so too should Londoners; according to the *Bolton Evening News*, 'The city that is too busy living to take much notice of life will surely spare a glance and a laugh here.'[98]

The point at which the relationship between North and metropolis merged into a more general sense of national community is difficult to locate. But in none of the identities being created in this reporting was there any sense of the North being *apart* from the symbolic nation of the Cup Final. The 'taking' of the capital was simply a projecting of Northern local and regional identities on a national stage, an opportunity to exploit momentary renown. Local and national converged naturally. This was never more evident than in the Cup Final of 1914, when the presence of the King provided an opportunity to parade and glorify the North's place in the nation. 'It was,' proclaimed the *Burnley Express* with pride, 'a Royal Lancashire Day', noting that it had been Lord Derby, the Northern aristocrat, who had been instrumental in persuading the King to attend. Red roses, the symbol of Lancashire, were to be worn by the royal party, in celebration not only of the Lancashire origin of the two teams – Liverpool and Burnley – but because the King was also Duke of Lancaster, and it was this title that the press appropriated as a way of linking the monarchy with local sentiment.[99] At the time of another impending war, 'Townsman' of the *Preston Guardian*, reporting North End's reception after their Cup win of 1938, was moved to portray the English crowd as a bulwark of decency in the face of threats from abroad. He contrasted the essentially humane, English good-naturedness of the vast crowd in Preston with the 'large, disciplined gatherings' to be found in continental Europe. The difference was pointed up when a woman in the crowd, on the point of fainting, passed her child to a policeman for safe keeping. This commonplace incident, with its comforting stereotypes of mother, child and friendly bobby, somehow gave 'Townsman' an insight into his community that revealed it to be much more than mere locality: 'for all our bickerings we are all one big family on these great occasions'.[100]

IV

Preston North End was the last of the clubs from medium-sized Northern industrial towns to appear in the FA Cup Final, in 1964. So much of the culture of the Final had been based on this type of community, and with its passing as a force in football during the 1960s and 1970s the meaning of the Final changed. With the increased frequency of appearances by big-city teams from London, Liverpool and Manchester, each with its clutch of internationally-famous players rendered into 'personalities' by press, radio and television, the Final has lost some of its local flavour. Wembley, too, has changed. The segregation of spectators to minimize crowd disturbances has seemed to accentuate divisions at the expense of the unity the stadium symbolized in former times. Even 'Abide With Me' was removed from the programme for a time when fans either ignored or sought to subvert it. And 'God Save the Queen' became 'God Save Our Gracious Team' in the 1970s. It is perhaps to the Wembley Finals of the lesser trophies that have proliferated since the 1980s, and to the recently-instituted 'play-off' system in the lower divisions of the Football League (where many of the former Cup-winning Northern clubs now reside), that we should look to recapture some of the old local fervour of Cup Final Day.

This occasion, in its broadest terms as both sporting and cultural event, has good claim to be seen as a cardinal element in Northern popular culture. Of course, it is not *uniquely* Northern: plenty of Midland and Southern clubs (an increasing number of the latter since the 1960s) have appeared in the Final, and their appearance has no doubt served to bind local identities in Wolverhampton, Watford, Islington and other places. But there is something peculiarly Northern about the Cup. It probably derives from the frequency with which Northern clubs have appeared in the Final and the way in which the festival aspect of Cup Final day has been embraced in Northern communities. In this way it has become an important site for the myths by which people live their lives. John Walton is surely correct in seeing these as an important subject for the regional historian.[101] Through the cultural practices and the text of the Cup Final were created and reproduced for many years ideas about the people of the North and their communities, and the wider community of which they were a part.

Ideologically, one of the most intriguing themes in all this that of the *unified* community. It is represented most clearly in the image of the crowd welcoming the local heroes on their return from London. This image, it might be suggested, sought a magical resolution of the many internal tensions and conflicts that in fact beset the communities. Though in many cases we are dealing with towns which possessed a dominant industry and therefore a marked uniformity of social class and occupation, frequently underpinned by the kind of solidarity produced through strong trades unionism, this had not invariably produced a sense of unified civic identity. In reality, divisions of gender, age, ethnic group, religion and status could provide powerful forces pulling against civic coherence. This was very clearly represented in the town of Burnley, for example, at the point when its football team won the Cup in 1914. Its politics manifested deep ideological and social divisions which had prevented the working-class uniformity of the town from being translated into a class-based political identity. Burnley, perhaps surprisingly, did not share in that emergence of Labour representation which was so noticeable in North West England in the few years before the First World War.[102] Similarly, perhaps in even more acute form, there were the religious tensions – Protestant and Catholic as well as intra-Protestant – that had afflicted these towns for at least three generations by the 1920s. The Irish and Catholic traditions of a town like St Helens were still marked after the Second World War, as was the quite different *English* Roman Catholic culture of Preston, in spite of the unifying leaven created in both towns through work and labour movement.[103] Parallel with these sectarian loyalties was the fundamental division of gender, whose existence is emphasized by the focus of this very study: football. There were few other pastimes which served more to generate a feeling of male sociability and exclusiveness than football, whether in its participant or spectating forms. It reminds us that British social life, especially working-class life, reproduced a sexual division of leisure, just as the world of work had its sexual division of labour, for the whole of the period under consideration.

Running alongside these identities was a discourse which counterposed an alternative sense of a united community of people. It took many forms and the story of the Cup Final was but one of them. Its principal creator and perpetuator was the local press. And what is most remarkable about this story of the Cup Final is its unchangingness, both across time and place. It is as if there was a journalistic model to which reporters had recourse, a narrative form which *structured* the story. It represented an 'imaginary constitution of the social order', as Joyce has termed it.[104] What it sought to assert, in the face of division, was a civic and national unity of seamless communities. Its abiding image nationally was that of Wembley and all it connoted in terms of a united social hierarchy. Locally it was the image, reproduced in so many local press photographs, of the physical presence of the town assembled to greet and laud its heroes (many of them not local men, of course) on their return from the Final. There was, perhaps, an element of wish-fulfilment in this. In the same way that some historians of the British cinema have suggested that the images of unity, and narratives in which social contradictions are magically harmonized and resolved, might have masked an underlying fear about discord in society,[105] so the story of the Cup Final might be seen as offering an idealized vision of community. There is no doubt that people of all sorts did turn out to welcome their teams home, but perhaps the wish to amplify this occasional event into a more generalized image of the authentic nature of community reveals an all-too-keen awareness of the actual disharmonies present in the everyday life of Northern towns. The image of the seamless community existed, perhaps, more readily in the imagination than in reality.

Notes

1. Patrick Joyce, *Visions of the People: Industrial England and the Question of Class* (Cambridge U.P., Cambridge: 1994 edn), p. 159.
2. Of the many publications commemorating the 'magic' of the Cup Final one of the most interesting, and one that has been very helful in preparing the present essay, is Tony Pawson, *100 Years of the FA Cup* (Heinemann, London: 1971).
3. Fred Inglis, *The Name of the Game: Sport and Society* (Heinemann, London: 1977), p. 37.
4. 'Deep play: notes on the Balinese cockfight', *Daedalus* 10. 1 (Winter 1972), pp. 1–37.
5. Donald Read, *The English Provinces c. 1760–1960: A Study in Influence* (Edward Arnold, London: 1964), pp. 231–2.
6. The 1970 Final was replayed at Old Trafford, Manchester.
7. Alfred Gibson and William Pickford, *Association Football and the Men Who Made It* (4 vols; Caxton Publishing Co., London: 1905), IV, p. 4.
8. *Bolton Evening News*, 30 April 1923; other accounts from *The Times*, 27 and 30 April 1923.
9. *Bolton Evening News*, 30 April 1923.
10. T. S. Eliot, *Notes Towards the Definition of Culture* (Faber & Faber, London: 1948), p. 31.
11. Tom Finney, for example, described how, for weeks before the Final of 1954, he was plagued by requests from Preston North End supporters for tickets. 'The allocation to each competing club is pitifully inadequate', he claimed: *Finney on Football* (Nicholas Kaye, London: 1958), p. 128.
12. See Pawson, *100 Years of the FA Cup*, pp. 203–4.
13. Geoffrey Green, *The Official History of the FA Cup* (Naldrett Press, London: 1949), p. 60.
14. David Watkins and Brian Dobbs, *The David Watkins Story* (Pelham Books, London: 1971), p. 138.
15. Harry Johnston, *The Rocky Road to Wembley* (Museum Press, London: 1954).
16. Gary Whannel, *Fields in Vision: Television Sport and Cultural Transformation* (Routledge, London: 1992), p. 3.
17. See Ilse Hayden, *Symbol and Privilege: The Ritual Context of British Royalty* (University of Arizona Press, Tucson: 1987), p. 27.

18. See David Cannadine, 'The context, performance and meaning of ritual: the British monarchy and the "invention of tradition", c. 1829–1977', in Eric Hobsbawm and Terence Ranger (eds), *The Invention of Tradition* (Cambridge U.P., Cambridge: 1984 edn), pp. 101–64.

19. See J. Wentworth Day, *King George V as a Sportsman: An Informal Study of the First Country Gentleman in Europe* (Cassell, London: 1935).

20. Football Association, *The History of the Football Association* (Naldrett Press, London: 1953), pp. 62, 262.

21. *The Times*, 27 April 1914.

22. See Robert Gate, *Rugby League: An Illustrated History* (Arthur Barker, London: 1989).

23. Rugby Football League (RFL), *Minute Book; Meeting of the Cup Committee*, 24 October 1928 (consulted by kind permission of the Chief Executive, RFL, Leeds). Wembley was chosen in preference to the Crystal Palace, probably because it offered a better financial deal, though the minutes are unclear on this point.

24. *Sporting Chronicle*, 6 May 1929.

25. *Yorkshire Post*, 6 May 1929.

26. Except that of 1932, played at Wigan because Wembley was not available at the earlier date when the RFL wished to stage the Final. The replayed Final of 1954 was held at Bradford and that of 1982 at Leeds.

27. Stanley Chadwick, 'The will of the north', *Rugby League Review* (13 May 1954). I am indebted to Robert Gate for drawing my attention to this article.

28. See Graham Morris and John Huxley, *Wembley Magic: A History of the Rugby League Challenge Cup* (Evans Brothers, London: 1983).

29. *Lucky 13* (Stanley Paul, London: 1964), p. 53.

30. See Asa Briggs, *The History of Broadcasting in the United Kingdom* (Oxford U.P., Oxford: 1979), IV, pp. 854, 861; Football Association, *History of the FA*, pp. 508–17.

31. *History of Broadcasting*, IV, p. 854.

32. Though Wolstenholme came from Bolton, he never developed a 'Northern' persona as a BBC commentator.

33. See, for example, Geoffrey Moorhouse, *At the George: And Other Essays on Rugby League* (Sceptre, London: 1990), pp. 44–5.

34. *The Times*, 30 April 1923.

35. Pawson, *100 Years of the FA Cup*, p. 215.

36. Noel Cantwell, *United We Stand* (Stanley Paul, London: 1965), p. 55.

37. Joyce, *Visions*, p. 159.

38. See Bob Bushaway, 'Name upon name: the Great War and remembrance', in Roy Porter (ed.), *Myths of the English* (Polity Press, Cambridge: 1992), pp. 136–67.

39. Simon Inglis, *The Football Grounds of Europe* (Willow Books, London: 1990), p. 99.

40. Sir Frederick Wall, *Fifty Years of Football* (Cassell, London: 1935), p. 167.

41. *The Times*, 5 May 1962.

42. *Nineteenth-Century Britain: Integration and Diversity* (Clarendon Press, Oxford: 1988), pp. 163, 168.

43. Alan Tomlinson, 'North and south: the rivalry of the Football League and the Football Association', in John Williams and Stephen Wagg (eds), *British Football and Social Change: Getting into Europe* (Leicester U.P., Leicester: 1991), pp. 25–47.
44. 27 April 1923.
45. 28 April 1923. Unfortunately, because of the poor organization of the event, many returned home without having seen the match, or having even got near the stadium because of the traffic congestion.
46. See, e.g., *Northern Daily Telgraph*, 25 April 1947.
47. See *Burnley Express*, 22, 29 April 1914.
48. *Rugby Renegade* (Stanley Paul, London: 1958), p. 78.
49. 25 April 1952.
50. Gibson and Pickford, *Association Football*, IV, pp. 41–2.
51. *Bury Times*, 22 April 1903.
52. Gibson and Pickford, *Association Football*, IV, pp. 41–2.
53. *Burnley Express*, 29 April 1914.
54. 4 May 1929.
55. *Huddersfield Examiner*, 6 May 1922.
56. *Northern Daily Telegraph*, 25 April 1947.
57. *West Lancashire Evening Gazette*, 2 May 1953.
58. *Bury Times*, 18 April 1900.
59. 30 April 1923.
60. *Bolton Evening News*, 28, 30 April 1923.
61. *Blackburn Times*, 11 April 1885.
62. *Bolton Evening News*, 30 April 1923.
63. *Huddersfield Examiner*, 6 May 1922.
64. e.g. *Dewsbury Reporter*, 1 May 1929.
65. *Workington Star*, 28 March, 25 April 1952.
66. *Prescot and District Newspaper and Advertiser*, 26 April 1956.
67. *Prescot and District Newspaper and Advertiser*, 3 May 1956.
68. 8 May 1937.
69. 7 May 1938.
70. *Northern Daily Telegraph*, 29 April 1947.
71. *Burnley Express*, 29 April 1914.
72. 6 May 1922.
73. *Rugby Renegade*, p. 80.
74. *Newcastle Journal*, 6 May 1952.
75. 7 April 1883.
76. *Blackburn Times*, 7 April 1883, 5 April 1884, 11 April 1885.
77. *Bury Times*, 25 April 1900, 22 April 1903.
78. *Huddersfield Examiner*, 6 May 1922.
79. *Sunderland Echo*, 3 May 1937.
80. *Newcastle Journal*, 6 May 1952.
81. See Martha Vicinus, *The Industrial Muse* (Croom Helm, London: 1974), p. 190.
82. 4 April 1952.
83. *Burnley Express and News*, 2 May 1962.
84. *Sporting Chronicle*, 4 May 1929.

85. 4 May 1929.
86. *Sporting Chronicle*, 4 May 1929.
87. *Dewsbury Reporter*, 11 May 1929.
88. *Newcastle Journal*, 3 May, 6 May 1952.
89. *Sunderland Echo*, 4 May 1937.
90. *Northern Daily Telegraph*, 25 April 1947.
91. 2 May 1953.
92. Compare the *Burnley Express* of 1914: 'Long before London itself woke up for business, the invaders had moved far afield. They took possession of the Strand, Piccadilly, Holborn and Regent Street before London had aroused itself' (29 April 1914).
93. 18 April 1952.
94. *Northern Daily Telegraph*, 26 April 1947.
95. *Northern Daily Telegraph*, 26 April 1947.
96. *Burnley Express*, 29 April 1914.
97. The Northern simpleton had been the stock-in-trade of the music hall artist George Formby Snr, whose character 'John Willie' from Lancashire 'embodied the gormless, guileless Lancashire lad adrift in the wicked city'; Colin MacInnes, *Sweet Saturday Night* (Panther, London: 1969), pp. 81–2.
98. 27 April 1923.
99. *Burnley Express*, 29 April 1914.
100. *Preston Guardian*, 7 May 1938.
101. 'Professor Musgrove's North of England: a critique', *Journal of Regional and Local Studies* 12 (1992), pp. 25–31.
102. See, for example, Jeffrey Hill, 'Social democracy and the labour movement: the Social Democratic Federation in Lancashire', *Bulletin of the North West Labour History Society* 8 (1982–3), pp. 44–55.
103. See Michael Savage, *The Dynamics of Working Class Politics: The Labour Movement in Preston, 1880–1940* (Cambridge U.P., Cambridge: 1987).
104. *Visions*, p. 213, and pp. 336ff.
105. See, for example, Tony Bennett and James Donald in *Popular Culture* (Open U.P., Milton Keynes: 1981), Block 2, 'The historical development of popular culture in Britain', pp. 79–85.

6. Churches, sport and identities in the North, 1900–1939

Jack Williams

Consideration of church-affiliated sports clubs is essential for an appreciation of sport and its social significance in the North of England before the Second World War. In many parts of the North a very high proportion, and at some times a majority, of those playing team ball games during the first four decades of the twentieth century did so for church clubs. Such clubs were not restricted to Northern England, but no other region had a greater concentration of them. This chapter discusses the extent of church-related sport and explores how the involvement of churches with recreational sport in the North of England between 1900 and 1939 reflected and helped to fashion identities centred upon gender, denomination and class. By deepening understanding of these cultural identities and their formation, analysis of church-based sport provides a further dimension for assessing debates about the nature of social and political relations in England during the first half of the twentieth century.

Although the impact of muscular Christianity upon sport in England before the First World War has been demonstrated by Mangan and Mason,[1] little attention has been devoted to the connections between churches and recreational sport after 1914, which, given the vast numbers of church clubs in the 1920s and 1930s, is a surprising omission from the historiography of English sport. The neglect of church sport in social histories of organized religion is equally perplexing, especially as the willingness of so many to play for church teams uncovers much about popular assumptions concerning the social functions of churches. What church sports clubs reveal about attitudes to the churches is highly pertinent to appraisals of the claim that English society was becoming more secularized before the Second World War.[2]

I

Although many church sports clubs had been formed before 1900, numbers of church teams were highest during the first four decades of the twentieth century. Throughout the period 1900–39 association football and cricket were the sports with most church teams. Table 1 illustrates what proportion of teams playing recreational cricket and football in a number of Northern towns and their surroundings in 1900, 1914, 1922, 1930 and 1939 were affiliated to churches or Sunday schools. Big cities are excluded from Table 1 because their local newspapers did not usually have such detailed coverage of the lower levels of recreational sport as those based upon county boroughs. Bolton, Burnley, Oldham, St Helens and Wigan, the five localities from Lancashire, were included in Table 1 because travelling to them in order to collect data was relatively easy. Barnsley, Halifax and Sunderland, the three areas outside Lancashire, were chosen because of their differing industrial structures. The sample years of Table 1 indicate that the numbers of church football teams rose between 1900 and 1914 and reached a peak in six localities in 1922. The number of church teams in 1930 was higher than in 1914 for six localities, whilst seven localities had fewer church football teams in 1939 than in 1914. The pattern for the numbers of cricket teams differed slightly. Half of the localities had more cricket teams in 1900 than in 1914. 1922 was the sample peak year for the number of church cricket teams in four localities, whilst 1900 was the sample peak year for one locality and 1930 for the remaining three. The highest concentrations of church teams were in Bolton, Burnley and Oldham and their surroundings.

Numbers of church-affiliated clubs playing other sports expanded between the wars, yet rarely approached those for football or cricket. Of the eight localities represented in Table 1, only Bolton had a tennis league specifically for church clubs, though probably some churches had tennis clubs which did not play in formal competitions and so were overlooked by local newspapers. The proportion of women's hockey clubs connected with churches was greater than that for men's hockey clubs. Of the localities in Table 1, Bolton had the highest number of women's hockey teams. In 1920 35 of the 38 women's teams playing hockey in the Bolton area were connected with churches, though by 1939, five of the 20 teams playing regularly were affiliated to churches. Bolton was a great stronghold of rounders, a sport played exclusively by women. In 1920 all eighteen of the teams playing in the Bolton area were affiliated to churches or Sunday schools. By 1939 the total number of teams had risen to 60, but included only eight connected with churches. Cricket as a sport for women grew modestly between the wars. By 1935 towns in Lancashire such as Bolton, Burnley, Crompton,

Heywood, Littleborough and Milnrow each had a women's club, but none was based upon a church. Women's cricket was stronger in Yorkshire. In 1935 Bradford had a women's cricket league of sixteen clubs. Only one was a church club.

Table 1 The numbers of church-based cricket and football teams in selected localities, 1900–1939

Locality	1900	1914	1922	1930	1939
Church-based cricket teams					
Barnsley	4(80)	3(61)	24(73)	14(101)	3(32)
Bolton	97(111)	42(111)	70(134)	77(168)	62(155)
Burnley	59(81)	49(60)	107(129)	79(145)	54(101)
Halifax	11(43)	31(100)	22(88)	29(117)	18(93)
Oldham	30(126)	81(139)	79(132)	94(169)	64(140)
St Helens	9(34)	5(32)	6(32)	11(44)	2(42)
Sunderland	8(53)	13(108)	20(103)	13(122)	9(121)
Wigan	13(43)	15(38)	17(41)	11(48)	10(43)
Church-based football teams					
Barnsley	0(36)	28(75)	69(143)	21(99)	1(69)
Bolton	26(65)	75(136)	167(255)	92(192)	63(127)
Burnley	7(20)	28(133)	69(136)	41(73)	23(51)
Halifax	2(11)	39(78)	3(30)	16(42)	20(54)
Oldham	7(42)	37(57)	115(199)	48(78)	22(35)
St Helens	6(29)	30(50)	55(88)	51(95)	24(80)
Sunderland	14(58)	40(226)	72(307)	60(189)	24(142)
Wigan	3(34)	27(41)	37(55)	59(72)	33(54)

Note: Numbers in brackets represent the total number of teams from each locality which were mentioned in local newspapers. Each locality represents the area for which local newspapers reported upon recreational sport. The geographical extent in the coverage of local sport scarcely changed between 1900 and 1939. Each locality included a county borough and its surrounding districts. Newspapers consulted for Tables 1 and 2 included *The Barnsley Chronicle, The Barnsley Independent, Bolton Evening News (Bolton Evening News), Cricket and Football Field (Bolton Evening News), The Buff, The Burnley Express, Halifax Daily Courier and Guardian, Halifax Evening Courier, Oldham Evening News, Green Final, The St Helens Newspaper, The St Helens Reporter, The Sunderland Daily Echo, The Wigan Observer.* The numbers of football teams are for the months January–April of the sample years. This note also applies to Table 2.

There was a considerable church presence in indoor sport, but this too varied between sports. Church teams in billiards leagues seem to have been more numerous in Lancashire than in Yorkshire or Durham. There were no church or Sunday school billiards leagues in Barnsley, Halifax or Sunderland in 1900, 1914, 1922, 1930 or 1939, though in 1922 seven of the 26 teams in the Sunderland and District Institutes Billiards League had been affiliated to churches. In 1930 there were three church-affiliated teams in the Halifax Institutes Billiards League and two in the Barnsley Temperance Billiards League. In Lancashire St Helens had a Catholic Young Men's Society Billiards League in 1914, whilst in the 1930s there was a Wigan and District Church of England Billiards League and a Free Church Billiards League containing eleven church teams and six connected with temperance organizations. In the Bolton area 80 of the 96 teams playing billiards in 1920 were connected with churches and 66 of the 120 in 1939. Numbers of church teams were also high in table tennis, a game which press reports suggest expanded between the wars, though as early as 1914 the thirteen teams playing in the Sunderland and District Ping Pong League were connected with churches. In St Helens four of the eight teams playing in table tennis leagues by 1929 were affiliated to churches. By 1939 the number of teams had grown to 47 with fifteen being church teams. The first table tennis league in the Bolton area was formed in 1932 by the Bolton Sunday School Social League. By 1939 Bolton had two table tennis leagues. 21 of their 35 teams were affiliated to churches. In Halifax fourteen of the teams playing in the two table tennis leagues in 1939 were church teams.

Some sports had very small numbers of church-affiliated clubs. Church golf and rugby union teams were rare. Newspaper references to church netball, athletics or boxing teams from the towns mentioned in Table 1 are unusual, though in big cities church youth clubs provided boxing facilities. As an amateur sport, rugby league, or northern union football as it was called until 1922, almost collapsed in the Halifax area between the wars, but even in 1914, none of its fourteen teams had been connected with a church. None of the 20 teams playing rugby league in Oldham in 1900 was affiliated to a church. By 1914 the number of teams in Oldham had dropped to five, which included two church teams. A revival occurred between the wars, but only three of the fifteen teams playing in 1924 and two of the sixteen in 1939 were based on churches. No amateur rugby league teams were mentioned by *The Wigan Observer* in 1900. One of the ten teams playing in the Wigan area by 1914 was a church team, and only one of the twelve playing in 1930 and two of the fourteen playing in 1939 were connected with churches. Billiards was the only sport played extensively in pubs which also had large numbers of church teams. Very few church teams played in darts leagues. The church presence in bowls was a little stronger, though usually church teams were far outnumbered by those connected with workplaces, political clubs, pubs and parks. By the late 1930s Wigan had a Catholic Young Men's Bowls League and a Protestant Churches Bowls League. Church and non-church badminton teams were rarely mentioned by newspapers from the towns listed in Table 1.[3]

The greatest concentrations of church teams were found at the lower levels of organized recreational cricket and football. No church clubs have played in the Lancashire League, the Central Lancashire League or the Bolton League, which are usually regarded as the most prestigious cricket leagues in Lancashire. The Durham Senior Cricket League included no church teams between 1900 and 1939, though Pudsey St Lawrence, a church club, played in the Bradford League, one of Yorkshire's leading cricket leagues. Church teams were equally rare at the highest levels of amateur football. Even in such a stronghold of church sport as Bolton, only two of the 34 teams from the Bolton and District Football League, generally considered to be the locality's leading amateur soccer league, were connected with churches.

Sunday school football and cricket leagues were usually regarded as having the worst facilities and lowest standards of play, though they produced some players of great skill. The cricket grounds and pitches of Sunday school cricket clubs were often particularly rough. Even after the Second World War the Burnley Sunday School Cricket League had a separate section for teams playing on cinder pitches. In the St Helens area some church clubs had grounds on waste land with shale wickets.[4] Those of the Radcliffe Sunday School Cricket League near Bolton have been remembered as having 'Grass, shrubs and all sorts in the outfield ... Important not to lose a ball ... For a ball lost in the outfield batsmen were allowed to run four runs.'[5] One ground was so small that on one side only two runs were awarded when a ball crossed the boundary. Low scores were a further indication of the poor quality of cricket pitches. The Radcliffe Sunday School League had an annual prize for the batsmen who reached double figures most often in a season and a side scoring 50 runs had a fair chance of winning.[6] On one occasion the whole of Brunswick United Methodist team from the Horwich Sunday School League, also near Bolton, were dismissed for nought, but five of the opposition were dismissed before the single run was scored to win the match.[7]

II

Because written records of church clubs are so scarce, interviews are usually the only method for establishing the social backgrounds of those who played for such clubs, though few of those who played before the 1930s are still living. Interviews show that those who played for church teams in the 1930s belonged predominantly to the working class and lower middle class. Most were blue-collar workers, often with some degree of skill, whilst many sides seem to have included between two and four white-collar workers such as teachers or clerks. The Mass-Observation Worktown archive shows that thirteen players from the Westhoughton Congregational Sunday School FC in the late 1930s included two clerks, four side piecers, two joiners, a railway worker, an apprentice fitter, a chemical worker, a rope splicer and one who was unemployed.[8] In the Bolton area the proportion of those with white-collar occupations who played for church cricket teams rose slightly in the 1930s.

Inclusion of the words 'Sunday School' in the titles of many church-based clubs and leagues did not mean that they were primarily for youths. The great majority of Sunday school sport clubs were for the men's sections of Sunday schools, though some Sunday school leagues had divisions for youth teams. The Bolton Sunday School Social League, which organized competitions for a variety of sports, was reputed to be the largest Sunday school sports body in England by the mid-1930s. In 1936 the majority of the 3000 who played in its wintertime competitions were over eighteen.[9] The nature of the game probably meant that most of those who played football for open age Sunday school football teams tended to be under 30. Westhoughton Congregational Sunday School FC included one player aged 35, ten aged between 20 and 24 and two aged 18, whilst the ages of players from Walkden Congregational FC were between 17 and 27.[10] Sunday school cricket teams often contained two or three players in their thirties or even forties and in general, the higher the level of competition at which a church club played, the higher the average age of its players tended to be. In 1938 the first eleven of the All Souls CC, which played in the Second Division of the Bolton and District Cricket Association, a relatively high level of recreational cricket, had two players in their forties and three in their thirties, whilst the second eleven contained one 50-year-old and three in their thirties.[11]

Oral evidence suggests that those who played for church-based sport teams between the wars came from the 'respectable' sections of the working and lower middle classes, though definitions of respectability were highly subjective. The recollections concerning one Sunday school team in Lancashire could have been applied to most others:

Almost certainly they belonged to the respectable working class. We had only one black sheep in the team. George. A boozer. A regular drinker. He had no friends in the team who went with him ... Good

hard working lads from working-class families in the main ... No
rough eggs. All had settled jobs. Good working families.[12]

Most players are remembered as being regular attenders at church or
Sunday school, which was often seen as a mark of respectability. 'Your
roughnecks', it has been pointed out, 'they didn't go to church.'[13]

The tiny numbers of church clubs competing at the higher levels of
local football and cricket, on the other hand, did not enforce rules
about players attending church regularly, especially where the survival
of a club at a high level of sporting competition meant that talented
players, regardless of their religious inclinations, had to be recruited.
This probably explains why the small numbers of church clubs playing
in prestigious leagues often severed the formal links with their parent
churches and became open clubs. In 1924, Walkden Congregational
Cricket, whose first team was playing in the First Division of the Bolton
and District Cricket Association, became an open club. Previously there
had been no requirement for first team players to attend church, but
those who played for the second team had to be members of the Sunday
school.[14] Syd Greenhalgh has recalled that when he became the professional of the Delph Hill Wesleyan club of the First Division of the
Bolton and District Cricket Association in the early 1930s 'Nobody
ever asked me about my religion or if I went to church. I didn't
go, no.'[15]

III

The sparseness of evidence about the origins of church-based clubs and
leagues means that explanations for the great numbers of church cricket
and football teams have to be expressed with caution. Because church-
based teams formed such a high proportion of all teams, factors
encouraging the growth of recreational sport in general overlap with
those stimulating the expansion of church sports clubs. Table 1 shows
that the greatest concentrations of recreational soccer clubs were in
areas where local clubs had been admitted to the Football League before
1914, which suggests a connection between a high level of interest in
professional football and the desire to play recreational sport, though
this does not explain why football clubs came to be based on churches.
County cricket may well have encouraged the playing of cricket in
Lancashire and Yorkshire, though in Lancashire the greatest concentrations of church cricket clubs were in those areas where league cricket
of a very high quality was played, and in Yorkshire the Bradford area
was a stronghold of high-quality league cricket and church-based
cricket. The relatively small numbers of teams playing recreational

rugby league in centres of professional rugby league have already been noted and indicates that interest in the first-class variant of a sport was not always accompanied by large numbers of recreational teams.

League competitions encouraged the formation of church clubs. The organization of recreational football and cricket into league compet-itions gathered momentum in the North of England during the Edwardian period, a development which probably owed much to the spread of leagues at the higher levels of association football and club cricket in the North during the 1890s. To remain viable, leagues needed usually a minimum of six teams. When leagues, and especially Sunday school or church leagues, were being formed, it was not unusual for churches without teams to be invited to form teams. When the Horwich Sunday School Cricket League was formed in 1922, all local churches were invited to enter teams, which resulted in three new church teams being established.[16] Some leagues, such as the Walkden Amateur Cricket League, insisted that each member club had to field a side in the reserve division, a practice which obliged some clubs to form additional teams. Occasionally league structures may have restricted the establishment of church teams. The Sheffield and Hallamshire Football Association usually insisted that new leagues could not accept clubs from existing leagues. In 1919 it refused to permit the formation of a Sunday school league in Wombwell after the Barnsley Football Union complained that its approval for the proposed league had not been obtained and that it was already making provision for Sunday school teams.[17]

The high numbers of church cricket and football teams reinforced assumptions that such teams should have been based upon churches and Sunday school. Mason has explained that churches, workplaces and pubs were the social institutions most likely to have spawned football clubs in the North and Midlands between the 1860s and 1890s,[18] but by 1900 church teams outnumbered those based on workplaces or pubs for all eight localities mentioned in Table 1. Very few football clubs were named after pubs between 1900 and 1939, though some clubs with district titles may have had strong informal links with pubs. Fishwick has shown that in Sheffield teams playing football but not affiliated to Sheffield and Hallamshire FA were often connected with pubs.[19] The extent of 'unaffiliated' football is difficult to estimate, but as it is not reported for the sample years by local newspapers for the eight localities of Table 1, which reported upon local sport in great depth, it seems probable that it was not very extensive. The difficulty of finding grounds, which limited the numbers of affiliated clubs, would have been an equally formidable problem for unaffiliated clubs. It is likely, of course, that teams based upon pubs may have played 'knockabout' matches on patches of rough ground. By 1913 licensed victuallers' leagues from Rotherham, Swinton and Sheffield had affiliated with the Sheffield and Hallamshire FA. In 1919 the Swinton LVL became the Swinton and District Football League. The Rotherham LVL was still playing in the early 1920s. In 1922 a Doncaster Clubs and Institutes League affiliated with the Sheffield and Hallamshire FA.[20] None of the eight localities mentioned in Table 1 had a licensed victuallers' football league in 1900, 1914, 1922, 1930 or 1939. A working men's clubs' football league was formed in Barnsley in 1922, but disbanded after one season.[21] There was a licensed houses' cricket league in Burnley in 1900 and another in Halifax in 1922, though neither survived for long. In the late 1930s Burnley had a club and institute cricket league. No evidence was found of pub-based teams of women playing tennis, hockey, rounders or table tennis in the towns listed in Table 1.

The strength of Sabbatarianism in the North, which reflected the role of organized religion in popular culture, restricted opportunities for some to participate in sport. Although recreational sport was played on Sundays in Southern England between the wars,[22] league football and league cricket were hardly ever played on Sundays in the North. Some who worked on Saturdays perhaps would have welcomed opportunities to play on Sundays, but acceptance of Sabbatarianism was such that no public demands for the playing of recreational sport on Sundays have been found in a wide range of Northern newspapers. One interviewee has said that playing football or cricket on Sundays was 'taboo. Just not thought of'.[23] Almost all towns had midweek leagues which played on early-closing afternoons and catered for groups of workers unable to play on Saturdays. Church clubs rarely played in outdoor sports midweek leagues, though the Burnley Sunday School Cricket League established a Tuesday section in the late 1930s.

IV

No firm connections can be made between the numbers of church sports teams and the economic circumstances of the working and lower middle classes. Playing for church clubs was not expensive, subscriptions rarely exceeding five shillings. Football clubs provided shirts, but not shorts or boots, whilst cricket clubs provided bats, pads and gloves. The numbers of both church and non-church football teams for most localities listed in Table 1 rose sharply between 1900 and 1914, though similar increases did not occur in the numbers of church and non-church cricket teams. It is usually claimed, however, that any gains in the living standards for most occupational groups in this period were at best slight.[24] For most of these same localities, the numbers of church and non-church cricket and football teams were lower in 1939 than 1922, though the figure for 1930 in some instances was higher than that for 1922. Most groups of workers experienced modest rises in their living standards in the 1920s and 1930s, yet all the localities except Halifax listed in Table 1 had high concentrations of either coal miners or cotton workers, two major occupational groups whose real wages remained stationary for most of the inter-war period. Rising levels of prosperity for those in work especially during the late 1930s, whilst no more than modest,[25] may have contributed to the declining numbers of church-based teams by increasing access to commercialized forms of mass entertainment.

Unemployment does not seem to have caused the number of church teams to fall. Unemployment was lower in 1939 than 1930, but in almost all of the localities listed in Table 1, numbers of church cricket and football teams were higher in 1930 than 1939. In the Bolton area unemployment reached its peak in 1931, but this was also the season of the 1930s with the highest number of church cricket teams, though even more church teams had played in 1927 and 1928, years of relatively low unemployment. After 1931 levels of unemployment declined each year in the Bolton area except for 1938, but the number of church cricket teams also fell each year with the exception of 1936. Oral evidence from the Bolton area shows that those who became unemployed did not stop playing for church cricket teams, though it is possible that being unemployed may have discouraged some from joining a club. Unemployed players from the Horwich Sunday School cricket league passed their time tending the grounds of their clubs. In the late 1930s the Westhoughton Congregational FC paid the expenses of its three unemployed players.[26]

Unemployment seems to have stimulated the playing of recreational soccer in the Sheffield area. Annual reports of the Sheffield and Hallam-shire County FA record the number of affiliated clubs for each season from 1923–4 until 1938–9, though, of course, these ignore those clubs which played and did not bother to affiliate with the Association. The number of affiliated clubs reached its peak for the 1920s in the 1926–7 season when the miners' strike had caused unemployment to rise. In 1926–7 the number of affiliated clubs was 748, compared with 671 for 1925–6 and 661 for 1927–8. The annual report for 1927–8 attributed the high number of affiliated clubs in 1926–7 to 'abnormal conditions prevailing during that season, many clubs being temporarily formed in the mining areas'. The first four years of the 1930s, times of high unemployment in the Sheffield area, saw the number of affiliated clubs rise each season from 1929–30 until a peak of 874 was recorded in 1933–4. A fall in the number of clubs for 1934–5 was attributed in part to 'improvements in trade'. By 1937–8 the number of affiliated clubs had dropped to 601, a figure lower than for any other inter-war season since 1923–4, and in the 1938–9 season the number of affiliated clubs was only 602, even though the second half of the 1930s is generally thought to have been a time of rising prosperity.[27]

House building caused the number of church teams to fall. Land-owners often found it profitable to sell sports grounds for house building and church sport clubs could rarely find alternative land to lease at affordable rents. A sports club usually collapsed when the lease of its ground was terminated. Sixteen cricket clubs, including fourteen based on churches from Bolton county borough alone, disbanded as a result of losing their grounds between 1924 and 1934.[28] The annual reports of the Sheffield and Hallamshire FA for 1934–5, 1935–6 and 1936–7 all stated that the loss of grounds through house building was a prime cause for the decline in the number of clubs and in 1939 the National Fitness Council pointed out that building around six West Riding towns had recently absorbed 130 football pitches.[29] Indirect evidence shows that church football clubs were hit disproportionately hard by the loss of grounds. The only annual handbooks of the Sheffield and Hallam-shire FA to have been found are those for 1933–4 and 1936–7. These do not list all affiliated clubs, but 525 clubs were named in that for 1933–34 and 526 in that for 1936–37, whilst the numbers of church clubs listed dropped from 99 to 58, which suggests that church clubs were among those most likely to have been affected by the sale of grounds for house building. The acquisition of more publicly-owned playing fields through the activities of the National Playing Fields Association compensated only partially for the loss of privately-owned sports fields.

Differences in industrial structures and in levels of support from firms for work-based sport clubs influenced the numbers of church-based sports clubs. Table 2 indicates the number of cricket and football teams based on workplaces for the eight localities mentioned in Table 1.

Table 2   The numbers of works cricket and football teams in selected localities, 1900–1939

Locality	1900	1914	1922	1930	1939
Works cricket teams					
Barnsley	11(80)	6(61)	5(73)	18(101)	6(32)
Bolton	1(111)	3(111)	5(134)	20(168)	31(155)
Burnley	3(81)	0(60)	2(129)	20(145)	21(101)
Halifax	3(43)	12(100)	3(88)	30(117)	24(93)
Oldham	0(126)	0(139)	2(132)	4(169)	1(140)
St Helens	4(34)	3(32)	4(32)	6(44)	10(42)

Sunderland	1(53)	12(108)	21(103)	31(122)	38(121)
Wigan	4(43)	1(38)	3(41)	5(48)	4(43)

Works football teams

Barnsley	3(36)	5(75)	8(143)	9(99)	28(69)
Bolton	4(65)	4(136)	13(255)	32(192)	34(127)
Burnley	4(20)	4(133)	5(136)	10(73)	16(51)
Halifax	0(11)	9(78)	2(30)	7(42)	13(54)
Oldham	2(42)	5(57)	10(199)	3(78)	3(35)
St Helens	1(29)	4(50)	3(88)	8(95)	19(80)
Sunderland	1(58)	10(226)	37(307)	62(189)	53(142)
Wigan	3(34)	4(41)	0(55)	3(72)	1(54)

Note: Numbers in brackets represent the total number of teams from each locality. The totals of work-based teams do not include those which were playing in interdepartmental works competitions.

For most of these localities numbers of workplace teams were highest in 1930 or 1939 and where the number of workplace teams rose in the 1930s, this usually coincided with a fall in the number of church cricket and football teams. The proportions of cotton firms with sports teams between the wars were less than those found in coal mining, engineering, ship building and other forms of metal working, which may have been because international trading conditions were especially harsh for the cotton industry during most of the 1920s and 1930s. The high number of mining company sports teams in Durham and Yorkshire was due to a substantial part of the Miners' Welfare Fund, financed by a levy upon coal production paid by colliery companies and disbursed by joint committees representing employers and mining unions, being devoted to recreation which included sport. In 1929, for instance, over £500,000 of the Miners' Welfare Fund income of £770,000 in the South Yorkshire region was spent on recreation and nearly £135,000 out of £337,000 in West Yorkshire.[30] The relatively weaker state of colliery sport in Lancashire may have stemmed from the decision of mining unions and companies to devote all their income from the Miners' Welfare Fund to a convalescent home at Blackpool. Between 1921 and 1938 99 miners' recreation schemes in Northumberland, 158 in Durham, 29 in Cumberland and 190 in Yorkshire had been granted aid from the Welfare Fund, but only one in Lancashire.[31] In 1928 the chairman of the Bolton Sunday Schools Social League noted that some who had played for Sunday Schools Social League teams were being tempted to works welfare teams because of their better facilities,[32] a tendency which probably occurred in other localities. The sporting facilities provided by the glass manufacturing company Pilkington Brothers could have been responsible for the decline of church-based cricket in the St Helens area during the 1930s. An interdepartmental league was launched in 1927 and for most of the 1930s it included at least ten teams. In addition, the St Helens Recs CC, for which all of the company's employees in St Helens were eligible to play, ran four teams for much of the inter-war period.[33] The strength of works sport in the Sheffield area probably contributed to the decline in the number of church football clubs. The rise in the number of works clubs named in the annual handbooks of the Sheffield and Hallamshire FA for 1933–4 and 1936–7 matched exactly the decline in the number of church clubs.

V

Evidence about the origins of church-based cricket and football clubs between 1900 and 1939 is so meagre that it is not possible to determine how often clerics were the prime movers in the establishment of such clubs. Cunningham has argued that in the 1870s and 1880s the costs of establishing football clubs may have meant that working men wishing to play football sought upper- or middle-class sponsorship, but that such sponsors were cast aside once clubs were firmly established.[34] It is not certain whether pressures from working men with a strong desire to play sport led to the formation of church teams between 1900 and 1939, but as only a tiny proportion of all church-based teams severed their links with churches in this period, it seems unlikely that working men used churches as sponsors of sports clubs in the manner which may have occurred in the late nineteenth century. Material regarding the beginnings of church-based leagues is also scarce. No clerics were involved in the creation of the Horwich Sunday School Cricket League in 1922. The great majority of teams which played in the Walkden Amateur Cricket League were connected with churches, but no clerics were concerned with its resuscitation in 1924. Whilst clerics often acted as honorary figureheads of church-based leagues and attended annual prize-giving ceremonies, they did not usually help with the routine administration of such leagues, which could mean that they had not taken key roles in the formation of such leagues.

Clerical support for church-based sport was more widespread than opposition, though the dominant attitude among most clerics appears to have been closer to indifference than fervent enthusiasm. Few clerics played regularly for church teams. Extensive searches through local newspapers from the Bolton area and more selective inspections of newspapers from other Northern towns have unearthed a few statements by clerics in support of church-based sport and only one of opposition. Such reports, however, are too infrequent to determine whether the intensity of clerical support for church involvement with sport varied between 1900 and 1939. The numbers of church-based clubs are indirect evidence that opposition among clerics to church sport cannot have been intense, though in 1928 the chairman of the Bolton Sunday School Social League complained of 'antagonism or lack of encouragement on the part of clergy and the heads of some Sunday schools'.[35] None of the five clerics who had worked in the Bolton area in the 1930s and who could be traced played regularly for church teams or recalled any of their colleagues being highly involved in church-based sport. Only one had a strong interest in sport. He played cricket for one of the area's prestigious clubs, yet was unaware that there had been a cricket club connected with his church before the start of his ministry and had made no attempt to establish cricket or football teams at the church.[36] It is likely that many clerics would have agreed with the reports of the Conference of Christian Politics, Economics and Citizenship, a gathering held at Birmingham in 1924 and attended by delegates of all major denominations, which called for more public playing fields, but also stressed that sport could use energies needed for other purposes and become a form of idolatry. The report of the Conference sessions on leisure claimed that:

> the church must not be secularised; in all her social obligations the spiritual side must come first. She is a social agency, but something more ...

and continued:

> neither the athlete nor his admirers would be the worse for a wider outlook. The tendency of the athlete to scoff at other forms of ability should be deprecated as silly.[37]

When they did advocate church involvement with sport, clerics usually stressed how sport could strengthen qualities compatible with Christian teachings. At the annual dinner of the Manchester YMCA in 1909 it was claimed that sports strengthened 'determination and purpose' whilst presenting 'unrivalled opportunities for social intercourse' and 'the development of unselfishness ... an effect the value of which could not be overrated'. Writing in *The Bolton Congregationalist* the Reverend Albert Peel argued that 'Modesty and patience, intellect and harmony, these are the things that make for success on the cricket field – and also in the game of life'. A. W. Nye, an Anglican vicar from Bolton, claimed that the great recreative value of cricket was that it schooled one to accept success or defeat, and when played in the correct spirit developed character.[38] Clerics rarely advocated church-based sport as a means of promoting church attendance.

Fragments of evidence suggest that clerical opposition to Catholic teams playing in interdenominational Sunday school leagues may have discouraged the formation of Catholic teams. Before 1914 and in the early 1920s some Catholic churches had teams which played in inter-denominational Sunday school football leagues, though more often Catholic teams competed in leagues not based on Sunday schools. Very few Catholic teams played in Sunday school cricket leagues. In the late 1920s and 1930s Catholic teams tended to withdraw from inter-denominational football leagues and Catholic football leagues were set up in Bolton, Oldham, St Helens and Houghton near Sunderland. It seems probable that this tendency for Catholic teams to withdraw from interdenominational leagues was influenced by fears among clerics that contact with other denominations could weaken adherence to the Cath-olic church. One priest has described the Catholic church as not 'going in for mixed bathing' between the wars.[39] The one Catholic church cricket team playing in Bolton beween the wars, however, was formed by one of its priests.[40]

Assertions about the interdependence of modernization and secular-ization have led to assumptions that society in England has become increasingly secularized in the twentieth century.[41] Although seculariz-ation is notoriously difficult to define or measure, fluctuations in the numbers of church-based sport clubs can help to gauge the spread of secularized attitudes. If convictions that the social role of churches should be restricted are taken as evidence of secularization, it would seem that the rising numbers of church cricket and football teams between 1900 and the 1920s do not indicate an increase in seculariz-ation. The decline in the number of church teams during the late 1930s may perhaps have meant that it was becoming expected that the social activities of the churches should be restricted, though many church clubs collapsed because of the loss of their grounds. If falling levels of church attendance are used as evidence of secularization, it can be argued that the decline in the numbers of church teams in the later 1930s was more a cause than a result of secularization. As will be shown below, church clubs stimulated church attendance. The demise of church clubs due to the loss of grounds removed one incentive for attending church.

If a decline in the influence of clerical teachings over conduct is regarded as an expression of secularization, the degree to which church-based cricket and football teams played in accordance with the expectations of clerical apologists for sport may help to chart the extent of secularization. Clergymen with an interest in sport often claimed

that it could develop character in a distinctly Christian manner by
fostering sportsmanship and unselfishness. There is evidence among
church teams of both sportsmanship and sharp practice, but unfortunately even highly localized data fails to show whether misconduct on
the part of church teams rose or fell between 1900 and 1939. Oral
evidence concerning cricket in the Bolton area suggests that church
teams played in accordance with clerical teachings in the 1930s. One
player whose cricketing career covered the full range of league cricket
never experienced a more competitive spirit than that found in the
Radcliffe and Bury Sunday School Leagues, but he has recalled that
there was 'no cheating'.[42] One who played in the Horwich Sunday
School League has said:

> I'm not trying to give myself wings. I always tried to be fair … There
> was swearing in matches. No vulgarities. Damn and blast, I've know
> parsons come out with that on a cricket field. No fights, never.[43]

Written evidence, however, shows that church teams were as likely to
resort to sharp practice and cheating as other teams. Reports in the
minute book of the Walkden Amateur Cricket League for the 1920s
and 1930s of playing unregistered players under false names, a player
threatening to strike another and of one team abandoning its innings
as a protest against the decisions of an umpire, though far from common,
all involved church teams. In the Horwich Sunday School League,
where it was felt essential to have umpires not connected with either
side, umpires complained of players disputing decisions and failing to
indicate when balls crossed the boundary.[44] Monthly meetings of the
Council of the Sheffield and Hallamshire Football Association from
1900 until 1939 always recorded instances of players from church clubs
being suspended for fighting, kicking opponents, inciting others to
violent conduct or insulting referees. The numbers of players suspended
from church clubs seems to have been at least proportional to the
numbers of church clubs. The fact that church cricket and football
teams did not play in a more sporting manner than non-church teams
can be regarded as a rejection of clerical teachings over one form of
conduct and consequently as evidence of secularized attitudes.

VI

Church sports clubs expressed distinctive gender identities and so
helped to bolster the social power of men. The playing of sport for
church teams by women may have promoted the emancipation of
women by undermining beliefs about the physical weakness of

women, but the fact that far more men than women played for church teams and that few sports had mixed teams probably reinforced assumptions about it being natural for the two sexes to have different social roles. As with other forms of recreational sport, church teams for men often depended upon the services of women. Kit was usually washed by women. Church cricket clubs observed the ritual of tea, but teas were invariably prepared by women.[45] The performance of these domestic-style duties by women reflected an understanding that such duties were the sphere of women, and as such perpetuated sexual inequalities. Whilst some men stopped playing sport because of family commitments, women hockey and rounders players from the Bolton area were almost always listed in local newspapers as 'Miss', which suggests that women were expected to cease playing team sports when they married. Church sport helped to maintain the social influence of the churches, but churches have not usually been seen as social institutions which were at the forefront of campaigns for women's liberation between 1900 and 1939. Male priesthoods and male-dominated authority structures within the churches seem likely to have strengthened beliefs that power should be exercised by men.

VII

Church clubs and Sunday school leagues invariably had regulations insisting that players attended church or Sunday school regularly, but such requirements were not always observed. In 1928 the chairman of the Bolton Sunday Schools Social League lamented that it was 'no uncommon practice' for players to be registered with the League who were not members of a Sunday school or church because of clerics or Sunday school officials 'not knowing to whom the registration referred, nor taking the trouble to discover', but added that church officials were being 'gradually educated to a fuller sense of their responsibilities'.[46] One respondent has remembered that 'a lot of ministers signed forms with a blind eye', especially where raising objections about non-attendance would have made it difficult to field a team and so prevented regular attenders from playing, though another minister has been described as 'a real tartar. He wouldn't sign a form with his eyes shut.'[47]

There is a much stronger body of evidence, however, which shows that church sports clubs encouraged regular church attendance, particularly in the 1930s. Interviews have confirmed that the comments of a Mass-Observation report on Harvey Street Methodist FC in Bolton applied to other clubs. The football club, it claimed:

brought more young men into the school – a rule compelling them to attend periodically, but this was seldom enforced because after playing football on Saturday, they sought out each other on the Sunday and used to meet at the school.[48]

Oral evidence has also shown that the competitive nature of church-based recreational sport meant that teams would complain to the authorities of Sunday school leagues about opposing teams playing non-church attenders. Interviews also indicate that the presence of young men at churches boosted the attendance of young women who in turn stimulated the attendance of young men who did not play sport. Those who played for church clubs were usually recruited from those who attended church or Sunday school which suggests that sports clubs were more effective in consolidating and prolonging church attendance among those who had been church attenders than in attracting non-attenders into a habit of church attendance, though a Mass-Observation report indicated that players of the Walkden Congregational football team had joined the Sunday school in order to play for the football team.[49]

For the localities listed in Table 1, Church of England cricket and football teams usually outnumbered those from any other denomination, but the strength within recreational sport of other denominations varied between localities. Hardly any Baptist churches in the Bolton area, for instance, had cricket clubs between the wars, whereas all six Baptist churches in Burnley had cricket teams at some time in the 1920s or 1930s, whilst the proportion of Wesleyan and Primitive Methodist churches with cricket or football teams in the Bolton area were far higher than in the Burnley area. Few Nonconformist churches in the Wigan area had cricket or football teams. The greater number of Church of England places of worship explains partly why Anglican teams out-numbered those of other denominations in most localities, but the ratio of teams to places of worship for other denominations was sometimes greater than that for the Church of England. In Lancashire Congreg-ational churches were usually among those denominations with the highest proportions of cricket and football teams to places of worship. Presbyterian teams in all eight localities of Table 1 were rare. The Cath-olic church was the denomination with the most marked disparity between the numbers of cricket and football teams. The proportion of Catholic churches with football teams was roughly equal to that of most other denominations, whilst Catholic cricket teams were comparatively rare in the Barnsley, Bolton, Burnley, Halifax and Sunderland areas, which may reflect the Irish origins of many Catholics in the North. Many towns had football clubs with the word 'Celtic' in their titles. These were primarily clubs for Catholics of Irish descent and perhaps had unofficial connections with particular Catholic churches. Although the number of church rugby league clubs was small, church-related rugby league clubs in Halifax, Oldham, St Helens and Wigan were usually either Catholic or YMCA teams.[50]

As the great majority of players attended the church or Sunday school with which their club was connected, playing for a church team expressed a denominational identity, though the denominational loyalties emphasized by church-based sport did not necessarily imply sectarian animosity. Most church cricket and football leagues were interdenominational. Throughout the period 1900–39 the number of church teams playing in interdenominational leagues always exceeded those belonging to leagues for single denominations. Of the eight localities listed in Table 1 there were separate Anglican and Nonconformist cricket and football leagues in Halifax and Sunderland. In the 1920s the Primitive Methodist and Congregational cricket leagues in Oldham contained teams from several denominations. The formation of separate Catholic football leagues in some parts of the North has already been mentioned. Although players were required to attend church or Sunday school regularly, some Sunday school leagues allowed players to play for the teams of churches other than those which they attended. Some clubs were prepared to play those who attended churches of other denominations. In the late 1930s the Walkden Congregational Sunday School FC had three players who attended an Anglican church. Those who attended other Protestant churches, but not Catholics, were allowed to play for the Westhoughton Congregational Sunday School FC.[51] Whether such prejudices against Catholics were common is not clear, though such practices, the formation of Catholic football leagues and the reluctance of Catholic teams in some areas to join interdenominational leagues strengthened assumptions that Catholics were a distinctive group in the North of England.[52]

VIII

Church sports clubs are relevant to debates about the nature of class identities between 1900 and 1939. Within recent years doubts have been expressed about the existence in late nineteenth-century Britain of a working-class consciousness based upon a sense of mass solidarity and a conviction that working-class interests were opposed to those of capital. Patrick Joyce has emphasized the depth of occupational divisions among working people and has argued that between 1850 and 1914 they subscribed to a notion of 'the people' which embraced other classes and did not necessarily involve a sense that the interests of working people were in conflict with those of other classes.[53] Postmodernist critiques of social relations have claimed that increasing social fragmentation stemming from ethnic and gender identities and post-Fordist methods of industrial production have undermined notions of a working-class mass solidarity in the late twentieth century. Yet if the notion of a mass working-class identity retains validity, it would seem to be for the first half of the twentieth century which witnessed the rise of the Labour Party as a major political force, though the reformist nature of the Labour Party and limited support for militant socialism for much of this period weaken suppositions about the existence of a fiercely confrontationist working-class consciousness.

As the great majority of those who played for church-based teams had occupations which are generally termed working-class with a minority from the lower middle class, playing cricket or football for church clubs reflected a desire to spend leisure time among those with similar backgrounds and can be interpreted as an expression of a working-class solidarity. Moreover, the highly competitive spirit in which the predominantly working-class church-based teams played cricket and football can be regarded as a rejection of the notion usually associated with bourgeois and clerical apologists for sport that playing a game in the right spirit was more important than winning. Yet although church sports clubs expressed a working-class identity, they also reveal a degree of fragmentation among working people and suggest that there was no overriding sense of working-class identity to which all working people subscribed. Church sport helped to reinforce gender divisions amongst working people and stressed divisions between respectables and non-respectables. Whilst church sport often encouraged interdenominational contact and showed that sectarian loyalties were often not a cause of animosity between different branches of Protestantism, it enhanced the consciousness that Catholics constituted a distinctive social grouping.

The extent of the church presence within recreational sport added to those cultural and social forces which inhibited the emergence of a working-class identity based upon a sense of mass solidarity. The expansion of church-based sport between the 1890s and the 1920s coincided with the rise of the labour movement as a major political force in the North of England. The extent of the churches' penetration of recreational cricket and football meant that it was very difficult for local branches of the Labour Party or trade unions to provide sports facilities on a similar scale. There was a strong presence of labour organizations in bowls and indoor sports such as billiards, darts and dominoes, and though this was often greater than that of Liberal clubs, it was usually no stronger than that of Conservative clubs. The fact that in some towns teams based on labour organizations played against Conservative teams shows that indoor sports even when played by labour organizations were not necessarily powerful agents in consolidating a confrontationist consciousness. The British Workers' Sports Federation and the National

Workers' Sports Association, both formed between the wars, indicate that some socialists hoped that sport could foster working-class cultural values sympathetic to socialism, but at the local level labour involvement with cricket and football did not usually rival that of the churches. Had labour organizations established cricket and football teams on a scale similar to that of the churches, this may have helped to strengthen a working-class political identity and, by extending the influence of such organizations into another area of social activity, could have encouraged a broader labour culture. On the other hand, the strength of the church presence within recreational cricket and football meant that Conservative and Liberal teams were as rare as those based on labour organizations, with the result that these sports could not be used directly to bolster support for political alternatives to the Labour Party.

The working-class identity expressed through playing for a church team was not based upon a consciousness that working-class interests were in conflict with those of other classes. Playing for church teams was a voluntary association with churches and although the churches may have been perceived as cross-class rather than bourgeois institutions, they were not working-class cultural establishments. Some churches may have had more working-class members than others, but the organizational structures of hardly any churches were controlled by working people, and they were not creations of the working class to the same extent as, say, trade unions or co-operative societies. Teachings of the churches upon social issues also meant that church sports clubs were unlikely to have promoted confrontationist attitudes among those who played for church teams. Though there were clerics in the North who condemned capitalism in a manner likely to have fostered a confrontationist working-class ideology,[54] local press reports of church gatherings and newspaper columns written by clerics usually showed an acceptance of capitalism though linked with calls for greater class understanding and for a more humane treatment of working people. At the local level the social teachings of churches would appear to have been compatible with support for the Conservative or Liberal parties or for the reformist elements within the Labour Party. The capacity of church cricket and football clubs to promote church attendance has already been noted, and whilst attendance at church or Sunday school was not in itself proof that all of the teachings of a church were accepted, it would have been difficult to square fierce antagonism to church teachings with regular attendance.

IX

It would be absurd to maintain that church-based sport is the key to unlocking the nature and complexities of social identity within the North of England during the first four decades of this century. Church-based sport was only one cultural institution which influenced senses of identity among working people. Wage levels, workplaces, the incidence of un-employment and the impact of other cultural forms such as the cinema no doubt did more to fashion social consciousness and focus senses of identity. Yet the perspective which church-based sport provides upon senses of identity among working people reveals much about their values and shows how these could be shaped through connections with cultural institutions such as the churches. Church-based sport not only demon-strates the varied and fragmented senses of identity among working people, but also helps to explain why the social consciousness of many working people did not express a mass solidarity which implied hostility to other classes or precluded co-operation with them.

Notes

1. J. A. Mangan, *Athleticism in the Victorian and Edwardian Public School* (Cambridge U.P., Cambridge: 1981), considers the connections between muscular Christianity and athleticism at the public schools; T. Mason, *Association Football and English Society 1863–1915* (Harvester, Brighton: 1980), chapter 1, discusses the contribution of muscular Christianity to the spread of association football.

2. A. Hastings, *A History of English Christianity, 1920–1985* (Collins, London: 1985), overlooks the role of churches and Sunday schools in providing opportunities for the playing of sports; even such localized studies of the social activities of the churches in the North of England as W. S. F. Pickering (ed.), *A Social History of the Diocese of Newcastle* (Oriel, London: 1981) and E. R. Wickham, *Church and People in an Industrial City* (Lutter-worth, London: 1957), do not discuss the churches and recreational sport. For a discussion of secularization in Britain between the wars, see J. Stevenson, *British Society 1914–45* (Penguin, Harmondsworth: 1984), chapter 13.

3. Data about the numbers of church teams playing different sports were collected from *The Barnsley Chronicle, The Barnsley Independent, Bolton Evening News, Cricket and Football Field, The Buff, The Burnley Express, Halifax Daily Courier and Guardian, Halifax Evening Courier, Oldham Evening News, Green Final, The St Helens Newspaper, The St Helens Reporter, The Sunderland Daily Echo, The Sunderland Echo, The Wigan Observer, Bolton Sports Federation Centenary Booklet 1890–1990* (Bolton, n.d.).

4. Interview with Mr A. (glass manufacturer's invoice clerk, later depart-mental manager, born 1908), 21 November 1984.

5. Interview with Mr B. (bank clerk, later bank executive, born 1907), 3 August 1987.

6. Interview with Mr C. (foundry worker, born 1917), 2 April 1987.

7. Interview with Mr D. (cotton mill office worker, later mill manager, born 1914), 14 July 1987.

8. Mass-Observation Worktown Survey, Box 20, File A.
9. *Bolton Journal and Guardian*, 5 June 1936.
10. Mass-Observation Worktown Survey, Box 20, File A.
11. Information supplied by Mr E. (towel designer, born 1911).
12. Interview with Mr B.
13. Interview with Mr F. (railway clerk, born 1922), 2 April 1987.
14. *The History of Walkden Cricket Club 1899–1949* (n.p., n.d.), p. 15.
15. Interview with Mr S. Greenhalgh (dye works operative and professional cricketer), 25 March 1987.
16. Horwich Sunday School Cricket League minute book.
17. Sheffield and Hallamshire Football Association Council minute book, 14 October 1919.
18. Mason, *Association Football*, pp. 24–31.
19. N. Fishwick, *From Clegg to Clegg House: The Official Centenary History of the Sheffield and Hallamshire County Football Association 1886–1986* (Sheffield: 1986), pp. 9, 10, 15.
20. The Sheffield and Hallamshire Football Association Council minute book, 22 July 1913, 8 April 1919, balance sheet for 1922–3.
21. Telephone conversation with Mr G. (bank manager, born 1915), who was quoting from the minute book of the Barnsley and District Football Association.
22. J. R. Lowerson, 'Sport and the Victorian Sunday: the beginnings of middle-class apostasy', *British Journal of Sports History* 1.2 (1984), pp. 207–18, discusses the factors which weakened Sabbatarian restrictions upon the playing of sport on Sundays in Southern England.
23. Interview with Mr F.
24. T. R. Gourvish, 'The standard of living, 1890–1914', in A. O'Day (ed.), *The Edwardian Age: Conflict and Stability* (Macmillan, London: 1979), discusses the difficulties of calculating real wages for the Edwardian period.
25. For calculations of fluctuations in the real wages of major occupational groups between the wars, see B. R. Mitchell and P. Deane, *Abstract of British Historical Statistics* (Cambridge U.P., Cambridge: 1962), pp. 352–3.
26. Interview with Mr D.; Mass-Observation Worktown Survey, Box 20, File A.
27. Sheffield and Hallamshire Football Association annual reports 1923–4 to 1938–9.
28. *Bolton Playing Fields Association Report and Statement of Accounts for the Period Ending 31 December 1932* (Bolton Playing Field Association, Bolton: 1935), p. 4.
29. *The Times*, 12 June 1939.
30. *Barnsley Chronicle*, 1 March 1930.
31. S. G. Jones, *Workers at Play: A Social and Economic History of Leisure 1918–39* (Routledge & Kegan Paul, London: 1986), p. 76; G. Preece, 'Pithead baths and the Miners' Welfare Fund in the Lancashire coalfield 1911–1947' (MA thesis, Manchester Polytechnic, 1988), p. 59.
32. *Farnworth Weekly Journal*, 10 August 1928.
33. *The Cullet*, the house magazine of Pilkington Brothers, provides details of the company's provision of sports facilities in St Helens; see also

J. Arnold, 'The influence of Pilkington Brothers (glass manufacturers) on the growth of sport and community recreation in St Helens' (MEd thesis, University of Liverpool, 1977).

34. H. Cunningham, *Leisure in the Industrial Revolution; c. 1780–c. 1880* (Croom Helm, London: 1980), pp. 127–8, 181.

35. *Farnworth Weekly Journal*, 10 August 1928.

36. Telephone conversation with Mr H. (Congregational minister), 14 November 1989.

37. *Leisure, Being the Report Presented to the Conference on Christian Politics, Economics and Citizenship at Birmingham, 5–12 April 1924* (Longmans Green, London: 1924), pp. 25, 38.

38. *Bee-Hive* (monthly magazine of Manchester YMCA) 29. 4 (April 1909), p. 9; *Bolton Congregationalist* (May 1924), p. 75; *Buff*, 19 November 1921.

39. Telephone conversation with Father I. (Catholic priest, born 1945), 7 January 1992.

40. Interview with Mr J. (railway clerk, later school teacher, born 1917), 20 February 1989.

41. R. Wallis and S. Bruce, 'Secularization: the orthodox model', in S. Bruce (ed.), *Religion and Modernization: Sociologists and Historians Debate the Secularization Thesis* (Oxford U.P., Oxford: 1992), considers the relationship of modernization and secularization.

42. Interview with Mr C.

43. Interview with Mr B.

44. *Buff*, 2 June 1934.

45. Interviews with Mr B., Mr C. and Mr F.

46. *Farnworth Weekly Journal*, 10 August 1928.

47. Interview with Mr F.

48. Interviews with Mr B., Mr C. and Mr F.; Mass-Observation Worktown Survey, Box 16, File B.

49. Mass-Observation Worktown Survey, Box 20, File A.

50. P. J. Doyle, 'Some problems for the regional historian of rugby league', *Journal of Local Studies* 1 (1980), p. 10, suggests a close involvement of Irish Catholics with rugby league.

51. Mass-Observation Worktown Survey, Box 20, File A.

52. For an assessment of how far Catholics saw themselves as a distinct social grouping, see S. Fielding, *Class and Ethnicity: Irish Catholics in England 1880–1939* (Open University Press, Buckingham: 1993).

53. P. Joyce, *Visions of the People: Industrial England and the Question of Class 1848–1914* (Cambridge U.P., Cambridge: 1991).

54. See C. J. Ford, 'The Revd. John Wilcockson (1872–1969): a case study between church, politics and industrial society' (MPhil thesis, University of Leeds, 1985), for a detailed assessment of the political activities of a socialist cleric in Farnworth, near Bolton.

7. Heroes of the North: sport and the shaping of regional identity

Richard Holt

Introduction

The North and the South reinvented each other in the nineteenth century. Beyond the broad geographical boundaries of the Wash and the Trent, deeper cultural territories were carved out as the pace and scale of Northern industrial growth left the South behind. The North was undeniably dynamic; the remote North of Macaulay's historical imagination, of the wild fells and desolate moors, was replaced by the image that took shape in the writings of early Victorians such as Carlyle, Chadwick and Engels. This new mental map of the North was elaborated by the young Disraeli, by Mrs Gaskell, and most famously by Dickens in *Hard Times*, with its caricature of stony-faced masters of the Manchester School lording it over a landscape ravaged by factories, mines and wretched settlements of desperate workers. This was a new country with a new culture and professional team sports were a key male component of it. Sporting heroes gradually came to represent a distinctive idea of the North, of how Northern men saw themselves and how they were seen by others, including Northern women.

North and South was an old story in Europe. All kinds of much mythologized differences accumulated around this idea of geographical opposition; the hard-working, efficient, direct Northerner opposed to the more relaxed, voluble Southerner embodied in the idea of Germanic and Latin peoples; the religious split between Protestant and Catholic which divided Germany; the cultural differences of the Nord and the Midi in France, of Flemish and Walloon in Belgium, of the great Northern cities of Milan and Turin and the peasant South of Italy. The North and the South was almost as universal a cultural notion as it was a geographical fact.

Great Britain and Ireland were no exceptions. There were several such ethnic, national and regional divisions in the UK both distinct and overlapping. There was the fiercely embedded Ulster and Irish divide, with the Protestant North threatened by what was perceived as an alien culture with roots in Rome; there was the England–Scotland rivalry in which a largely Presbyterian smaller Northern nation had been politically absorbed by a larger Southern one and had to assert its distinctive identity; and finally the North–South cleavage within England itself, the personification of which in the lives of famous sportsmen is the subject of this essay. The South had a powerful and enduring myth of the poverty and backwardness of the North, especially between the wars when the North became synonymous with unemployment and deprivation. This was underpinned by familiar images and by social inquiry: the miner with his flat cap and false teeth and his whippets, the cobbles, chimneys and slag heaps of the dreadful North. The despair of Orwell's North in *The Road to Wigan Pier* and the stoicism of Cronin's Durham miners in *The Stars Look Down* combined with the more public display of Northern suffering in the Jarrow March to define the North for much of this century. A Southern England rooted in an ancient ecclesiastical geography where Durham and York were Anglican outposts of Canterbury saw the North as poor and uncivilized. Southerners, especially Londoners, patronized Northerners, who would descend on London in their tens of thousands for the football or Rugby League Cup Final. The North in contrast saw itself as more hard-working, honest and direct than the snobbish, sedentary South with its landed prejudice against things industrial; the Northern self-image was of a fairer, more genuine, friendly and industrious people whose misfortune it was to be governed by the aristocratic, agrarian South where so much was perceived to depend on public school and family connections.

Such images were not fixed or uniform but they were fairly well understood. Of course, our knowledge of them is necessarily speculative and somewhat confused, mixing up regional identities with wider ideas of class culture. Cockney dockers presumably found polite suburban London as unfriendly as the North found the South; and miners were hardly disposed to see mine owners as part of the Northern community. Yet, imprecise and approximate as they were, Northern and Southern stereotypes were very powerful, especially in sport. As old ways of playing were transformed into new organized sports, so they took over and reinforced emergent patterns of regional culture. This was particularly true of football, rugby and cricket, the three dominant modern team sports which form the bulk of this study. Although of Southern elite origin, these team sports spread very rapidly to the North in the second half of the nineteenth century and were more potent in creating a strong sense of geographical and cultural identity than individual sports like tennis and golf, which in any case were too narrowly confined to the middle classes to conquer the North. Athletics and even boxing also failed to carry the same symbolic power and meaning as collective ball games. The rapid spread of team sports was accompanied by a series of cultural changes which made Northern sport rather different from Southern, promoting professionalism and adopting distinctive ideals of masculinity. But worship of the team, the collective symbol of place and pride, did not mean neglect of the individual; individual team players rather than those who played individual sports were the new Northern heroes. A great batsman or a brilliant footballer could turn a game for his team and their supporters but he could not do it alone; he was part of a group with a collective identity, part of a civic community and, despite intense local rivalries, part of the North.

Northern sport was even more male-dominated than Southern, although both discriminated powerfully against women. Hence this essay deals with the Northern hero and not the heroine. Female achievements were ignored. Animals were more readily accepted than women as the objects of sporting admiration.[1] Greyhounds and pigeons were the favoured creatures of mining communities. Horses could be heroes, especially if they won the Grand National, which stood as a great Northern race, requiring supreme courage and strength from horse and rider, as opposed to the Southern flat-racing world revolving around social events like the Derby, Ascot and Goodwood. Red Rum pounding along the sands at Southport was an image to warm the hearts of Northern punters, but Northern men did not want their women to appropriate the grit, competitiveness and guile that they saw as belonging to themselves or their animals. Northern sporting heroes were supposed to define a distinctive kind of Northern masculinity to set against the 'moral manliness' of the public school so strong amongst the Southern elite. Northern heroes had to be tougher competitors, more dedicated, less stylish perhaps but with more substance. Winning *was* important as Yorkshire County Cricket Club, for example, showed only too well, dominating the sport from the later nineteenth century to the Second World War; they played to win, fielding sides that often contained only one amateur against Southern counties like Somerset, Hampshire or Middlesex who had more Gentlemen than Players. Northern sport was not a form of moral education in the way it was said to be amongst Southern amateurs. Even middle-class Northerners tended to accept this more openly competitive ethic. The long-standing captain of Yorkshire, Lord Hawke, came to be seen as an embodiment of the Northern approach to sport despite mixing socially with Southern Corinthians like C. B. Fry, who saw good sportsmanship as part of a wider code of chivalry and imperial idealism. Such notions were not apparent in the Northern hero.[2]

Sharing a national sport did not mean sharing a national culture. Football did not reconcile North and South. Nor did cricket. Rugby even split along a North–South axis in the 1890s, although the roots of the split were social rather than strictly regional. Cricket run from Lord's came nearest to an English national sport but only Lancashire, Yorkshire and Nottinghamshire – admittedly very important counties – were clearly Northern; the popular league form of the game, which was especially successful with workers in the Lancashire cotton towns, was considered beyond the pale by the gentlemen of the Marylebone Cricket Club. Cricket's social and geographical divisions were not exactly co-terminous, they were significantly overlapping.

Of course, Northerners were normally more interested in their own area in particular than the 'North' in general. North and South, despite being powerful images, had only partial and intermittent public resonance. North and South were not historical or official categories in the sense of the parish, the city or county; the North was not a nation or even a coherent region, as the historic cleavage of East and West, of the Red Rose and the White, illustrated. This was a fierce but not a bitter rivalry in the sense that many Lancashire and Yorkshire supporters ultimately preferred a Roses county to win than Surrey or Middlesex. Of course, the North was a big and varied area and 'Northernness' was a moveable feast. Yorkshire was a vast county of four million or so and tended to see the North as synonymous with its own peculiarly intense sense of itself as a 'a race apart'. But in Newcastle, somewhere like Sheffield or Doncaster could seem quite far South, and places like Nottingham or even Manchester only marginally Northern. Throughout the North locality was what mattered most and Northernness was contained within it rather than existing as a separate or distinctive allegiance. When Yorkshire played its 'grudge' match against Middlesex, the members of the MCC took on the mantle of the privileged South, who had to be beaten. When Northern professionals pitted themselves against Southern amateurs, as often happened in the Gentlemen and Players match, the edge to the event was real; class differences sharpened the sense of Northern identity and almost all Northern sporting heroes came from the ranks of manual workers. Northern heroes did not *have* to be born in the North – as we shall see, West Indians, Welshmen, Scots and even Australians could become heroes of the North if not strictly Northern heroes – but there were no Southerners. Northerners sometimes went South, especially to play football, but Southerners rarely went North.

Not surprisingly the sporting heroes of these two mythic lands were rather different; not many Northerners seem to have taken much interest in the great Carthusian, Corinthian and England centre-forward of the 1890s, G. O. Smith, who appropriately went on to run a prep school in the Home Counties; whilst rugby inhabited a world of even greater mutual ignorance and institutionalized contempt. The burly heroes of northern union, as rugby league was called until after the First World War, were unknown in the South. Likewise the hero of Edwardian rugby union, Adrian Stoop, of Oxford University, Harlequins and England, was not a name likely to have been heard much in Featherstone or Keighley. What follows here is an attempt to look at Northern values as expressed through the lives of those who became famous in the North (or parts of it) as sportsmen. After reviewing the lives of early Northern heroes, clustered around the more traditional sports like pugilism or rowing, the role of cricket, football and, to a lesser extent, rugby league will be examined in turn to see how heroes were made and the images of the North which their performances and personalities conveyed.

Traditional sports

Who were the first Northern sporting heroes? Very little is known before the later eighteenth century and the beginnings of a national and regional sporting press. A case could be made for the bluff hunting squire as an early heroic type, the fictionalized 'John Peel' figure, although the fame of huntsmen was too confined to the 'country' they hunted and the field more generally for them to figure prominently as popular urban figures, except in song. A stronger case can be made for pedestrians, rowers, and most importantly boxers or 'pugilists' as they were known.[3] Nottingham had a particularly fine run of them in the early nineteenth century. London, with its large market for sport and its wealthy patrons, aristocrats with a tradition of gaming loosely linked into what was called the 'Fancy', took up men like John Shaw, a farmer's son from Wollaton, Nottinghamshire, born in 1789, who enlisted as a private in the Life Guards in 1807, having established a local reputation as a fighter when still a boy. The officers of his regiment took him up, setting him against a series of opponents, including the famous Captain Barclay, a great gentleman rider, pedestrian and sportsman of the age. A challenge was issued against any man in England in 1815 just as Shaw was ordered into action. Refusing the offer to buy him out, Shaw, who was also a fine swordsman, set off for Waterloo where he died in the heat of battle whilst seizing the enemy standard and striking down nine of the Frenchmen surrounding him.[4]

Shaw was an intriguing mixture of the hero as soldier and the sportsman as hero. His fame came from his heroic end tinged with a sense of athletic promise unfulfilled. He was a hero from the North rather than a Northern hero. The mythology of the industrial North had not really taken shape and even a generation later it was only beginning to get a firm hold, as the careers of two prominent early Victorian Nottinghamshire pugilists reveal. William Thompson, one of triplets popularly called Shadrach, Meshach and Abednego (vulgarized as 'Bendigo'), rose from local fame in Nottingham to 'national' celebrity through issuing a challenge in *Bell's Life in London*. Bendigo's greatest bouts were against another Nottingham man, Ben Caunt, in the 1830s and 1840s for a 'champion's belt' bought by subscription amongst the 'Fancy'. Caunt later took the Coach and Horses in St Martin's Lane but was taken back to the village of Hucknall Torkard in Nottinghamshire to be buried. Bendigo took the pledge and became a local dissenting minister. He died at Beeston near Nottingham in 1880, a man still famous locally but with a town in Australia named after him into the bargain.[5] Yet Bendigo and Caunt did much of their fighting in and around London, and were probably more famous amongst the metropolitan Fancy than the North.

If the early pugilists from the North were too cosmopolitan to be distinctively Northern, those who played traditional games were too parochial – local figures in a local landscape. Take the Northumberland coalfield studied by Alan Metcalfe. The old sport of road or 'potshare' bowling threw up men known throughout their communities and thriving into the period more conventionally associated with new association and rugby forms of football. Two Newbiggin bowlers, Tommy Thompson and George Armstrong, were great favourites in the Edwardian years, drawing crowds of between four and ten thousand.[6] But few outside the North East had heard of them. More widespread, especially North of the Trent and in Lancashire and Yorkshire, was crown green bowling, which had its championships in Blackpool, drawing large entries and conferring a rather wider fame upon its best players.

These are the forgotten Northern heroes who await their historian. Another, happily rediscovered by Alan Tomlinson, was Billy Baxter, the 'World Champion' of knur-and-spel, a traditional sport in the cotton towns of north-east Lancashire around Colne involving the striking of a ball (the knur) suspended by a device (the 'spel') with a wooden headed stick resembling a golf club. Crowds would assemble on the moors to watch the 'laikers' or 'tippers', the most celebrated of whom between the wars was Billy Baxter, who worked at one mill for 20 years and another for 35. On one occasion three thousand spectators paying sixpence each attended and 'there'd be a lot climbin, over the walls. They'd 'ave nothin yer see,' remarked Baxter with the honesty of a performer who had stayed true to his own world.[7] Different pubs would have their champions 'an there was allus a bit o' rivalry among 'em.' The sport was an institution in and around

Colne, creating in 'Burly' Billy and his like what Tomlinson calls a 'core of self-endowed celebrity'.[8] A careful ethnography of England would no doubt throw up many more such figures, North and South, Cumbrian or Devonian wrestlers like Abraham Cann, for instance, who was honoured by Palmerston amongst others.

A common pattern of geographical rivalry before the Football League and the County Championship institutionalized North–South alignments was the regional challenge to London. This sometimes happened in horse racing when a noble Northern owner or trainer challenged the dominance of the South at the Derby, but also in boxing and rowing. There was nothing like a local man going up to the metropolis and bringing home a cup or a belt. Harry Clasper, for example, was a Geordie hero. Born in 1812 and growing up illiterate by the banks of the Tyne, doing odd jobs, he learned to row and, despite being only five feet eight and under ten stone, his skill both as an oarsman and a builder of boats brought him victory over Robert Coombes, the leading Thames oarsman, on several occasions. Clasper was part of a wider Geordie dynasty whose fame was sung in the music halls and pubs, culminating in a public testimonial in 1862 at which that anthem of Tyneside, 'The Blaydon Races', was first performed. Clasper's family, several of whom rowed with him, were the backbone of the fours that made his name.

His 'pupils' in the single sculls were almost as famous. First there was Robert Chalmers, who beat the London challenge first in 1859 and four other times and called forth these lines from Geordie Ridley, the music hall poet: 'O, ye Cockneys all,/Ye mun think't very funny,/ For Bob he gans and licks ye all/An collars all yer money.'[9] 'Honest Bob' died young in 1868 and was followed by James Renforth, who thrilled the Tyne by winning the national sculling championship in 1869 and the self-styled professional championship of the world the following year in Canada, only to collapse and die the year after whilst defending the title. A short glorious career or an exceptionally long one, the tragic cutting short of a life or the flouting of the ageing process itself – these were the two most certain routes to an honoured place in the folk memory. So it was with Chambers and Renforth and with Clasper, whose deaths following so close upon each other were occasions of mass mourning with grand funeral monuments erected by public subscription. Clasper's funeral 'was held on a Sunday "to meet the convenience of numerous bodies of working men" and crowds of between 100,000 and 130,000 lined the streets'.[10]

Cricketers

If pugilists were arguably the first sporting heroes, cricketers were unquestionably the second; key Northern figures who became nationally known as modern sport matured at the end of the nineteenth century. Cricket was the only sport followed with more or less equal enthusiasm in both halves of England. Even though the North had only a few first-class counties, they produced a remarkable number of outstanding players who became widely known in the South, although it was a Southerner who became the first national hero. It was deepest Gloucestershire, an 'Angleterre profonde' of county towns and country doctors, that supplied the first undisputed national sporting hero. Grace, who played more like a professional than an amateur and whose girth called up avuncular images of an older England of squire and parson, was not a public schoolboy, sometimes not quite a gentleman, and possibly more acceptable in the North because of it.[11] Yet he remained a Southerner and a member of the MCC and it was there he had his most avid following. The North had its own cricketing heroes before Grace.

The folk heroes of the White Rose and the Red, whose antagonism came to epitomize Northern cricket, were preceded by men such as William Clarke, a bricklayer and publican born in Nottingham in 1798, who played an enormous part in the history of cricket. Taking up with a widow, who owned the Trent Bridge Inn, he laid out an excellent cricket field, organizing in 1840 a Notts versus Sussex match and later bringing together an All-England Eleven that subsequently toured the country making use of the newly completed rail network. Clarke, who was known by the players as 'Our General', was a slow underarm bowler and a good batsman but it was as an entrepreneur rather than a performer that he was most famous. He was the pioneer of organized professional cricket in the North and as such responsible for bringing to a wider public several of the greatest players of the age.[12]

Of these none was better known and more popular than George Parr, 'The Lion of the North', who played for Notts from 1844 to 1871. Parr played his last match for the Players in 1865, the same year that Grace first played for the Gentlemen and *Wisden* observed 'that his style of play has long ranked him the best batsman in England'.[13] He was from yeoman farming stock, one of nine children whose family had worked land rented from the Earl of Manvers for over two hundred years. Parr, then, was not a poor factory boy who rose modestly in the world in the manner of many of the sporting heroes to come. He was, like Grace, a link with an earlier age, a countryman who was said to prefer 'one day's shooting to a season's cricket'.[14] He stood five feet nine and weighed nearly thirteen stone, a robust, rustic man who could throw a ball over a hundred yards. Parr's prowess as well as his management of the All-England Eleven after Clarke's death in 1855 made him very widely known. Southern professionals broke away from the All-England side in 1864 and a series of North–South matches were played in the 1860s in which Parr had a major role. 'The Lion of the North' was probably the first sportsman to build up a following beyond the local or county level in the North and the newly completed rail network enabled him to tour often in the South. As for Parr, the greatest batsman of his generation, turned his back on cricket, asking nothing more than to be allowed to get on with country sports. The hero as coach, columnist, pundit and keeper of Northern sporting lore was still to come.

Parr was the first of a trio of Nottinghamshire cricketers who had a mass following as the game shifted from less regulated to more modern forms. Next came Alfred Shaw, the son of a handloom weaver, a trade which despite mechanization survived sporadically into the later nineteenth century and was associated with sport partly because of the opportunity to catch up playing time by frantic night work. Shaw put to good use the family enthusiasm for cricket, first joining Grantham as a professional and then Nottinghamshire, for whom he bowled his slow medium deliveries from 1865 to 1887, playing at Lord's for the North of England in June 1873 against the MCC, when he took all ten wickets for 73 runs. Shaw began as a typical local hero, taking a pub in his home village, but moved to London, travelled to America (where he took 178 wickets for 426 runs) and coached for Lord Sheffield in Sussex.[15] Yet he remained a Northern figure and went back to Nottinghamshire to take another pub and retire. Shaw was a great devotee of the Gentlemen and Players match. He played in a remarkable 28 of these games, memorably dismissing seven of the Gentlemen for 17 at the Oval in 1880 and six for 19 the following year at Brighton. Northern professionals beating Southern amateurs aligned class and region in a temporary suspension of county rivalries. As time passed, there was a better geographical mixture, with more Northern Gentlemen and Southern Players, but the occasion kept something of its nineteenth-century North–South symbolism.

Shaw's contemporary at Nottingham was Arthur Shrewsbury, the best professional batsman of the late nineteenth century, heading the averages five times between 1885 and 1892. The Mayor of Nottingham presented him in 1887 with an illuminated address together with a purse containing 72 sovereigns subscribed by the 'noblemen and gentlemen residents of the town' whose names were appended. This loyal address to a local hero praised 'not only his great ability as a cricketer' but 'his straightforward and honourable conduct which has won him universal respect both in his native county and throughout the cricketing world'.[16] Here surely was an incontrovertible hero, following a well-trodden path to wealth and fame, a loyal local man around whom the full spectrum of county society could coalesce. Or was he? For what is most remarkable about this Northern hero is how little he has been remembered. Of course, he lived on in the memories of committed cricket fans and county members but his clashes with authority both at county level and with the MCC followed by a tragic suicide in 1902 blighted his public image. He was a hard competitor, shrewd and solid, but Nottingham-shire lacked the special sense of identity of Yorkshire which could have turned his way of playing into an expression of regional character. By contrast, the ordinariness of Jack Hobbs, who followed Shrewsbury as England's greatest professional batsman, was used to build a Southern myth of the decent chap, the cricketer as suburban hero. Hobbs became a much loved national figure and Shrewsbury was forgotten, save for the phrase attributed to Grace when asked to choose his favourite opening partner: 'Give me Arthur'.[17]

The press had a central role in the making and unmaking of heroes. In the era before newsreels and television, Saturday's deeds were mulled over on a Sunday or Monday morning and men compared their view of what they had seen or heard with what the paper said. The most influential of the new breed of sports journalists in the North were those working with the big regional papers, who not only reported the facts but embellished them with a sense of place and character. A few became particularly famous, the appointed spokesmen of their tribes. A. W. Pullin, who as 'Old Ebor' covered cricket from the late nine-teenth century to the 1930s for the *Yorkshire Evening Post*, was one such maker of legends, who died on the top of a bus on the way to a Test match and became a kind of Yorkshire hero himself. He was so moved by a terse reply to a question about the whereabouts of John Thewlis, an early Yorkshire player ('Think dead; if not, Manchester'), that he wrote a series of articles on pioneer Yorkshire figures.[18] J. M. Kilburn, who took over from Pullin in 1934 and wrote his cricket column until 1976, was a careful man, neatly writing out his daily match reports in fountain pen, well known for getting the facts right, but also espousing the view that:

> cricketers are products of their environment and grow as they do grow because of the impulse of their setting ... To know Woolley at the crease is to know the calm maturity of sunlit Kentish meadows ... to contemplate Arthur Mitchell in the acquisition of an unsmiling, purposeful century is to appreciate the hard, unyielding Yorkshire hills.[19]

Mitchell was a classic Yorkshireman – 'grim as a piece of stone from Baildon Moor' as Sutcliffe said – 'dour, hard and patient', a great slip fielder who growled at a young man beside him, somersaulting and tossing the ball high in the air, after a superb diving catch: 'Gerrup. Tha's makkin an exhibition o' thisen.'[20]

Yorkshiremen revelled in their reputation as tough competitors. The most famous of cricket writers, born across the Pennines in Manchester, loved to play on this and joined Kilburn in stoking up the flames of the Roses rivalry, which began in the 1880s. Neville Cardus embellished these images of Yorkshire grit and the 'spiky antagonism' of the Roses match, held on a Bank Holiday, always a sell-out, a world closed to the Southerner. 'Keep thi' clipper shut. This game's got nowt to do with thee', a Londoner commenting on the climax of a Roses match in Huddersfield was brusquely reminded.[21] The Roses tradition may have been invented but it was also spontaneously popular; 'Park Avenue, Bradford, August 1923. Part of the 26,000 crowd for the Roses match. An estimated 50,000 were locked out' reads the terse caption of a crowd photograph, which revealed not only a sea of caps and bowler hats but a good sprinkling of summer bonnets.[22] Northern women watched cricket in larger numbers than football but as yet there is no proper estimate of their role and by extension the types of play and personality that appealed to them.

A gritty, unadorned, indomitable masculine style, blending courage and patience with a certain cunning was the stuff of Northern cricket. Sutcliffe, Hutton and Washbrook admittedly could play with amateur panache when they wished, but two men born in the 1870s in the same bleak Pennine industrial village of Kirkheaton were more typical: Hirst and Rhodes. 'George Herbert', as Hirst was known, managed 100 wickets and 1,000 runs in no fewer than fourteen seasons. Wilfred Rhodes took over 4,000 wickets and made 40,000 runs in a career that included a successful recall for a key Test match against Australia at the age of 48. Rhodes was the South's typical Northerner, short, unsentimental, running to fat in his later years yet keeping a fierce competitive edge. 'Give 'em nowt' and 'we doan't play cricket in Yorkshire for foon' were oft repeated aphorisms – the latter a rebuke to a young team-mate who had dared to attack the bowling on his debut with fours off the first two balls.[23] Truth and fiction became hopelessly mixed in the mythology that surrounded a man who played for Yorkshire from 1898 to 1930 and became almost as famous for his Yorkshireness as for his cricket. Hirst and Rhodes never really got on; George was one kind of Northern male, kindly and jokey; Wilf was another, tart and dour. Both were lured as coaches later in life into the heart of the amateur beast at Harrow and Eton, where Hirst's warmth predictably produced better results than Wilfred's terseness. Wilfred did not suffer fools gladly, especially not privileged young Southerners with pretensions to play cricket, but he was not above taking their money.

The fierceness, the edge, the hunger to win regardless of whether or not the public was vexed or pleased with the manner of victory was what made Northerners different from Southerners; and if you were in Yorkshire what made Yorkshiremen different from everyone else. Sporting heroes displayed different styles of masculinity which varied according to social class and cultural tradition. Of course, there were striking exceptions; Douglas Jardine may have looked and behaved socially like the Winchester and New College man that he was but on the field he was a ruthless competitor and captain. Part of the argument against allowing professional captains was that the Northern will to win would kill good cricket. The Northerner would avoid defeat at all costs, sticking in for a draw rather than going down in style: a way of playing familiar to the many fans of Geoffrey Boycott. Trying to explain the long uneventful build-up of the Tour de France, Geoffrey Nicholson observed that the French accept it with 'the stoicism of a Headingley cricket crowd watching the slow construction of an opening stand'.[24] Robertson-Glasgow, the cricket writer and celebrated Somerset amateur, said of Maurice Leyland, the inter-war Yorkshire all-rounder, that 'he would disappear into the haze of Bramall Lane, where a sterner sort of game was being played under the name of cricket and entrench himself among the sawdust and the smoke and the off-breaks and appeals and do his raw, tough work in silence'. Here was a Southern view of the North which the North itself could recognize.[25]

Of course, image and reality became endlessly confused as men tried to live up what they thought their image was supposed to be and journalists tried to catch what they took as true Northernness. This was famously true of Emmot Robinson, 'a grizzled, squat, bandy-legged Yorkshireman' pressed into service at the age of 36 just after the Great War and staying on beside the ageing Rhodes until he was 48.[26] He was a handy bowler and made a few runs but what made him into a hero was the way Neville Cardus in particular 'invented' him as a Yorkshire stereotype, 'created one day by God scooping into the nearest acre of Yorkshire soil at hand, then breathing into it saying, "Now lad, tha's called Emmott Robinson and tha can go on with the new ball at t' pavilion end".'[27] Emmott was famous for being a character and played up to the image that the Lancastrian had given him. He even wrote a cricket column later in life, from which he could perpetuate on paper an image on the pitch that had itself been partly a journalistic creation. Such was the symbiotic relationship between the press and performer which created a distinctive Northern sporting and cultural identity.

Lancashire never had as well defined an image as Yorkshire but they had plenty of great players, a few of them as cussed or comic as any across the Pennines. Sydney Barnes was one, perhaps the greatest Test bowler of all time, who by choice played most of his cricket with

Staffordshire in the Minor Counties. Though a Midlander by origin, his choice of teams and his resentment of the Southern establishment made him culturally a Northerner. Barnes could have been a Lancashire hero but fell out with Archie MacLaren, the great England amateur batsman and captain of the county in the early years of the century. MacLaren was a rare example of an amateur achieving heroic status in the north of England – Lord Hawke was arguably another – but despite the awe his batting inspired he was not the object of great public affection. That privilege went to Cecil Parkin, who ironically only just failed to qualify for Yorkshire by being born a few yards into Durham. Parkin was both outspoken and entertaining and a great favourite of the Lancashire crowd in the 1920s. One of only two players ever to open the bowling and the batting for England, he criticized the England captain's tactics openly in a Sunday newspaper and was duly disciplined for getting above his station. Parkin's Northernness was not confined to criticizing amateur team selection; he took the bull by the horns demanding to know why Jack Hobbs had not been made England captain – which must have alarmed as quiet and deferential a Southerner as 'The Master' – adding that 'the class distinction that exists between amateur and professional should not be expressed *in public*'; 'Cec', as Andrew Sandham, the Surrey professional who partnered Hobbs, remarked, 'was a bit too independent for the powers that be'.[28] But not for the Lancashire public, who seemed to appreciate his bluntness on the subject of Southern class bias. He remained popular when he moved back to league cricket which was a fertile source of Lancashire heroes ignored in London.

But this is only one side of the story. Some Northern cricketers did succeed in Southern terms and changed themselves in the process. The late flowering of Jack Hobbs, the hero *par excellence* of English cricket after Grace, was greatly enhanced by Herbert Sutcliffe in their great partnerships of the mid-1920s against Australia. Sutcliffe was Yorkshire through and through. He grew up in Pudsey, played for Yorkshire and embodied the concentration and courage which Northern heroes were supposed to have to match the fluent beauty of Hobbs, the son of a Cambridge college servant who had watched his first cricket at Fenners. Sutcliffe was probably the first Northern professional cricketer to win a large following amongst the Southern public. But it was not until Sutcliffe's protégé, Len Hutton, also from Pudsey, broke the record of the highest Test score at the Oval against Australia in 1938 that the North had a hero who was fully recognized in the South, going on to be the first professional captain of England in the twentieth century and receive formal acknowledgment of national standing with a knighthood; the first professional cricketer after Hobbs to be so honoured.[29]

In the course of their professional careers Sutcliffe and Hutton, modest sons of the same small Yorkshire town, moved up the social ladder – Sutcliffe's Leeds sports shop was especially successful, bringing him a grand house and a Rolls. But they distanced themselves from their roots in the process. Sutcliffe physically stayed put but changed his accent so completely that C. P. Snow remarked after a speech at the Guildhall in 1930: 'one would never know you had not been to public school and Cambridge'.[30] Sutcliffe, in fact, sent his son to Rydal and as an ex-public school boy Billy Sutcliffe got the county captaincy that had eluded his father. Hutton, too, changed his accent and sent his eldest son to Repton and Cambridge before he in his turn played for Yorkshire. Sir Leonard settled eventually in that bastion of Home Counties suburbia: Kingston upon Thames. Both were attractive, successful men who appealed to female spectators. They began as provincial figures whose origins and work ethic commended them to the Yorkshire faithful but whose playing style, appearance and business success made them more nationally known.[31] Sutcliffe's biographer calls him a cricketing Clark Gable: 'with his glossy black hair and twinkling deep set eyes he was worshipped by the girls'.[32]

The camera was starting to wrench great performers from their roots in a regional male community closed to outsiders. The media made Northerners better known, but did it make them less Northern? In the case of Hutton perhaps it did but this was not usually the case. Fred Trueman and Geoffrey Boycott, the most recent embodiments of the Yorkshire spirit, have become nationally known, especially with the vast expansion of television coverage, and yet they remain rooted in their Yorkshireness, which has turned out to be quite a saleable commodity; Trueman known for his 'fiery' outbursts and Boycott for his famous indifference to time and his own team when building an innings. They have kept their accents and played up their origins, partly to stay true to themselves, partly in a self-conscious Northern pastiche that has proved popular with the general public. The journalist and television personality Michael Parkinson has made a career of recounting sporting tales of his Barnsley and Yorkshire heroes to a national audience.

Footballers

If cricket shows up the differences between North and South most clearly, it is football that is most deeply Northern. The professional game originated in Lancashire and until the inter-war years was predominantly played in the North, but unlike cricket lacked a more literary and middle-class element to celebrate its culture and distinctiveness. In the Roses counties football had to share the winter with the even more self-consciously Northern sport of rugby league; it was only in the North East that football reigned supreme, its heroes unchallenged by cricketers and rugby players. If one Geordie hero stands out from the many who followed the Victorian oarsman Harry Clasper, it must be 'Wor Jackie'; Jackie Milburn, a tall young pitman from the mining community of Ashington north of Newcastle, who played for United from 1945 to 1957 including the three victorious Cup Finals of 1951, 1952 and 1955. He was not the greatest centre-forward to play for Newcastle; that honour must go to the little Hughie Gallacher, the greatest of many gifted Scottish players to play in the North East. Considered by many the finest of all British centre-forwards, hard-drinking, irascible Hughie was certainly a legend on Tyneside but not an emblematic Geordie or Northerner and not the kind of 'canny lad', the decent young miner, that Milburn represented. 'Wor Jackie' was a big, open-hearted, ordinary man in the tradition of other great northern centre-forwards like Dean, Lawton and Lofthouse, the weakest with his head but the fastest of all; the sight of him tearing after a through ball and shooting on the run from long range thrilled a post-war generation of men who could still find work in the mines and shipyards. The Milburns were a footballing dynasty in Ashington over three generations and Jackie's cousin, Cissie Charlton, became celebrated in her own right as the mother and first trainer of two of the greatest figures in recent English football. Jackie's death in 1988 brought the city to a stop and his statue stands in the city centre.[33]

The old rivalries of the Tyne and the Wear passed quickly into the new world of professional football as the mutual hostility of Sunderland and Newcastle United. Derby games at St James's and at Roker Park often drew crowds of fifty and sixty thousand. These industrial cities defined themselves through and against each other. The wider regional identity of the North East counted for something, especially when a Southern team was visiting, but the city always came first. There was not much evidence of a Northern solidarity with teams from Liverpool, Manchester or Nottingham. Sunderland in fact established themselves first, winning the championship four times and being runners-up three times between 1892 and 1902. Newcastle United's great era followed this with the League title in 1905, 1907 and 1909 and the Cup in 1910. Between them the North East had a great influence on the first era of professional club football. Sunderland's fortunes rose again in the 30s with Raich Carter, an outstanding inside-forward and a local boy playing before and after the Second World War. The son of a an ex-professional player turned publican, 'Raich' (short for Horatio) was devoted to Sunderland but sold to Derby after the war and later became player-manager with Hull. What the Sunderland public or Raich himself wanted did not seem to matter.

Heroes had few rights. Raich lived on in the folk memory of the fans but felt let down by his club.[34]

As Raich was to Sunderland, Wilf Mannion was to Middlesbrough. Mannion, a diminutive blond-haired ball-playing inside-forward, was a sensational player both for England and for the otherwise unglamorous club to which he brought a touch of flair and greatness. He grew up in South Bank, an area settled by the descendants of the Irish immigrants, who had built the iron and steel works. 'Football was the only way out', Mannion remarked in a later television documentary of his life.[35] But Wilf never really left, ending up with a labouring job in the steel works near to where he was born and to Ayresome Park. Like Raich Carter he felt badly treated by the club. On one occasion against Blackpool, in a performance engraved in local memory, all the 21 other players lined up and clapped him off the field. However, he was not even given a testimonial or a job and drifted through the lower divisions. 'The only place for a retired footballer', he remarked, 'is the knacker's yard.'[36] In a sense this made him even more popular. He remained an ordinary man, a worker whose efforts to make his way after football had failed, who had stayed close to his roots and been poorly used by his employers. There was something innocent, almost sacrificial, about Wilf Mannion that made him easy meat for the Middlesbrough board-room. Yet it was this very ordinariness as well as the memory of that astonishing body swerve – fans could still imitate it thirty years on – that gave him the stamp of Northern authenticity.

Mannion made next to nothing out of football whilst a man whose boyhood idol Mannion had been made a fortune. Don Revie enjoyed his own period of playing celebrity with Manchester City but it was his years as manager of Leeds, bringing late football glory to a great Northern city, that made him a hero and the England manager after Sir Alf Ramsay. Then came a sudden fall from grace as he deserted the national team and took a vast sum of money to go to the Middle East. When Revie died in 1989 there was none of the outpouring of Northern or national feeling that usually accompanies such an event. Revie was remarkable in how far and how fast he fell. The same has been true of another outstanding player and great manager, Brian Clough, a self-confessed blunt Northerner, whose heroic status at Nottingham has recently been tarnished with allegations of profiteering. Combining wealth and popular esteem has until recently been difficult but Revie's lanky centre-half at Leeds, Jack Charlton, a man with all Revie's toughness and realism but shot through with humour, seems to have done it.

Jack Charlton is a new kind of hero, his brother Bobby is the older sort; yet both have gone on to transcend the regional origins of their fame in ways that their uncle, Jackie Milburn, never did or sought to do. Men like Milburn in Newcastle or Lofthouse in Bolton stayed put, legendary figures in the clubs where they spent their lives as players or elder statesmen. Perhaps most notable in this regard was Tom Finney, the Preston plumber, whose life has been devoted to North End. Matt Busby and Bill Shankly – the Scottish manager as hero is a striking sub-theme of Northern sport that lives on in Alex Ferguson and Kenny Dalglish and demonstrates the greater willingness of Northerners to take Scots rather than Southerners to their hearts – proclaimed Finney the greater player than Matthews. Stan and Tom, who played as wingers together in the England team many times, shared the same reserve, the lack of bombast, the same uncompromising blend of virtuosity and ordinariness. Percy Ronson, a well-known amateur with Fleetwood, asked Finney to play at his testimonial and the great man agreed. According to Ronson's son, as the match approached, his father, anxious that fans might be disappointed if Finney did not appear, hesitantly phoned him up. 'I've said I'm coming' was the blunt reply; and so he did, along with his England partner, Stan Mortenson. Generous acts like this enhanced a player's standing as word spread through pub and club that he was a decent bloke for all his fame. Finney has remained synonymous with Preston and still lives there.

Loyalty is important in sport, especially for a hero; perhaps more so in the North than in the South as Stanley Matthews, the first footballer to get a CBE and later a knighthood, found when he moved from Stoke after the war to Blackpool. Matthews, the son of a famous boxer turned barber, played his first game for Stoke in 1932 at seventeen and returned home for his last in 1965 at the age of fifty when his intervening sojourn in Blackpool was finally forgiven. For he was very much a Potteries figure, their claim to fame, and the intensity of local feeling for their man was displayed when the question of his transfer first arose in the late 30s. A public outcry backed by local manufacturers kept Matthews in Stoke. But after the war, this most delicate player, frail-looking but super-fit, went to Blackpool, the holiday Mecca of the North still in its pre-Costa Brava heyday. He was the first footballer to become a national hero. But this was a slower process than today. It was not until the Blackpool–Bolton Cup Final of the Coronation Year, when Stan was nearly forty and still without the elusive Cup Winner's medal, that he was declared 'a superb artist, a football genius beyond compare' in *The Times*.[37]

A generation earlier Everton's 'Dixie' Dean's amazing 60 goals in a season had not conquered the South in the way that Stan's quickness and longevity would eventually do. Dean's fame was largely confined to Merseyside. He was born in Tranmere and died at Goodison Park in 1980 watching Everton play Liverpool. If one player stood for Merseyside it had to be 'Dixie' but he was selected only sixteen times for England despite scoring eighteen goals. Maybe the South was not ready to accept a blunt Liverpudlian who liked a bet. Northerners were convinced their men were unfairly treated by the Southern-based FA. As the national team became more important in English life – a gradual process which accelerated in the 30s with the challenge to English supremacy from Italy and Austria – so the great Northern players became more famous throughout the country. Tommy Lawton, who began at Burnley, followed Dean in the Everton and England shirt and was well known in the South for exhibition matches during the Second World War. Nat Lofthouse, a Bolton miner, was the next in the line of big England centre-forwards and is still much loved in Bolton. Regional radio and television have made men like Lofthouse and Finney known to a new generation – the electronic media enhancing the heroic aura that before had come down by word of mouth from father to son and on the shopfloor.

Nat was a nice man but he was not above knocking a goalkeeper into the net to win a Cup Final. His courage in an international against Austria led to the nickname the 'Lion of Vienna'. 'Like a centurion tank was our Nathan' began a bit of club doggerel.[38] Nat was the acceptable face of Northern football hardness. He began as a player like many others working a full shift in the pit before a game. But there was an unacceptable face as well. Not all Northern heroes were nice; some were famous for their willingness to be sent off for injuring the opposition. Clubs like Barnsley, fed by miners from the nearby coalfield, abounded in stories, polished in the telling, of men working double shifts and walking 20 miles to play a match. These men did not like to lose, especially if there was a hefty side bet illegally placed on the outcome. There was a self-conscious cult of Northern aggression, which applauded the violent antics of some players, especially a centre-half like Frank Barson, a former blacksmith, who boasted as battle scars his four broken noses and two serious back injuries.[39] Barson was a hero of sorts and well paid for his labours. Bought for a record fee for a defender by Manchester United in 1922, he expected special treatment and extra money in an envelope. 'Where's the doin's?', he roared at the trainer on one occasion before a match, 'I'm not taking my bloody coat off till I get it.'[40]

Barson was not alone. Plenty of teams had a hard man but some clubs, it was widely believed, made a fetish of aggression. When Barnsley played Swindon in a Cup semi-final in 1912 Barnsley deliberately kicked Harold Fleming, the star Swindon player, until he had to go off seriously injured and the local press jeered at the soft Southerners for making an official complaint.[41] These hard men were never heroes in the sense of commanding wide admiration as athletes but there was a side of Northern masculinity that admired anyone who could 'do the business'. Being able to give and take punishment was universal, part of the male ethos of football. When Nat Lofthouse bundled the Manchester United goal-keeper, Harry Gregg, into the net along with the ball for Bolton's second goal in the post-Munich Cup Final of 1958, there were few complaints. 'These days it would be considered GBH, but I didn't talk about it and Nat is a close friend', Gregg remarked recently, adding 'I'd given a lot of thumps in my time, so I had to take them.'[42] Honest and open physical aggression was accepted: even the fierce charge on Ray Wood in the Cup Final of the previous year by Aston Villa's Peter McParland, which had left the United goalkeeper concussed with a fractured jaw and unable to continue, was more or less condoned. Jackie Blanchflower, who took over from Wood in the United goal in the era before substitutes, simply observed 'Peter was a naive lad. Villa told him Woody was suspect and to "get in and let him know you're there".'[43]

Of course, it would be absurd to suggest that Southern teams were free of hard men. Arsenal's Ted Drake was a fiercesome sight in the 30s, mauling the Italian 1934 World Cup winners at the Battle of Highbury, knocking goalkeepers and goals – seven past Aston Villa for an individual record – into the net. Tommy Lawton, who followed Dean as England and Everton centre-forward, said Dixie's legs were black and blue and Drake likewise picked up some bad injuries. Partly out of male pride, partly from a prudent fear of losing their place, professionals tended to play down their injuries.[44] Whilst open charging and crunching tackles were seen as integral to the game, particularly in the North, shirt pulling, elbowing, spitting at opponents, kicking and punching off the ball and behind the referee's back were not acceptable to most fans. The North was always tough but rarely vicious – that at least was its self-perception – and the fairly orderly behaviour of crowds before the 1960s seems to bear this out. A Northern football crowd was not a quiet place; there was always some drunkenness, swearing and the odd punch; but good humour prevailed to a very large extent on and off the field and policing problems were minimal before the hooligan generation that emerged in the 1960s. The point is not that the North was necessarily more aggressive but that it was perceived and presented as such both in the South and by plenty of Northerners themselves.[45]

The later 1950s saw a marked shift in the heroic image of the Northern footballer. This was bound up with the rise of Matt Busby's young Manchester United side. The spread of television brought the 'Busby Babes' into the living rooms of the nation and made them a focus for the future of English football so recently and roughly shoved from international pre-eminence by the likes of Hungary. Manchester United became the first Northern team to have a following in the South as names like Pegg, Coleman, Taylor, Viollet, Whelan, Charlton,

Edwards and the rest began to capture the youthful English imagination as they went into the new European Cup to play Real Madrid and the other great European sides. It was returning from just such a game on 6 February 1958 that their plane crashed taking off in snow from Munich, killing eight of the team and badly injuring several others.

Apart from Whelan, a Dubliner, the players killed outright in the crash were Northerners: Tommy Taylor, Mark Jones and David Pegg from Yorkshire and Byrne, Colman and Bent from around Manchester. They were local boys whose lives and whose deaths became national property. Duncan Edwards, still only 21, possibly the greatest all-round player ever seen in England, the youngest player to win an England cap, the inspiration of the 'Babes' who won the League in 1956 and 1957, died after more than a week fighting to live. Edwards was already a national rather than a Northern hero, a boy from the Black Country where his bereaved parents kept his room untouched, a fan of the famous Wolves team of the 50s, buried in Dudley where there is a stained glass window in the church to his memory. Just as Matthews was famous for playing so long, so the legend of Duncan Edwards was built around its sickening brevity. Busby and Charlton recovered to become the most famous survivors of the Munich disaster, sanctified in the public imagination both by their association with the tragedy and their success in building a great side to replace the Babes and win the European Cup. Bobby Charlton became a national hero, playing 606 games and scoring a record 198 goals for his club and appearing 106 times for England and scoring 49 goals – another record. But it was not just statistics that have made him one of the best-loved Englishmen of his time. The nephew of Jackie Milburn, taught the game in Ashington Park, Bobby was 'as near perfection as man and player as it is possible to be' according to his manger.[46]

Charlton, alongside Matthews, has achieved the status of revered national figure – the embodiment of all that is best about English sport officially endorsed by a knighthood, a model of what the South expected of the ideal Northerner. But this had its price. Bobby was not the 'King' of Old Trafford. The Stretford End gave that title to Denis Law, the quick-tempered blond Scottish striker, the pioneer of the clenched fist salute, 'Denis the Menace', who was sent off so many times and still managed to score almost as many goals as Charlton in half the number of games.[47] Law settled in Manchester and is one of its favourite sons. Law's career began just before the 60s turned footballers loose on the fashion and gossip pages of the tabloid press. George Best's coincided with this; not just his playing genius but his looks, style and sex appeal and appetite for alcohol were a gift for the press. Plenty of gifted players had gone his way before but none so publicly; the age of obscurity was over. That and their genius, if nothing else, was something Duncan Edwards and George Best were doomed to share. Television and the new tabloid press were turning Northern heroes into national icons of popular culture.[48]

Rugby League

Rugby league was the only sport that split explicitly along North–South lines. It was Northern in a way no other team sport could claim to be; it was played only in the North. Northern union, as it was known at first, was concentrated in the woollen textile towns of the West Riding and in South Lancashire beyond Manchester in a pattern *The Times* called 'sporadic and curious'.[49] However, it was not so much a sense of Northern identity itself that caused the schism of 1895 with the Southern-dominated Rugby Union as the sharp class differences between players. The Southern amateur elite tradition clashed with the working-class acceptance of payment to compensate for lost earnings. The majority of Northern rugby players were working-class and, though some of the more middle-class rugby union clubs remained in the North after the schism of 1895, the fifteen-a-side game lost its hold. Yorkshire went 30 years before winning the Rugby Union county championship that it had dominated before the split. Northern union was an inward-looking class game in terms of its players and public, and was run for the most part by small businessmen living locally who shared the enjoyment of collective force that was the most distinguishing feature of a game whose greatest players were also fast and tricky. These men tended to be local, often working in a nearby pit or mill, well known in their close-knit communities. Rugby league was still small enough for 'face to face' relationships between the players and the fans; this was a world where great players were known personally, seen in the streets and in the pubs even more frequently than footballers, who played in bigger towns and travelled further.

If anything defined a popular image of the North, it was the bruising, muddy world of rugby league, which David Storey described in *This Sporting Life*, probably the most successful novel to deal with the question of sport and Northern identity, written by a man who had tried the game himself and knew the scarred and toothless heroes of the post-match bath and massage bench at first hand. The opening passage of the novel brings out sharply the hardness of the sport.

> I had my head to Mellor's backside, waiting for the ball to come between his legs. He was too slow. I was moving away when the leather shot back into my hands and before I could pass a shoulder

came up to my jaw. It rammed my teeth together with a force that stunned me to blackness.[50]

But this was male violence touched by comradeship and a deep sense of belonging. 'I was big, strong and could make people realize it', says the central character, who briefly becomes a local hero, listening 'to the tune of the crowd', trying 'to conduct it'.[51]

The heroes of rugby league who survived its unrelenting physical demands and 'conducted' the crowds were little known in the South. Like Roses cricket, rugby league was a predominantly Lancashire–Yorkshire affair. Joe Ferguson was a great forward, who joined Oldham in 1899 and played 677 games until his retirement in 1923 at the age of 44. He reached the final of the Challenge Cup in five consecutive seasons, scoring a drop goal from the half-way line against Swinton in 1910 to snatch the game 4–3 which was talked of for many a year.[52] What was in effect a Northern 'national' side won an international match in Sydney with only eleven men. This side was captained by Harold Wagstaff of Huddersfield, a prodigy of the Northern Union, playing at fifteen and capped at seventeen, inventor of the 'standing pass', a star in the North but probably better known in New South Wales than in the leafy suburban London heartlands of the RFU.

Alongside Wagstaff, there was Billy Batten, a great winger of the early years with Hunslet, Hull and Wakefield; two brothers were also famous players and the Batten dynasty continued with Billy's three sons, who again played at the top level with Eric appearing in a record eight Challenge Cup finals. The North even moved South to press home their claim to national recognition with the holding of the Challenge Cup final at Wembley from 1929, seven years after the Northern Union had changed its name to the Rugby League. Tens of thousands of Northerners began an annual invasion of London like the Scots in their 'Wembley clubs'. Train loads of mill hands and miners 'up for the Cup' took the game into the London suburbs not so far from the headquarters of the English Rugby Union at Twickenham. The League Final was not quite a new national institution like the Cup Final but it was a major event and a purely Northern one at that. There was no Southern team wresting the highest honours from the great Northern clubs as Arsenal eventually did in football. What could have been a more Northern, or a more quintessentially Yorkshire, crowd than the 95,050 who saw Halifax play Bradford at Wembley in 1949, a game in which Eric Batten fractured a shoulder but played on and scored a try – an incident that seemed to sum up the decent Northern hardness that the game stood for.[53]

Several of the greatest rugby league players, of course, were not Northern at all. Providing they were not Southerners, this did not really matter. Australia provided Albert Rosenfeld, who scored 80 tries for Huddersfield in 1913–14, and Brian Bevan, the record try scorer, with 796 in a career spanning almost 20 years from his debut in 1945–6 whilst on naval service in England. The loss from the Welsh game of Jim Sullivan at seventeen just after a cap for the Barbarians – the youngest ever – was an enormous gain for the League in general and Wigan in particular where 'Sully' spent his playing days. Lewis Jones, the 'Golden Boy', signed for Leeds in 1952 and had a brilliant career with them. 'Gone North' was a frequent complaint in the Welsh valleys, especially in times of economic recession when jobs were scarce. Rugby league scouts in the Rhondda were about as popular as Churchill's strike breaking or the Assistance Board inspector. It was another native of Cardiff who became the undisputed hero of the next generation of Wigan fans. Billy Boston scored 100 tries in only his first 68 games and played from 1953 to 1968.[54]

Billy Boston was also the first black star of Northern rugby; more recently Ellery Hanley and Martin Offiah have led the way towards a new kind of multicultural Northernness. Attitudes have changed dramatically – and for the better – since 'Dixie' Dean's well-known self-consciousness and loathing of a nickname that derived from his curly black hair and slightly dark skin. Until recently being black and Northern were considered incompatible. Learie Constantine's wonderful spell with Nelson in the Lancashire League in the 30s was both an exception and a taste of things to come. 'Connie' was both an exotic attraction and a familiar Northern figure – one of the world's great batsmen who chose to play in the cotton towns – and as the local paper put it 'he has, to all people, both living in and out of Nelson, been Nelson'.[55]

Television has played a major part in spreading awareness of rugby league beyond the North, though only recently has it begun to shake off its older image of stocky men bumping into each other on a Saturday afternoon in front of a few thousand locals. Rugby league games were a boon for the BBC looking to fill their Saturday schedules before the football results without spending much. This turned out to be a mixed blessing, both raising the profile of the game and making a parody of it. This happened in part through a man who came to be one of the best-known figures in television sport with a turn of phrase and an accent that was a gift to impersonators: Eddie Waring. For most of the English, certainly the Southern BBC audience, Eddie *was* the epitome of the Northern man, with his 'oop and oonders' and the brisk way he would dismiss a flurry of punches between two stocky props as 'a little disagreement'. Eddie, who had made a name as an outstanding manager in wartime Dewsbury, with his trilby and his false teeth, enlivened even the most dour encounter with remarks like 'if that thing in the mud moves, it'll be his 'ead not the ball'.[56] All this shot him to celebrity, a pie and chips pastiche, more of an attraction to many than the game itself, a television producer's dream but disliked by some devotees, part of a wider re-packaging of Northern culture for mass consumption, from the Beatles and Merseybeat to the Likely Lads and the Tyne.

Conclusion

Being a Northern sporting hero was really only possible in those sports the North called its own or appropriated on its own terms, as in the case of cricket. Fred Perry was a Northerner – his father was a Labour MP for Stockport – and his origins clearly told against him, as the slighting attitude of Wimbledon towards the man who won the Singles for three consecutive years revealed. Perry became rich and was eventually welcomed back to Wimbledon as a great man. But Perry was not a Northern hero. Being Northern was far less important to him than the American identity, accent and status he later assumed and tennis was a suburban, Southern sport not much followed in the North outside of the leafy suburbs the big cities.

Individualistic sports like athletics or swimming seem to have been rather more appreciated in the South, where the Olympic ideal made more of an impact among the gentlemen amateurs. Although a sense of place was important in the South too, it was in the North that the idea of a team as the embodiment of civic or county identity and loyalty was most deeply held. Yorkshire took this furthest, confining their choice of players (but not of amateur captains) to those born in the county, dismissing middle-class Middlesex with the jibe that 'anyone who'd been through the toilets at Charing Cross' was eligible. Before the 1950s almost all Northern heroes were born in the North, the few exceptions being mainly Scots in football and the Welsh in rugby league. Like Scottish teams who would not buy English players, Northern English teams refused to buy Southerners. To have done so would have been an admission of defeat. Talent in football or cricket was something bred in the bone; something the North had more of than the South despite being poorer and less powerful. Northerners – like the Scots in soccer – had a superiority complex about sport which compensated for a sense of inferiority in other respects. Alongside this need for the hero to define and assert a sense of place, there was the underlying question of the relationship of Northern sport to the culture of hard and skilled manual work. The North was, after all, the heartland of heavy industry. The hero was someone who not only made a man proud to belong to a particular place but who had certain physical skills with which the audience could identify if not emulate. Big strong forwards were certainly admired in football and rugby league in particular. Strength, especially, in the sense of endurance was important and appreciated by those who worked with their bodies. But strength was combined with team-work, where the skill and guile of an individual could inspire the team. A man like Wilfred Rhodes was like an old master craftsman who kept his secrets to himself and for the greater glory of Yorkshire. Football and cricket were trades in which even the most talented young men entered as apprentices emerging in the fullness of time as master craftsmen. These were men with whose appearance and attitudes other Northern males could identify. Few could look like C. B. Fry but many resembled a Rhodes or a Matthews. Being a perfect physical specimen was not required. Of course, as Ross McKibbin and others have stressed, the cultural meanings of leisure activities are speculative and contradictory. Some men might see sport as an extension of work, others as a compensation for it. Tough miners on the football field might also be the gentle breeders of racing pigeons. Northern men had elements of both and the attempts to make precise links between the nature of work and Northern sporting culture are at best tentative.[57]

Northern heroes, then, came in three kinds: the strictly local figure, probably but not necessarily involved in traditional sports; the new urban hero, often a footballer like Milburn or Carter with roots in his community but recognized outside it; and finally the national figures like Hutton or Matthews whose Northernness was partially eclipsed by their fame. The composite Northern hero was a tough competitor with a strong work ethic, not always a great stylist but highly effective; grit and competitiveness were very important as well as a debunking, blunt sense of humour that showed skill in dialect rather than received pronunciation. Few outstanding sportsmen had all this – Maurice Leyland and Cecil Parkin came close.

This, of course, was a world of male virtue from which women were effectively excluded. Men and women had their separate worlds and in the North this division of time and space was particularly sharp. Women might watch big cricket matches and make the tea at club games but the pub and the pitch were closed to them. In such places where men congregated to be men, free of female surveillance or criticism, the sporting hero showed men how to be men. Sportsmen did things; they spoke through actions not words; they kept their feelings in check; they had mates rather than friends, communicating through the discipline of a physical performance. Limits on their earnings kept most of them in touch with their roots and made them morally credible in a way that today's players are not.

Northern heroes scarcely exist nowadays in this earlier form. They tend to be rich and deracinated, nationally famous with a temporary or free-floating local following in their chosen city or region; so much now depends on the whims of an ever more volatile transfer market which can as easily bring a Londoner to Newcastle as a Frenchman to Manchester. To stay close to a chosen place, to build a life and a family around a career with one club seems increasingly difficult for good players, even in rugby league. The public still want their heroes but they are stars rather than heroes in the older sense. Talented young players seem increasingly to feature nationally in the dozens of glossy new football magazines as well as in the press and on television. The star players may now be less specifically local or Northern but the urban identities that attach to them seem as strong as ever. The big clubs are sold out. Local passion rages as fiercely in the all-seater stadia as it did on the terraces, even if poorer fans can no longer afford to go. Urban identity remains, adjusting to the new media, exploiting it and exploited by it. What has gone is the classic incarnation of the North and the heroic ideal of Northern masculinity that went with it.

Notes

I am grateful to Bert Moorhouse for his helpful and perceptive criticisms. I also wish to acknowledge the help of the editors, Jeff Hill and Jack Williams, in suggesting the topic, correcting errors and supplying ideas. The papers presented at the British Society for Sports History conference in 1995 were also useful, especially the valuable discussion of 'Yorkshireness' by Dave Russell. Alan Tomlinson kindly provided me with information about Wilf Mannion as well as his work on Billy Baxter and thoughts on Burnley.

1. I have set out my views on male working-class sporting culture more fully in R. Holt, *Sport and the British: A Modern History* (Clarendon, Oxford: 1989), part 3, pp. 135–202; for a case study of male/female Northern leisure patterns, see A. Davies, *Leisure, Gender and Poverty: Working Class Culture in Salford and Manchester 1900–1939* (Open U.P., Milton Keynes: 1992).
2. This theme is fully discussed in the work of J. A. Mangan, especially his *Athleticism in the Victorian and Edwardian Public School* (Cambridge U.P., Cambridge: 1981) and subsequent work.
3. D. Brailsford, *Bareknuckles: A Social History of Prize Fighting* (Lutterworth, Cambridge: 1988).
4. *Dictionary of National Biography*, XXII, pp. 1213–14.
5. *Dictionary of National Biography*, XIX, p. 708; III, pp. 1240–1.
6. A. Metcalfe, 'Potshare bowling in the mining communities of East Northumberland', in R. Holt (ed.), *Sport and the Working Class in Modern Britain* (Manchester U.P., Manchester: 1991), p. 31.
7. A. Tomlinson, 'Shifting patterns of working class leisure: the case of Knur and Spel', *Sociology of Sport Journal* 9 (1992), pp. 192–206.
8. Tomlinson, 'Knur and Spel'.

9. E. Halladay, *Rowing in England: A Social History* (Manchester U.P., Manchester: 1990), pp. 19–20.

10. A. Metcalfe, 'Organized sport in the mining communities of South Northumberland', *Victorian Studies* (Summer 1982), p. 24.

11. W. F. Mandle, 'W. G. Grace as Victorian hero', *Historical Studies* (April 1980), pp. 357–8.

12. R. Sissons, *The Players: A Social History of the Professional Cricketer* (Kingswood, London: 1988), pp. 20–2.

13. Sissons, *The Players* p. 23.

14. Sissons, *The Players* p. 26.

15. *Dictionary of National Biography*, XV, pp. 353–4.

16. P. Wynne-Thomas, *'Give me Arthur': A Biography of Arthur Shrewsbury* (Arthur Barker, London: 1985), pp. 98–9.

17. Wynne-Thomas, *'Give me Arthur'* p. ix.

18. D. Hodgson, *The Official History of Yorkshire County Cricket Club* (Crowood, London: 1989), p. 22.

19. J. M. Kilburn, *In Search of Cricket* (Pavilion, London: 1990 edn with introduction by M. Engel), p. 9.

20. Hodgson, *Yorkshire CCC*, p. 119.

21. C. Brookes, *His Own Man: The Life of Neville Cardus* (Unwin, London: 1986), p. 92; see also Cardus cited in Holt, *Sport and the British*, p. 177.

22. Hodgson, *Yorkshire CCC*, p. 113.

23. Hodgson, *Yorkshire CCC*, p. 72.

24. G. Nicholson, *The Great Bike Race* (Methuen, London: 1977), p. 35.

25. Hodgson, *Yorkshire CCC*, p. 115.

26. Brookes, *His Own Man*, p. 107.

27. Brookes, *His Own Man*, p. 107.

28. Jeff Hill, 'Reading the stars: a post-modernist approach to sports history', *The Sports Historian* (14 May 1994), p. 48; M. Marshall, *Gentlemen and Players: Conversations with Cricketers* (Grafton, London: 1987), p. 25.

29. G. Howat, *Len Hutton: The Biography* (Mandarin, London: 1990 edn) provides a full picture of his career; also Len Hutton, *Fifty Years in Cricket* (Stanley Paul, London: 1984).

30. A. Hill, *Herbert Sutcliffe: Cricket Maestro* (Simon & Schuster, London: 1991), p. 87.

31. Howat, *Len Hutton*, p. 203.

32. Hill, *Herbert Sutcliffe*, pp. 97–8.

33. M. Kirkup, *Jackie Milburn in Black and White: A Biography* (Stanley Paul, London: 1990).

34. *The Footballer*, Feb./March 1995, pp. 41–2.

35. 'Wilf Mannion', written and produced by John Mapplebeck, BBC2, 4 September 1981.

36. T. Pawson, *The Goal Scorers: From Bloomer to Keegan* (Cassell, London: 1978), p. 64.

37. Tony Mason, 'Stanley Matthews', in Holt (ed.), *Sport and the Working Class*, p. 172.

38. D. Pickering, *The Cassell Soccer Companion* (Cassell, London: 1994), p. 188.

39. S. Wagg, *The Football World: A Contemporary Social History* (Harvester, Brighton: 1984), p. 62.
40. S. Jones, 'Economic aspects of Assocation Football in England, 1919–39', *British Journal of Sports History*, Dec. 1984, p. 294 (now *International Journal of the History of Sport*).
41. N. Fishwick, *English Football and Society 1910–1950* (Manchester U.P., Manchester: 1989), p. 84; also Holt, *Sport and the British*, p. 175.
42. *Independent on Sunday*, 14 May 1995, p. 9 (Sport).
43. E. Dunphy, *A Strange Kind of Glory: Matt Busby and Manchester United* (Heinemann, London: 1991), p. 214.
44. Tony Mason and Richard Holt, 'Le football, le fascisme et la politique etrangère brittanique', in P. Arnaud and A. Wahl (eds), *Sports et Relations Internationales* (Metz: 1994), p. 80; Fishwick, *English Football*, pp. 82–3.
45. Historical attempts to look at football hooligansim do not reveal any particular regional pattern; see E. Dunning, P. Murphy and J. Williams, *The Roots of Football Hooliganism: An Historical and Sociological Study* (Routledge and Kegan Paul, London: 1988).
46. Cited in Pickering, *Soccer Companion*, p. 64.
47. R. Holt, 'King across the border: Denis Law and Scottish football', in G. Jarvie and G. Walker (eds), *Scottish Sport and the Making of the Nation* (Leicester U.P., Leicester: 1994) on the fate of Scottish players in England; and H. B. Moorhouse, 'Shooting stars: footballers and working-class culture in twentieth-century Scotland', in Holt, *Sport and the Working Class*, pp. 179–97.
48. Dunphy, *Strange Kind of Glory*, pp. 238–9.
49. D. Russell, '"Sporadic and curious": the emergence of rugby and soccer zones in Yorkshire and Lancashire, *c.* 1860–1914', *International Journal of the History of Sport* 5.2 (September 1988), p. 192.
50. David Storey, *This Sporting Life* (London: 1962), p. 7.
51. Storey, *This Sporting Life*, p. 22.
52. R. Gate, *The Guinness Rugby League Fact Book* (Guinness Publishing, Bath: 1991), pp. 34–5.
53. Gate, *Rugby League Fact Book*, pp. 70–1.
54. Gate, *Rugby League Fact Book*, pp. 126–7, 144–5.
55. Hill, 'Reading the stars', p. 50.
56. Geoffrey Moorhouse, *At the George and Other Essays on Rugby League* (Hodder, London: 1989), p. 45; a book shot through with a travel writer's acute sense of place.
57. R. McKibbin, 'Work and hobbies in Britain, 1850–1950', in J. Winter (ed.), *The Working Class in Modern Britain* (Cambridge U.P., Cambridge: 1983).

8. Sport and racism in Yorkshire: a case study

Brian Holland, Lorna Jackson, Grant Jarvie and Mike Smith

Over the past two decades many historians and cultural critics have commented upon the way in which sport has embraced racism and race relations in various historical, social, political and economic contexts.[1] It is a subject which has recently gained considerable coverage in the British media. During September 1991 a Channel 4 documentary commented upon the experience of racism in British football; subsequently the comments from that programme hit the headlines of our national newspapers. Only a week earlier another sports documentary programme *On the Line* asked the question why was there only one British Asian footballer playing in the English Football League. The Scottish Football Association received complaints from both Mark Walters (Glasgow Rangers FC) and Paul Elliot (Glasgow Celtic FC) about racism on the terraces and indeed action was taken against a number of Glasgow Rangers fans. A further series of programmes during January 1991, on the experiences, opportunities and culture of both Afro-Caribbean and Asian communities in Britain, suggested that while sport played a significant part in the life of some groups of people, sport itself was not free from racism. During the early 1990s reports by the London Strategic Policy Unit, the London Council for Sport and Recreation, the Local Government Training Board, the West Midlands Council for Sport and Recreation, Stirling District Council and the Commission for Racial Equality have all addressed the assertion that British sport reproduces forms of racism.[2] More specifically, one writer commented on the opening of the 1994 football season by asserting that 'When the premier league season kicks off on Saturday, there will not be a single professional footballer of Asian origin on the field around the country'.[3]

While black players currently make up almost 20 per cent of the 20,000 professionals playing in the English football leagues Asian players have remained largely invisible. At the beginning of the 1994 season there were approximately 60 Asian footballers playing with semi-professional or high-level amateur teams. Across Britain there are an estimated 300 Asian football teams. Many were formed in the mid-70s by temples and community centres who sought to protect youngsters from the racism they experienced with white teams. According to one young Asian footballer who had trials with a leading Premier League club:

> From the moment I got on the pitch I didn't stand a chance. I got abused by other players and was played out of position by the coach. Maybe I didn't have the talent to make it but how could I know when I was never given fair treatment? [4]

At grass-roots level football, according to a recent Sports Council report, is more popular amongst Asian youngsters than among their white peers.[5] The report indicated that 60 per cent of Bengalis, 43 per cent of Pakistanis and 36 per cent of Indian youngsters regularly played football.

In comparison with other regions of the North of England Yorkshire has, perhaps belatedly, awoken to many of the charges of in-built racism within sport in Yorkshire. In cricket the Yorkshire tradition of fielding only Yorkshire-born players (a policy which was only abandoned in the late 1980s), was for some time viewed as a whites-only policy. Some have argued that the popularity of Yorkshire's first two overseas professionals, the Indian batsman Sachin Tendulkar and the West Indies' captain Richie Richardson, helped to challenge the assumption that Yorkshire folk could only appreciate their own.[6] Others have been less sanguine about the way in which those on the terraces have welcomed certain sporting heroes and heroines in Yorkshire. The Gloucestershire and England fast bowler David Lawrence described the hostility he met from the local Yorkshire crowd in the late 1980s:

> It makes me sick when I hear Yorkshire committee members saying they have the best, most loyal supporters in the world, that there weren't any racist fans in the crowds. It's absolute rubbish. I was standing on the boundary line and there was a whole section calling me all the names under the sun. They call me nigger, black bastard, sambo, monkey, gorilla, they threw bananas and I had to take these insults.[7]

If Salman Rushdie was in the early 1990s the most hated figure within Bradford's Asian community, then Brian Close, the former chairman of Yorkshire CCC Cricket Committee, was also far from popular with some members of the community. Although he apologized afterwards, Close talked of 'bloody Pakistanis' and 'our lads teaching them how to play' on a BBC Inside Story documentary *The Race Game*.[8] He went on to explain that Yorkshire had done everything it could for young

Asians. In the same programme he added 'We sent out 1,000 invitations to Asian youth groups to send their lads up to a special training session – and do you know how many turned up? Six.'[9] This is a view that was perhaps shared by Norman Tebbit who in 1990 suggested that by supporting the countries 'they were from rather than England many immigrants would fail the cricket test'.[10] The same man was to lead a Commons revolt against the granting of British passports to Hong Kong Chinese. Delivering the first Nicholas Ridley Memorial Lecture Tebbit expressed his concern at the 'substantial and growing Muslim minority' within Britain.[11]

Such sentiments do not take us very far in terms of understanding either the experience of Asian Muslim children living in Bradford or how Islamic beliefs influence aspiring cricketing talent within the Asian communities in Yorkshire. Cricket is not important for many Islamic groups living in Bradford or Yorkshire and it is therefore crucial not to provide sport with an overdetermined degree of political significance. Arnu Misra, a former cricketer from Manningham, explained that he gave up the game after six years while he gained a degree from Bradford University.[12] It is a typical pattern supported by much ethnographic research in which Asian families want their children to succeed in education, to become doctors and lawyers and not to waste their time with cricket. Mohammed Saddique, founder and former leader of the Muslim Youth Movement of Great Britain, was also critical of those cultural areas such as sport which deflected attention from 'the more fundamental traditions and culture according to the Islamic fashion'.[13] To be fair this was an attitude that was also adopted by many leading classical Marxist writers who viewed sport as a diversionary activity from political activism.[14] However, the bread-and-circuses stance adopted by the likes of Miliband and Hobsbawm was a view that was not shared, for example, by the Independent Labour Party through to the Communist Party, who saw working people in the 1930s and 1940s improving themselves through sport, education and political work.[15]

Nor do the views expressed by Brian Close, Norman Tebbit and others in positions of power in sport and in government help to explain or understand the day-to-day experiences of racism in the lives of many young Asians in Bradford and Yorkshire. Certainly for many Asian women and young girls, family life militates against the same experience of sport enjoyed by other sectors of the community. Many have to work long hours helping with the family business and going to the mosque. Yet as one young Asian Leeds United fan explained:

When I go to watch Leeds United I feel a sense of antagonism. They don't attack me because they know I'm a Leeds fan. But they stare and they say things if they meet you in the toilets. Once a gang of supporters shouted Death to the Ayatollah to me when I was on the bus.[16]

During the 1940s and 1950s the position of newly arrived black communities in Britain can be seen in terms of a pattern of exclusion and marginalization from the British political system.[17] Black organizations or groups during this period had little or no resources to affect what the state did. This does not mean that there was an absence of political involvement or action but it was not until the 1960s that a number of black groups and individuals started to challenge this exclusion and to invoke fundamental issues of citizenship and equality. During the 1960s Afro-Caribbean and Asian migrants launched a series of local and national organizations that sought in various ways to challenge the exclusion of blacks and other communities from equal participation in British society.[18] Such organizations included the already established Indian Workers' Association, the Campaign Against Racial Discrimination (CARD), the West Indian Standing Conference and other ethnically based groups.

From the early 1970s there has been a noticeable growth in the levels of political involvement and mobilization among Afro-Caribbean and Asian communities. In practice there always has been a rich and complex diversity of political and cultural expression. This diversity can be seen at the level of electoral politics, community mobilization, political party involvement and the level of parliamentary politics. Campaigns against racism in sport have figured little in the history of Afro-Caribbean and Asian struggles in Britain. In comparison with the 1968 Black Power demonstrations at the Mexico Olympic Games, political mobilization through sport has not been high on the agenda of community groups in Britain. The actions of Tommie Smith and John Carlos had a profound effect on black peoples around the world. Having won the 200 metres Olympic gold and bronze medals both Tommie Smith and John Carlos stood on the Olympic medal rostrum and staged a political protest against the violation of black people's rights in America. In an interview Smith explained:

> I wore a black right hand glove and Carlos wore the left hand glove of the same pair. My raised hand stood for the power in Black America. Carlos' raised left hand stood for the unity of Black America. The black scarf around my neck stood for black pride. The black socks with no shoes stood for black poverty in racist America. The totality of our efforts was the reclaiming of black dignity.[19]

Many other examples could have been given in an attempt to illustrate that sport and racism do not exist in some sort of social, or historical vacuum. Just as historical examples of racism in sport change over time, so too do the ways in which different discourses attempt to explain the relationship between sport and racism. It is not our intention to provide a lengthy account of various attempts to explain race relations through social or historical frameworks. Discussions of racism have been prominent not just within sociology but within many interdisciplinary fields such as cultural studies, black studies and science itself. Racism has been broadly defined as a set of beliefs, ideologies and social processes which discriminate against others on the basis of their supposed membership of a particular racial group.

Racism itself is not the property of any individual or group and, just as people move through different identities, so too do people experience different forms of racism. While individuals may be conceptualized as belonging to different groups, people also move through different groups and identities. We can for example think of identity at different levels. People may: (1) know an identity exists; (2) not understand what that identity involves; (3) believe in what that identity involves; (4) not allow that identity to affect their behaviour; (5) make a particular identity one of their main identities and (6) see any one identity as more or less important over time. Many members of the Asian community or Afro-Caribbean community also see themselves as members of other communal groups or frames of reference, such as being male, Catholic, Welsh, female, English, British, Protestant, Sikh etc. Hence, if figurations of people identify themselves as Asian or Afro-Caribbean, this does not preclude their actions from also being part of the broader struggle to determine what it means to be a twentieth-century Englishman or Englishwoman. Indeed some of the most stimulating work that has recently emerged has been the intervention in many fields by black British feminist writers who have published around the notion of black as a political colour. Yet the overall point that is being made here is that it is impossible to identify uniform patterns of racism or prejudice or race relations and therefore it is perhaps at a concrete historical or contemporary level that a better understanding of sport, racism and identity should be grounded.

Clearly the emergence of the Leeds United football fans' campaign against racism has not had the same influence as the Black Power demonstrations at the 1968 Mexico Olympic Games. Yet it is to the emergence of this campaign that this study now turns: a campaign which essentially addressed issues of racism, masculinity and youth culture during a particular period, a campaign which was rooted in a particular Yorkshire community.

The emergence of a sporting campaign against racism

The city of Leeds celebrated its hundredth birthday in 1993. One of its slogans during its centenary year was 'Leeds: the City of Sport'. Leeds can certainly boast a regular menu of sporting activities with football, both codes of rugby and, of course, cricket, featuring regularly at all levels and in all districts of the city throughout the year. Two of the most famous sporting venues in Leeds are Headingley, the home of Yorkshire cricket and Leeds Rugby League, and Elland Road, home of Leeds United Football Club. Of these two venues it is the culture of Elland Road that is the focus of attention in this chapter. The club acquired a reputation in the 70s for unruly and racist behaviour by its fans and an aggressive style of play on the pitch. It is an image that the club and the city have found difficult to shed. As Haynes describes:

> Leeds have had to endure two decades of derision and scorn from within the football world, among supporters, and in the media, ever since Don Revie assembled one of the greatest teams in English football, bringing the name of Leeds United into the broader public domain. 'Hardness' has long been associated with not only the style of play, but also with the temperament of Leeds fans in general.[20]

This image was firmly in place by 1982 when Martyn Harris focused on the behaviour of certain Leeds fans and the emergence of a fighting gang known as the 'Service Crew'. Harris particularly reminded us of the pitch invasions back in 1971 which led to the Elland Road stadium being closed for three weeks and the club's ban from European competition football in 1975 following riots in Paris.[21] The ground's reputation sank to further depths during the 80s, with the football club not only losing its first division status, but also the ground becoming a recruiting venue for fascist groups such as the National Front and the British Movement. Both of these fringe parties used the ground throughout the ten-year period from 1977 to 1987 to sell literature and encourage membership into their ranks. By 1987 the Leeds United club and the Elland Road stadium had become synonymous with violence, fascist activity and racist behaviour during matches. It was also in the same year that a small group of fans calling themselves the Leeds United Fans Against Racism and Fascism emerged.

The growth of modern racism at Elland Road

An early incident of collective racial chanting during a Leeds United football match at Elland Road occurred in December 1977. The victim was the then Nottingham Forest player, Viv Anderson, and choruses such as 'Kill the fucking nigger' were witnessed on that occasion.[22] The

1977–8 season was Anderson's fourth in the First Division of the Football League and within eleven months of this incident he was to become the first black player to be selected to play for England. At that time Leeds United did not have a black player on their books although, ironically, they had been one of the first clubs to do so when they signed Albert Johanneson and the lesser known Gerry Francis during the period 1961–70. Anecdotal evidence[23] suggests that Johanneson was the victim of racial abuse at Elland Road. Dave Hill provides evidence that the player was the victim of taunts at the hands of Everton supporters at Goodison Park in the mid-60s:

> In 1964 a British made movie, 'Zulu', went on general release, detailing the resistance of British troops to a bunch of African 'savages'. That season Johanneson turned out for Leeds ... The Merseyside fans, taking their cue from the film, bombarded Johanneson with their version of Zulu chants.[24]

After these two South African-born players left Leeds in 1970 – Johanneson moving to York City FC and Francis returning to his home country – it was nearly ten years before a black player pulled on a Leeds United shirt. By November 1979 Leeds-born Terry Connor had made his debut and stayed for four seasons. There was then another gap of some five years before Vince Hillaire and Noel Blake both transferred from Portsmouth in 1988. Since then there have been a number of black players at the club, including Chris Fairclough, Chris Kamara, Chris Whyte, the Wallace brothers from Southampton, David Rocastle, Brian Deane and Carlton Palmer.

Notwithstanding the comings and goings of black players in and out of the Leeds United team, there is ample evidence that collective racial chanting in the form of the infamous 'monkey chants' and individual abuse had been a regular terrace phenomenon since at least the late 1970s. August 1979 saw the first attempt by anti-racist activists to challenge the racist element at the ground. As one Leeds magazine mentioned at the time:

> The ANL [Anti Nazi League] are appealing to as many anti-Fascists to make an effort to go down to Elland Road when Leeds are playing at home to counter the presence of the NF and BM.[25]

The National Front and British Movement appearances at the ground reflected a trend at that time, with fascist groups using a number of football grounds, particularly in London, to recruit and hand out literature. Leeds and Newcastle were the two most popular Northern venues. Such activities signalled a change of strategy, particularly by the NF, which switched its tactics during 1979 from an electoral to a street-based campaign. Moreover, this reflected a changing power base in which the youth wings of the two parties became more influential in terms of controlling matters of strategy. Thus, the Leeds United ground became a venue for NF newspaper sellers to target young people and the place to buy the monthly edition of the Young National Front's infamous newspaper, *Bulldog*. Indeed, the content of *Bulldog*, and particularly its regular reference to the football scene, was a tactic and an appeal that was to be later taken on board by the anti-racists who emerged in 1987. As early as 1982, Harris discovered that copies of *Bulldog* were circulating in some Leeds public houses on match days [26] and were read avidly by members of the 'Service Crew' fighting gang which formed around this time. Harris spoke to one member of the gang who said that about two hundred fans formed the 'core' of the chanters in the 'Kop' during matches and these included supporters of the NF as well as the gang itself.[27] In fact, these chanters, at Elland Road and at other grounds up and down the country, were elevated to positions of considerable status in *Bulldog* where their activities were ranked in a racist 'league' table. Leeds United fans often held a top three position in this 'league'.

By 1983 Terry Connor had left the club but racial abuse and collective chanting remained in full public view every Saturday. In September of that year, one incident provoked particular outrage in the local press. This was when the black Manchester City goalkeeper, Alex Williams, was pelted with bananas and taunted with Nazi-style salutes by the 'Kop' fans. After the match a Leeds United Board Director made a statement to the press, saying 'I don't think this is anything to get too excited about. This sort of thing happens from time to time'.[28] A month later, the *Bulldog* magazine was clearly in a confident mood and sensed little resistance to the anti-black campaign at the ground. It argued that 'Leeds United supporters are proud to be called racists and are determined to make the NF stronger than ever at Leeds United this season [and] if you're not British don't come to Elland Road'.[29]

The following season racial chanting was still directed towards black players. On one occasion a Portsmouth player, Noel Blake (who was to sign up for Leeds some four years later) was the victim of racist taunts which were again well publicized by the local *Evening Post*.[30] In the eighteen months between September 1984 and February 1986, the political dimension to the racism at Elland Road had probably reached its height. A climax was perhaps reached in May 1985 at an away match between Leeds and Birmingham City. On that occasion, major public disturbances occurred and later became incorporated into Justice Popplewell's public investigation (which was perhaps better remembered for its enquiry into the Bradford fire disaster). At that game a teenage supporter died when a wall collapsed on top of him. 200 fans were arrested during a pitch invasion and prior to the game some Leeds United fans were seen selling NF newspapers, giving Nazi-style salutes and wearing swastika armbands. Those observations were offered as evidence before the Popplewell inquiry [31] and led to much public speculation about the extent to which groups such as the NF were directly influencing the behaviour of the Leeds fans. Such was the concern and interest around the Leeds area that two *Yorkshire Post* investigative journalists went undercover in 1985 and infiltrated the local Leeds NF branch. Their revelations appeared as good copy for the *Yorkshire Post* in February 1986 and publicly exposed the NF's crude tactics.[32] The journalists' exposé forced the club to make an official response, but the tone was totally inappropriate:

There may well be National Front elements who start the chanting [but] the Front is entitled under the law to sell its newspapers ... I would say to them 'please don't come to Elland Road' if I thought it would do any good, but I don't think it would.[33]

Such comments and expressions of resignation were even more amazing when it is considered that only three months earlier in November 1985 the *Yorkshire Post* had reported that:

Leeds United's Elland Road ground could be closed if the fascist salutes and racist taunts that marred Aston Villa's 3–0 victory, are repeated in future, Football Association Chairman, Bert Millichip warned today.[34]

The extent of the club's total complacency at this stage is well summarized by a report from a Commission of Inquiry into Racial Harassment in south Leeds near to the Leeds ground and based on research carried out in the period 1985–6:

It is apparent that the club does not consider there to be any particular problems at its ground. It adopts a 'low key' approach and admits that all it is doing is keeping a lid on any problems ... Only token efforts have been made to tackle racist activity.[35]

However, during March 1987 the Leeds club was again forced onto the defensive but this time from an unexpected quarter. It was following a game involving Leeds and Crystal Palace that a Palace black player, Andy Gray, went public to complain about the Leeds supporters. As he told *The Sun* after the match:

They are thugs and their racist abuse is aimed at coloured guys like me ... Elland Road is the worst ground of the lot. I've played there twice. The first time was my debut and I was taken off – and I was glad to come off. I couldn't handle the abuse: black bastard and things like that.[36]

The club gets its act together

Within weeks of the above comments being exposed in this national newspaper, the club at last made some real effort and circulated 18,000 leaflets with their match programmes, condemning racism. However, six months later this new-found anti-racist stance was completely under-mined, and their commitment severely tested, when the Leeds Trades Council launched its own campaign leaflet in October 1987. The club's subsequent over-reaction was bizarre and consumed with indignation over the Trades Council's use of 'Leeds United' in the campaign slogan: 'Leeds United Against Racism and Fascism'. The club's view appeared in the local press as follows:

> Leeds United today made it clear the club had no connection with the anti-racist leaflets distributed before Saturday's home match ... the club secretary, Mr David Dowse, said 'They had nothing to do with us. We don't like our name being used like this and [the leaflets] carried the club's logo giving some people the impression that they had official standing.' [37]

Clearly, the club was upset by the Trades Council initiative. The club did not want to be associated with a Trades Council sponsored campaign which it probably regarded as being overtly 'political'. However, the consequence of this was that on a public level the fans were being given ambiguous messages about the club's view of racism at Elland Road. Indeed, this was a pity because behind the scenes Leeds United were making genuine efforts to curb the racist chanting. For example, around that time the club voluntarily amended its ground regulations to ban formally racist behaviour. In addition, there were moves to make greater use of the law by the police and for the club to sign its own black player.[38] However, on the public stage there was confusion over the ownership of the anti-racist campaign at the ground. The club was publicly hesitant and the Trades Council was poised to seize the initiative. It was at this point during the 1987–8 season that a small number of white fans were getting restless and becoming increasingly angry at the lack of direction to eliminate the racist behaviour of many of their fellow supporters.

By March 1988 the club had finally decided to deal with the issue. Following yet another incident (at a Leeds United v. Aston Villa game on 9 January 1988), the club was forced to enlist an explicitly anti-racist stance. The Villa game had seen fans in the 'Kop' throw bananas and taunt the two black players during the 'warm up' session. Local MP Derek Fatchet intervened and on 15 January a meeting was finally held between the Leeds Trades Council and the club. On the Saturday the Trades Council distributed its leaflets and a few weeks later on 19 March the club handed out its own leaflets which included a statement, signed by all the first team players: 'Let's clean up our image totally and cut out any four letter words, racist taunts and noises and abuse.'[39] The two parties agreed to some degree of cooperation and the club, in particular, was now apparently less hesitant and more confident of its position. But the abuse and racist 'monkey chanting' still continued well into the 1989–90 season. For example, on 23 September 1989 a researcher visited the Elland Road ground to observe a match. On entering the turnstiles, the researcher had to pass NF newspaper sellers casually touting for business. Once inside the ground, separate incidents of both racist and non-racist abuse-chanting were targeted at three black players on the pitch, Jon Gittens and Fitzroy Simpson of Swindon and Chris Fairclough of Leeds United. The researcher heard some of the fans call Simpson a 'fucking coon' and both Swindon players received five doses of 'monkey chanting'. Overall, the breakdown was as follows:

Table 1 Abusive incidents at Leeds v. Swindon match

Type of incident	Frequency				Totals
	Against Leeds players		Against Swindon players		
	White	Black	White	Black	
Non-racial incidents	2	1	18	5	26
Racial incidents	0	2	0	18	20
	2	3	18	23	46

It will be noticed that 20 incidents out of a total of 46 (43 per cent) were racial in content. Moreover, irrespective of whether the abuse was racist the most abused players were the two black Swindon players who between them received 23 of all the 46 abusive incidents recorded (almost 50 per cent). If we take into account the fact that all three black players only made up 13.6 per cent of the total number of players on the pitch it is worth considering the respective burden on each of them. Thus, because there were 46 incidents in total, this means that the average burden on each of the 22 players was 46 divided by 22 = 2.09. If the direction of the 46 incidents is taken into account, the burden on each black player is fully exposed. Thus, the distribution of the burden was as follows:

Table 2 Distribution of incidents against the players

			Burden on each (%)
Leeds	White	2 incidents received by 10	0.2
Leeds	Black	3 incidents received by 1	3.0
Swindon	White	18 incidents received by 9	2.0
Swindon	Black	23 incidents received by 2	11.5

The above pattern is merely illustrative but it establishes that black players were subject to racial abuse at Elland Road during the 1989–90 season.[40] From these observations it can be seen that in a comparative sense black players received a disproportionate amount of racial abuse and harassment.

The fans make their move

What the researchers observed during trips to Elland Road in the 1989–90 season was also being tolerated by the supporters themselves and, indeed, had been tolerated for over ten years. A regular fan during those years was 'Paul'. Referring to the situation in the mid-1980s, 'Paul' made the following comment during a 1991 BBC TV *Sportsnight* programme:

> Leeds had reached a very low point in terms of the behaviour of the crowd – it was a very violent atmosphere at Elland Road and a very racist atmosphere ... a very unpleasant place to watch football. People were behaving very badly and we felt as a group of Leeds fans that we could no longer tolerate this behaviour.[41]

On a more personal note, 'Paul' also made the following point:

> I love football but I am not prepared to stand next to people going 'ooh, ooh, ooh' in the name of my team.[42]

However, 'Paul' and the other fans were conscious that any move to resist racism needed to be carefully considered and their enthusiasm to do something was tinged with apprehension:

> [We] started to think how to oppose it. We were shit-scared when we started because for ten years the culture had created an intimidating atmosphere and we weren't happy about having to oppose it ... First of all we had to raise the issue – the issue of not being racist.

Paul and his group of fans were conscious of how little had been done before 1987 to combat the racist atmosphere at Leeds matches:

The club were doing nothing; the Labour Council that own the football ground were doing nothing [although] players had not been reticent about criticising the Leeds fans [and] normally they are reluctant because it's seen as a sign of weakness.

'Paul' and others recognized that the situation at Leeds matches had acquired a political dimension with the NF regularly selling their literature outside the ground. For 'Paul', such targeting by fascist political groups was understandable:

football crowds are mainly working class people and for the fascists ... that's their target audience and especially the younger working class blokes. The [fascists] work on emotion, they work on violence, they work on atmosphere.

Referring to the youth magazine *Bulldog* produced by the NF and already discussed, 'Paul' sensed the appeal of that publication:

Bulldog was effectively the first football fanzine because it used humour – sick humour – and violent images [but] no-one was opposing this at the time. Official club programmes were useless [and] people want something to read on the terraces whilst they're waiting. Football is about humour and atmosphere and the NF tapped into that in the late '70s. More recently fanzines have struck that chord but in a positive and non-racist way.

Another member of the group, 'Dave', recalls the atmosphere of Elland Road and the Kop singing racist songs such as the following, sung to the tune of 'Brown Girl in the Ring':

... Brown Nigger on the Pitch,
Tra, la, la, la, la
He looks like a fuckin' lump of shit.[43]

'Dave' says that the whole ground seemed to be ringing with the song and he recalled the club manager's reaction:

Jock Stein's response at the end of the game – he was manager at the time – 'I was a wee bit disturbed by the attitude of some of the crowd to some of the coloured lads'.[44]

By the 1987–8 season fans such as 'Paul' and 'Dave' had become committed to some form of intervention. In that season, around 100 volunteers, organized at that time by the Leeds Trades Council, distributed leaflets. Fans such as 'Dave' and 'Paul' were involved in those exercises, but they recognized the limitations of handing out leaflets and stickers and felt the need to offer something more appealing.[45] The idea of the LUFARF fanzine *Marching Altogether* gradually took shape towards the end of the 1987–8 season. As Paul comments:

> For the first time, we were offering an alternative ... the unique thing about the fanzine is that it is free. There is a certain sort of person that buys the football fanzine – the younger, articulate and probably more progressive type. The older and the very young school kids aren't so ready to buy fanzines and it was the younger ones that were precisely the ones we wanted to get through to.[46]

Indeed, around 1988, the fanzine movement was beginning to gain ground having been given a lead by national fanzine publications such as *Off the Ball* and *When Saturday Comes*, first published in 1986. The fanzine formula is described by Vic Duke thus:

> The main ingredients ... common to most of them [are] a healthy sense of humour, constructive criticism of the players/management/ directors, unofficial news on club matters plus the occasional serious article/letter.[47]

The LUFARF fanzine *Marching Altogether* clearly falls in this tradition. It was one of six fanzines produced by fans supporting the Leeds United club, though it was the only one that was free and exclusively anti-racist in content as well as tone.[48]

However, when *Marching Altogether* was launched there was little, if any, support from the Leeds club and because of the alleged threat to sue Leeds Trades Council for using the ambiguous slogan 'Leeds United Against Racism and Fascism', even some apprehension concerning its possible response. Up to December 1993 a total of eighteen issues had been published, averaging between three and four issues per season. The tone of the fanzine is clearly provocative, humorous and thoughtful. As 'Paul' says:

> If you see people walking away from you and laughing then you know you are winning – we've undone the racism by humour, by making people think and not by ramming it down their throats.[49]

The first issue of *Marching Altogether* appeared in November 1988 with a front cover that showed a white Leeds United player standing with two black players: Vince Hillaire and Noel Blake. The first editorial clearly set out the objectives of the fanzine:

[It is] a fanzine produced by and for ordinary fans of Leeds United. The aim of this fanzine is to provide a place for discussion, comment and humour amongst Leeds fans ... [and] to repair the damage done by a small minority of violent and racist individuals. Leeds United, and Leeds fans, have had a terrible reputation over the last few years thanks to the behaviour of the morons who have shouted abuse at black players ... *Such behaviour is illegal and unacceptable and it has come close to permanently ruining our great club.* [Original emphasis] [50]

Included in the first issue of the fanzine was the first of many features on Leeds United's black players and on this occasion the spotlight fell on Noel Blake. Blake had been the victim of racial abuse whilst a Portsmouth player playing at Elland Road. As noted earlier, Blake signed for Leeds at the start of the 1988–9 season to coincide with the launch of *Marching Altogether*. The fanzine lost no time in portraying him in a positive light. Under the heading 'Home Grown Talent', the fanzine alluded to the fact that:

Noel Blake has been one of the best signings Leeds have made in years ... Leeds snapped him up and we haven't looked back since – our defence looks 100% better with Noel at the heart of it. Last season the defence panicked easily and had the speed of a tortoise, but Noel Blake has changed that. However, there are some so called fans who can do nothing better than threaten or insult him.[51]

The feature continued by making reference to the NF newspaper sellers outside the stadium on match days. This led on to a debate about a common racist argument that black people should be 'sent back to where they came from'. The feature debated the absurdity of the proposition and said:

where are we supposed to send black footballers back to? A survey of Britain's black footballers provides some interesting results.[52]

The article then provided a list of fourteen First and Second Division black players, thirteen of whom were born somewhere in Britain. And thus the argument continued:

This list clearly shows that all this 'send them back' stuff is a complete load of crap ... Noel Blake and Vince Hillaire have made Leeds United a better team and more attractive to watch. They are just as much British players as John Sheridan or Mervyn Day, so next time you hear any fans insulting or abusing black players because of their colour, make your views known to the morons – *Let's reclaim the game* for ordinary fans. [Original emphasis] [53]

Indeed, the slogan 'Reclaiming the Game' became a common one and appeared frequently in later issues.

The second issue was to see the introduction of a regular cartoon featuring 'The Adventures of Eric the Hooligan'.[54] Sometimes 'Eric' was depicted alone and on other occasions with a mate. On one occasion he was seen getting involved in silly capers and expressing racist-sentiments. He followed the latest football fashions in dress and hairstyle. Gradually, over the years, however, 'Eric' tempered his behaviour and became more intolerant of racist ideas. Thus by November 1989 'Eric' is prepared to confront a racist friend and, indeed, punches him for making 'monkey' noises and throwing bananas at a black footballer.[55]

The adventures of 'Eric' took on a greater significance in the 1991–2 season when the club signed Eric Cantona, the French international footballer. In one of its issues, *Marching Altogether* went French and captured the mood and the League championship success of that season. The issue of April 1992 was thus temporarily retitled '*Marchons Ensemble! Le Fanzine Officiel de la Lutte Anti-Raciste et Fasciste de Leeds Uniffiée*'. In this issue Eric the hooligan's status was uplifted and enhanced: he realized that the success of Cantona meant that 'being called Eric is Cool'. But perhaps more importantly, *Marching Altogether* highlighted the 1991–2 season by declaring the 'total end of Nazi Filth at Elland Road'.[56]

Another successful and popular cartoon had been the series '101 Things To Do with a Klu Klux Klansman'. The first cartoon appeared in December 1990 following reports that someone wearing a Klu Klux Klan hood had been seen during the riot on 5 May 1990 at Bournemouth FC at the end of the 1989–90 season. It was the last game of that season and Leeds needed to win to be promoted to the First Division. They won the game and the Second Division championship with it but the match is most remembered because of the disorders in the streets of Bournemouth. This 'KKK' character thus entered the pages of *Marching Altogether* early in the following season. Suggestions of what could be done to a 'Klansman' were as follows:

Kill him (slowly) and hang him upside down from the scrap metal bits on the roof of the Lowfields seats, with a Meat hook.[57]

Send him to change a bulb in the Floodlights without switching off at the mains.[58]

Drown him down the evil smelling men's bogs on Lowfields Road.[59]

Hang the Bastard from that nice new stand for away fans, preferably when we're playing Everton.[60]

Guillotine the bastard – Thanks to Eric's Countrymen for the idea.[61]

Set Fire to the Bastard, to see how he likes it.[62]

These cartoons clearly provided hard-hitting and direct messages to their readers. However, whilst 'Eric the hooligan' and '101 Things To Do with a Klu Klux Klansman' had become regular features, other 'one-off' items had become equally direct. For example, the issue of February 1993 asked 'Who is the dickhead in the Lowfields seats?', and illustrated this with a diagram of the Lowfields seating area and an arrow directed at a position near the front. Under the caption 'Dickhead spotted here!' the feature went on:

Who was the dickhead at the Spurs match who started singing 'Spurs are on their way to Belsen' [and] all that anti-Jewish, gas chamber, Hitler shit? Spurs are niggling trendy, time wasting Cockney bastards with bad haircuts, but you don't sing that sort of shit to anyone. So who was it? If you know him or if you are that dickhead the message is Fuck off and Die.[63]

Indeed the theme of 'dickhead in the crowd' became a new series after May 1991. This marked a watershed in the standing of the fanzine. It represented a growing confidence and an assertiveness to the extent that the fanzine felt able to confront not only groups of racist fans but also individuals, who were held up to ridicule. The fanzine also turned its attention to the racism that had been observed at other football grounds which Leeds United fans had reported to LUFARF. Thus in 1989 and 1990 respectively *Marching Altogether* named the Barnsley and Everton fans as 'Racist Scums of the Year'. Indeed, following the publicity of Barnsley for the unprestigious title in November 1989, the following issue revealed that Barnsley FC had placed an article in their official match programme admitting and condemning the racist behaviour of some of its fans.

However, the fanzine had always had Elland Road as its priority and not least its attempts to undermine the overtly fascist activities at the ground. The issue of April 1989 had a front cover showing NF newspaper-sellers with the caption 'The Nazis Are Still Among Us – Time To Go'.[64] By April 1992 the fanzine was claiming to have emptied the ground of such newspaper-sellers.[65]

Indeed, the question of the impact and progress of the fanzine's campaign was an important element for the credibility and motivation of those involved. A real boost was achieved in September 1991 when the Channel 4 documentary, *Great Britain United*, focusing on the plight of black players, referred to the Leeds campaign. In the film, Arsenal's black player, Ian Wright, provided an acknowledgment of their efforts:

> We went to Leeds the other week it was brilliant. They've got a thing down there petitioning against the noises and racial abuse black players take. I think it's a giant step because Leeds were really bad ... it's changed a lot.[66]

Obviously the fanzine made capital from such quotes and gave the TV documentary full coverage in the October 1991 issue. In fact, not only did black players refer to Leeds, but in addition 'Paul' and some of his colleagues appeared on the Channel 4 film along with Chris Fairclough and Howard Wilkinson, the Leeds United manager.[67] Whilst *Marching Altogether* almost exclusively aimed to present and articulate anti-racist themes, the fanzine maintained its credibility as a publication concerned with other football-related issues. For example, the controversial issue of all-seater stadia raised in the Taylor Report and the equally controversial question of identity cards were discussed.

Overall, the evidence suggested that the fanzine campaign had a relatively positive impact on the behaviour of fans at Elland Road. However, as the research revealed, racism at matches has not been totally eliminated. Indeed 'Paul' is the first to recognize the limitations of his group's efforts and the fact that racism has not totally disappeared. However, the style of the fanzine, aimed directly at the young fan, has proved to be a credible tool in the resistance to racist chanting and fascist political activities at the stadium.

The fanzine is produced by less than a dozen volunteers. Their finances come from voluntary donations and subscriptions. The members are committed anti-racists and anti-fascists. They are still viewed with suspicion by club officials. Clearly, for many the style and content of *Marching Altogether* is too hard hitting and crude (not to say rude). But this is the humour and culture of terrace life – a life not always understood or recognized by those sitting in centrally-heated executive boxes. The campaign recognizes the realities of terrace life and attempts to re-channel and re-script the racist feelings and sentiments of some fans. By 1993, 'Paul' was reasonably content with the way the campaign had developed over a five-year period, but he remained a realist:

> Elland Road is now a positive place in which to watch football but we're aware that it may not last; when things go wrong for the team,

some fans still fall back on the first racist insults that come to mind. Supporters have the power to defeat racism in football but it's vital that we continue to speak out; if we're silent it will never go away.[68]

Concluding remarks

A number of factors have influenced the thinking behind this study. First, there is no simple explanation of the relationship between sport, racism and ethnicity but rather a sustained effort to comprehend the circumstances which give rise to past and present formulations of racism. Those who have sought to explain the relationship between sport, racism and ethnicity have tended to rely upon a number of common arguments: (1) that sporting institutions are themselves inherently conservative and help to consolidate patriotism, nationalism and racism; (2) that sport itself has some inherent property that makes it a possible instrument of integration and harmonious race relations; (3) that sport as a form of cultural politics has been central to the process of colonialism and imperialism in different parts of the world; (4) that sport itself has contributed to unique political struggles which have involved black and ethnic political mobilization and the struggle for equality for black peoples and other ethnic minority groups; (5) that stereotypes, prejudices and myths about ethnic minority groups have contributed to both discrimination against and under-representation of ethnic minority peoples within sport; (6) that the study of sport and racism cannot be simply isolated, since racism articulates with other ideologies and discourses such as feminism and nationalism; and (7) that sport is a vehicle for displays of prowess, masculinity and forms of identity, many of which are racist in orientation.

It has not been possible to address all of these themes in this study. Indeed that has not been our concern. A wide range of sociological and historical literature has been produced to explain the relationship between sport, racism and ethnicity in different social and historical contexts. What is clearly evident from this literature is that a great deal of painstaking research needs to be undertaken if we are to understand the specificities of the ways in which racism influences people's sporting experiences. Such research will take us much further forward than a concern for broad generalizations and explanations. This is not a plea for empiricism but rather a suggestion that terms such as 'race', 'ethnicity' and 'sport' are not uniform and have to be specifically 'unpacked' in terms of content, time and place. It is an account of one particular campaign against racism which has formed the substantive part of this study.

The issue of identity is itself full of contradictions and complexities, and many would deny that any form of common identity is possible in a region or nation which displays a wide range of cultural diversity. How can a white male from Halifax, a supporter of rugby league, a member of the NF, have a common identity with a young Asian cricketer from Bradford who follows the principles of Islam and the Qu'ran? To pose such a question is to misunderstand the point and to assume wrongly that people have but one identity. In answer to the question 'who do I think I am?', individuals and groups may identify and shift between a number of reference points such as home and family, locality, nationality, sport and faith, to name but a few, all of which contribute to what it means to be, for instance, a twentieth-century person from Yorkshire. If one were to think of identity in terms of a history of complex loyalties then it is not impossible to imagine a powerful sense of being Asian, male and Islamic going hand in hand with a powerful sense of being male and English, all of which contributes to what it means to be British and from Yorkshire, and to be a Tyke in the late twentieth century.

Finally, it is important not to attach too great a degree of importance to the emergence of football fanzines as some democratic initiative in football. In many cases those who have written about football fanzines have tended to generalize rather than be specific about such an argument. The account of a campaign against racism in sport provided in this study, while it may have some affect at a local level, will not have the same impact as those who stood on the medal rostrum at the 1968 Mexico Olympic Games. We have not claimed that sport or football is some phenomenal equalizing agent; it clearly is not. Yet the Leeds United campaign against racism in football clearly, for a short period, influenced the opinion of some football supporters, helped Elland Road become a more tolerant place for black players and was conditioned and influenced by a very specific set of structures at a particular time and in a particular place. It might be that forms of racist behaviour merely shifted territory from the football terraces to elsewhere.

Notes

1. See, for example, the work of Ernest Cashmore, *Black Sportsmen* (Routledge & Kegan Paul, London: 1982) and *Making Sense of Sport* (Routledge, London: 1990). A useful comparative sociological account of racism can be found in Grant Jarvie, *Sport, Racism and Ethnicity* (Falmer Press, Brighton: 1991).
2. See, for example, *Equal Opportunity? Sport, Race and Racism* (West Midlands Sports Council: 1991), and *Talking Back: Combating Racism in British Football* (Stirling District Council: 1992).

3. Vivek Chaudhary, 'Asians can play football, too', *The Guardian*, 7 September 1994.
4. Chaudhary, 'Asians can play football, too'.
5. Chaudhary, 'Asians can play football, too'.
6. J. White, 'Yorkshire's biggest test', *The Independent*, 26 May 1990, p. 29.
7. White, 'Yorkshire's biggest test'.
8. White, 'Yorkshire's biggest test'.
9. White, 'Yorkshire's biggest test'.
10. S. O'Hagon, 'When respect is the goal', *The Independent*, 5 December 1993, p. 8.
11. Chris Searle, 'Race before wicket: cricket, empire and the white rose', in *Race and Class* 31. 3 (1990), pp. 31–48.
12. White, 'Yorkshire's biggest test'.
13. White, 'Yorkshire's biggest test'.
14. See, for example, the work of Scott Fleming, 'Sport, schooling and Asian male youth culture', in Jarvie (ed.), *Sport, Racism and Ethnicity*, pp. 30–57.
15. See S. Jones, *Sport, Politics and the Working Class* (Manchester U.P., Manchester: 1988).
16. White, 'Yorkshire's biggest test'.
17. J. Solomos and L. Black, 'Black political mobilisation and the struggle for equality', *Sociological Review* 39. 2 (1991), pp. 215–37.
18. Solomos and Black, 'Black political mobilisation'.
19. H. Edwards, *The Revolt of the Black Athlete* (Free Press, New York: 1969), p. 104.
20. R. Haynes, 'Marching on Together', Working Paper, Unit for Law and Popular Culture, Manchester Polytechnic, 1991, p. 1.
21. M. Harris, 'Leeds, the lads and the meeja', *New Society*, 25 November 1982, p. 337.
22. Leeds Trades Union Council and Anti-Fascist Action, *Racism and Fascism in Leeds and West Yorkshire* (Leeds Trades Council, Leeds: 1987), p. 4.
23. We are grateful to a colleague and former Leeds United fan, Steve Webster, for his recollections of Albert Johanneson's experiences whilst playing for the club.
24. D. Hill, *Out of his Skin: The John Barnes Phenomenon* (Faber & Faber, London: 1989), pp. 70–1.
25. *Leeds Other Paper*, 110 (August 1979), p. 7.
26. Harris, 'Leeds and the meeja', p. 338.
27. Harris, 'Leeds and the meeja', p. 338.
28. Leeds United director Maxwell Holmes, quoted in Leeds Trades Council, *Racism and Fascism in Leeds*, p. 8.
29. Quoted in *Racism and Fascism in Leeds*.
30. *The Yorkshire Evening Post*, 17 September 1984.
31. See Home Office (1985) *Committee of Inquiry into Crowd Safety and Control at Sports Grounds: Interim Report* (HMSO, London: 1985), para 5.5, p. 39.
32. See reports by Tony Watson and Richard Donkin in *The Yorkshire Post* issues of 17 February 1986, 18 February 1986 and 19 February 1986.
33. Maxwell Holmes quoted in *The Yorkshire Post*, 19 February 1986.
34. *The Yorkshire Post*, 1 November 1985.

35. Leeds Community Relations Council, *Racial Harassment in Leeds: 1985–1986* (Leeds CRC, Leeds: 1987), p. 50.
36. *The Sun*, 23 March 1987.
37. *The Yorkshire Evening Post*, 28 October 1987.
38. This information is revealed in correspondence between the club and the Football League and the West Yorkshire Police.
39. Leeds United FC press release statement dated 19 March 1988.
40. See B. Holland, 'Evidence on racial attacks and harassment in and around football grounds', submission to Home Affairs Committee, Dept of Social and Economic Studies, University of Bradford, 1993, para 2.5.
41. 'Paul', speaking on BBC *Sportsnight* programme, 21 January 1991.
42. 'Paul' during a speech to the Greater Manchester Football Supporters Association on 21 January 1991. The following quotations are also taken from this speech.
43. 'Dave' during a speech to the Greater Manchester Football Supporters' Association on 21 January 1991.
44. 'Dave' speaking during the documentary *Great Britain United*, Channel Four Television, 12 September 1991.
45. *Great Britain United* documentary.
46. Interview with LUFARF group, 18 February 1991.
47. V. Duke, 'Sociology of football: a research agenda for the 1990s', *Sociological Review* 39. 3 (August 1991), p. 638.
48. Duke, 'Sociology of football'.
49. 'Paul' during a speech to Greater Manchester Football Supporters Association on 21 January 1991.
50. *Marching Altogether* (November 1988).
51. *Marching Altogether* (November 1988).
52. *Marching Altogether* (November 1988).
53. *Marching Altogether* (November 1988).
54. *Marching Altogether* (November 1989).
55. *Marching Altogether* (January 1989).
56. *Marching Altogether* (April 1992).
57. *Marching Altogether* (March 1990).
58. *Marching Altogether* (April 1990).
59. *Marching Altogether* (November 1991).
60. *Marching Altogether* (January 1993).
61. *Marching Altogether* (February 1993).
62. *Marching Altogether* (April 1993).
63. *Marching Altogether* (April 1993).
64. *Marching Altogether* (April 1989).
65. *Marching Altogether* (April 1992).
66. *Great Britain United* documentary.
67. *Great Britain United* documentary.
68. *Marching Altogether* (January 1993).

Index

Afro-Caribbeans 165, 166
 local and national organizations
   168
 see also black sportsmen; racism
Althusser, Louis 85
Anderson, Viv 170
Anglican sports clubs 130, 131
animals as sporting heroes 139
annual celebrations
 in mining villages 22–3, 24–7, 35
 see also galas
Anti Nazi League 171
Armstrong, George 142
Asians
 Asian sports leagues 9
 in cricket 166–7
 in football
  non-professional 165–6
  number of players 165, 166
  professional 10, 165–6
 local and national organizations
   168
 traditional divisions between 9
 see also racism

Bairner, Alan 4
Bale, John 4
Baptist sports clubs 130
Barnes, Sydney 148
Barson, Frank 154
Barthes, Roland 3
Batten, Billy 158
Batten, Eric 158
Baxter, Billy 142
Bedlington Hoppings 26–8
Bergman-Osterberg, Martina 68
Best, George 156–7
Bevan, Brian 159
billiards 116

black sportsmen
 Black Power and 168, 169
 in football 9–10, 165
  Leeds United 167–8, 178, 179
 as managers 10
 in rugby league 9, 159
 sporting heroes 159
 see also racism
Blanchflower, Jackie 155
Boston, Billy 9, 159
bowls 117
 see also potshare bowling
Boycott, Geoffrey 148, 150
British Movement 170
broadcasting *see* radio; television
Broadhead, John 55
Bulldog see National Front
Busby, Matt 153, 155

Cadbury, Edward 60
Cadbury's 62, 74
Campaign Against Racial
  Discrimination (CARD) 168
Cardus, Neville 147, 148
Carlos, John 168
Carter, Raich (Horatio) 151, 152,
  161
Catholics
 church-affiliated sports clubs
   113, 114, 127, 128, 129, 130
  see also church-affiliated sports
  clubs
 English 107
 football and 107
 Irish 107
Caunt, Ben 142
Chalmers, Robert 143
Charlton, Bobby 151, 152, 155
Charlton, Jack 151, 152

Child, John 64
children
  in mining villages 35–6
    galas 25–6, 36
Church of England sports clubs
    130, 131
church-affiliated sports clubs 8–9,
    113–36
  Anglicans 130, 131
  Baptists 130
  billiards 116
  bowls 117
  Catholics 116, 117, 127, 130,
    131, 132
  cheating and 128
  church attendance and 126,
    129–30
  clerical opposition to 125, 126
  clerical support for 125–7
  Congregationalists 118, 119, 122,
    130, 131
  cricket 113–36 passim
  facilities 117
  fair play 126, 127, 128
  football 113–36 passim
  gender divisions 128–9
  golf 116
  house building, effects of 123
  indoor sports 116, 132
  interdenominational leagues 127
  leagues 120, 124, 127, 131
  local newspapers and 114, 115,
    125–6
  membership costs 121
  misconduct by 128
  mixed teams 129
  Nonconformist 130, 131
  numbers of teams 113, 114–15,
    120–4
    decline in 127
    reasons for 119–21
  Presbyterians 130
  Primitive Methodists 130, 131
  rough play 128
  rounders 114, 129
  rugby union 116
  Sabbatarianism and 121
  sectarian loyalties 107, 130, 131
  secularization and 113, 127–8
  social class and 118–19, 131–3
  sports grounds 117
    loss of 123
  standards of play 117
  subscriptions 121
  Sunday school teams 117–18,
    120, 124
  table tennis 116
  tennis 114
  unemployment and 122–3
  Wesleyan Methodists 119, 130
  women and 7–8, 128–9
    women's cricket 114
    women's hockey 114
  working-class consciousness and
    131–3
  see also pub teams; workplace
    teams
Clarke, William 144
Clasper, Harry 20, 36, 143, 151
class consciousness see social class
Clegg, Charles 41, 50
Close, Brian 166, 167
Clough, Brian 152
Collet, Clara 60
Colls, Robert 4, 5
communal celebrations, in mining
    villages 19–20, 22–8, 35
community
  characteristics of 14–15
  defining 16–18
competitiveness
  in cricket 144–5
  masculinity and 137
  women and 69
Congregationalist sports clubs 118,
    119, 130, 131
Conservative Party sports teams
    132, 133
Constantine, Learie ('Connie') 9,
    159
Coombes, Robert 143
Crerand, Pat 93
cricket
  church-affiliated clubs 113–36
    passim
  competitiveness in 147–8

County cricket 119
Englishness and 4
Gentlemen and Players match
    140, 145
Islam and 167
in Lancashire 118, 140, 148–9
local newspapers and 146, 148
masculinity and 147
North–South divide and 137,
    138–9, 140–7
in Nottinghamshire 144–6
pub teams 120–1
racism in 166–7
sporting heroes of 140–7
television and 150
women and 128, 147, 161
    women's clubs 70, 114
workplace teams 123–4
in Yorkshire 118, 139, 140,
    146–7, 148–9, 157, 166–7
culture, language and 2–3
Cunningham, Hugh 73, 125
Cup Finals 7, 44, 46–7, 50, 85–11,
    138
    'Abide With Me' 92–3, 106
    costs of attendance at 95
    at Crystal Palace 47, 87, 90, 92
    excursions to 46–7, 94–5, 103–5
    Football Association and 88–9
    'ghost towns' 98
    'hooliganism' 92
    mythology of 88, 98, 102
    as national events 87–93
    newspaper reports 86, 90–1, 92,
        93, 94
        local newspapers 86, 91, 94–5,
        96, 97, 98, 99, 102–5, 106
    on Northern supporters 47–8
    Northern presence in 7, 43–4,
        46–7, 86–7, 94–102, 106
    radio commentaries 92, 98
    reception of homecoming teams
        98–102
    royalty and 88, 89–90, 92
    rugby league 7, 85, 86, 91, 92,
        96, 157
    supporters at home 49, 94, 97–8
    television coverage 92

venues 47, 87, 88, 89
violence at 92, 97
at Wembley 87, 88, 89, 90, 106

Davin, Anna 61
Dean, 'Dixie' (William) 151, 153
    154, 159
Dellheim, Charles 62
discourse, role of 2
    see also language
Dodd, Philip 4
Dolling, Reverend Robert 59
Drake, Ted 155
Duke, Vic 178
Dyhouse, Carol 58

education
    gender and 54, 62–3
    physical education for women
        67–71
    sport as moral education 139
Edwards, Duncan 156
Eliot, T.S. 88
Elliott, William 20
Englishness
    cricket and 4
    Cup Finals and 93

FA Cup Finals see Cup Finals
fanzines, football 182
    Marching Altogether 178–82
femininity
    conventional notions of 8
    ideology of motherhood 61
    in mining villages 36
    models of 53–4
    see also gender; women
Ferguson, Joe 158
Finney, Tom 153, 154
Fleming, Harold 154
flower shows 24–5, 36
football
    aggressive play 154
    Asian players 9, 165–6
    association 6
    behaviour of supporters 46–7,
        50, 92

black players 9–10, 165, 170–1,
  178, 179
broadcasting of 106, 154, 155
centres 48
church-affiliated clubs 113–36
  passim
collective/co-operative game 48
communal solidarity and 33–4
Cup Finals *see* Cup Finals
dribbling 48
FA *see* Football Association
fanzines 182
  Marching Altogether 178–82
Football League 45
forward pass, development of 48
forwards 48
gate-money, introduction of 45
gender and 107
half backs 48
heading the ball 48
history of 42–3
  player formations 48
  positions 48
  styles of play 48–9
'hooliganism' 92
individualist game 41, 50
local rivalries 31–2, 35, 46
masculinity and 36
middle-class sponsorship of
  teams 125
in mining villages 20, 29–32,
  33–4, 35, 36, 151
Munich disaster 155–6
as national game 91
newspaper reports
  local newspapers 42–3, 44–5,
  46, 50
  on Northern supporters 47
North–South divide in 41–52,
  137, 149–55
passing game 48
player formations 47–8
professional 6, 44–6, 48–50, 148
  legalization of 44–5, 50
pub teams 120–1
racism in 9–10, 165–6, 167–86
  see also Asians; black sportsmen;
  Leeds United; racism

rough play 48–9
school teams 30–1
sectarian loyalties 107, 130, 131
social class and 85
as spectator sport 41, 46, 47
sporting heroes 149–55
styles of play 48–9
teamwork, development of 48
television and 106, 152, 154
university clubs 42
violence on the pitch 154–5
wing as specialist player 48
working classes and 85
workplace teams 120, 123–4
Football Association (FA)
  formation of 42
  Lancashire FA 43
  legalization of professionalism
  44–5, 50
  Sheffield FA 43
  see also Cup Finals
Football League
  admission to 119, 120
  formation of 49

galas 23, 33, 35
  children's 25–6, 35
  see also annual celebrations;
  mining villages
Gallacher, Hughie 151
Geertz, Clifford 2, 86
gender
  church-affiliated sports clubs and
  128–9, 131–2
  education and 53, 61
  identity 7
  ideology of motherhood 61
  sexual division of leisure 54–7,
  107
  social processes and 1
  sporting heroism and 139, 161
  see also femininity; masculinity;
  women
Gillis, John 54
Girls' Friendly Society 58
Gledson, Robert 28–9
Grace, W.G. 144, 146
Gregg, Harry 155

Hanlan, Ned 20
Hanley, Ellery 159
Hargreaves, Jennifer 7, 8, 71
Harris, Martyn 170, 172
Haynes, R. 170
heroes *see* sporting heroes
Hirst, George ('George Herbert')
    147
historiography 2, 3
history of sport *see* sports history
Hobbs, Jack 146, 149
hockey
    women's clubs 69, 114
Holt, Richard 5
horse racing 139, 143
horticultural shows 24, 25, 36
Hutton, Len 149–50, 161

identity 1–2
    cultural activity and 2
    Englishness *see* Englishness
    language and 2
    national 1
    Northernness *see* North–South
        divide
    race and 183
    social class and 2
    in Victorian England 2
    white identity 9
    see also racism
ideology 3, 85
Indian Workers' Association 168
indoor sports
    church-affiliated clubs 116, 132
    political organizations and 129
Inglis, Fred 85
Inglis, Simon 93
Islam, cricket and 167

Jardine, Douglas 148
Jarvie, Grant 4
Jewell, Helen 5, 42
Johanneson, Albert 171
Johnston, Harry 89
Jones, Lewis 159
Joyce, Patrick 3, 4
    on class consciousness 131
    on class relations 2

on Cup Finals 85, 93, 107
on identity 2
on language and culture 2
on 'linguistic turn' 2

Karalius, Vince 91
Kilburn, J.M. 146
knur-and-spel 142
Labour Party sports teams 132,
    133

Lancashire cricket 117, 140, 148–9
Lancaster, B. 5
language
    constitution of the 'self' and the
        'social' 2
    culture and 2–3
    identity and 2–3
    'linguistic turn' 2–3
    role of discourse 2
Law, Denis 156
Lawrence, David 166
Lawton, Tommy 151, 154, 155
Leeds United
    Anti Nazi League and 171
    black team members 170–1, 178,
        179
    British Movement and 170, 171
    fans' campaign against racism
        176–83
        Leeds United Fans Against
            Racism and Fascism
            (LUFARF) 170, 178, 181
        Marching Altogether 178–82
        'Reclaiming the Game' 180
    growth of modern racism at
        Elland Road 170–74
    National Front and 170, 171–3,
        175, 177, 179, 181
        Bulldog 172, 177
    official responses to racism 172,
        173, 174–6, 177, 182–3
    racial abuse/chanting 171, 172,
        173, 174–5
    'Service Crew' 170, 172
    Trades Council's initiative
        174–5, 178
    Yorkshire Post investigation 172

leisure
  men's 55–8
  rational recreation 60, 73–4
  sexual division of 55–8, 107
  women's 58–60
  see also Rowntree Cocoa Works
Leyland, Maurice 148, 161
Liberal Party sports teams 132, 133
local councils, recreation grounds
    and 33, 36
local newspapers 13, 28, 29–30,
    42–3
  church-affiliated sports clubs and
    114, 125–6, 129
  cricket and 146, 148
  Cup Finals and 7, 86, 93–4, 95,
    96, 97, 98, 99, 100, 102–5
  dialect tradition 103, 104
  football and 42–3, 44–5, 46, 50
  racism in sport and 172
  rugby league and 91
  sporting heroes and 146, 147
  see also newspapers

Lofthouse, Nat 151, 154
McCrone, Kathleen 8, 69, 74
McKibbin, Ross 161
McLaren, Archie 149
McParland, Peter 155
Mangan, J.A. 113
Mannion, Wilf 152
Martin, Stephen 16, 33
masculinity
  competitiveness and 139
  cricket and 147
  football and 36
  in mining villages 36
  models of 55, 55
  'moral manliness' 139
  North–South divide and 7, 138–9
  sporting heroes and 7, 139,
    145–6, 160
  team sports and 138–9
  see also gender
Mason, Tony 1, 2, 3, 6, 113, 120
Matthews, Stanley 153, 156, 161
Mechanics' Institutes 14, 15, 25,
    32, 33

media see local newspapers;
    newspapers; radio; television
Metcalfe, Alan 142
Methodism
  in mining villages 14, 15, 23
  sports clubs
    church-attendance and 127
    Primitive Methodist 130, 131
    Wesleyan Methodist 119, 130
    see also church-affiliated sports
      clubs
Milburn, Jackie 151, 161
mining villages 13–40
  annual celebrations 19–20, 22–7,
    35
  athletic events 20, 23, 24, 25, 26,
    27
  Bedlington Hoppings 26–7
  bond system 17, 34
  children in
    galas 25–6, 35
    importance of 35
  churches/chapels 18, 32, 33
  coal companies 18, 32, 36
  coal mine, influence of 18–19
  collective action 19–20, 34
  colliery officials 18, 32, 36
    on local councils 32–3
  communal celebrations 19–20,
    22–8, 35
  composition of 17
  as constructed communities
    17–18
  development of 15–19
  ethnic groups in 16, 17
  flower shows 24–5, 36
  football 20, 29–32, 33, 35, 36,
    151
    colliery officials and 32
    communal solidarity and 31–2
    local rivalries 31–2, 35
    outside competition 30–1
    regional identity and 30–1
    school teams 30–1
  galas 23, 33, 35
    children's 25–6, 35
    see also annual celebrations
  horticultural shows 24–5, 36

influxes of miners from outside
    16, 17, 33
instability of populations 16–17, 34
international sports competitions
    20
lack of homogeneity in 15
landowners and 18
local councils and 32–3, 35–6
as male domains 36
masculinity in 36
Mechanics' Institutes 14, 15, 25,
    32, 33
Methodism in 14, 15, 23
movement of miners between 17
national sports competitions 20
Northumberland Miners' Union
    19, 34
parks 33
physical layout of 17–18
picnics 23–4
pit shaft, influence of 18–19
poets of 21–2
populations of 17
potshare bowling 21, 28–9, 35,
    36, 142
public houses 18
quoits 20, 21, 22, 27, 28, 29
races 20, 26, 27
    120-yard handicap 23, 24, 27
recreation grounds 32–3, 36
rowing 20
schools 18
sponsored picnics 23–4
sporting heroes 20, 21, 28–9, 35,
    36, 141
sprint races 20
status in 15
strikes 19
Sunday schools 25
Temperance groups 33
traditional festivities 19–20, 22–7
women in 36
Working Men's Institutes 14, 25
workplace teams 123
wrestling 33
yearly bond 17, 34
YMCAs 32
Misra, Arnu 167

Moorhouse, Bert 4
moral education, sport as 139
Mortenson, Stan 153
Mosforth, Billy 41
Munich disaster 156

National Front 170, 171–3, 175,
    177, 179, 181
    Bulldog 172, 177
nationalism, resurgence of 1
newspapers
    Bulldog 172, 177
    Cup Finals and 86, 90–1, 92, 93,
        94
    inception of daily newspapers 34
    local *see* local newspapers
    on Northern football supporters
        47
    role of 4
    rugby league and 157
    sporting heroes and 4, 106, 153,
        157, 162
Nicholson, Geoffrey 148
North–South divide 4–6, 41–2,
    137–41
    aggression and 154–5
    cricket and 139–40, 144–50
    football and 44–50, 150–7
    history of 5, 41–2
    horse racing and 139
    male-domination of sport and 139
    masculinity and 7, 139
    rugby 49, 89, 138, 157–9
    sport as moral education 139
    sporting heroes and 137–64
    team sports and 138–9
Northern union football *see* rugby
    league
Nottinghamshire cricket 144–6

Offiah, Martin 159

Parkin, Cecil 149, 161
Parkinson, Michael 150
parks 33
Parr, George 144–5
Pearson, Ruby 75
Perry, Fred 160

ping pong 116
political organizations, sports teams
    and 132–3
Popplewell inquiry 172, 173
Porter, Roy 4
potshare bowling 21, 28–9, 35, 142
    see also bowls
Powell, Enoch 9
Presbyterian sports clubs 130
press see local newspapers;
    newspapers
Priestley, J. B. 5
Primitive Methodist sports clubs
    130, 131
Protestants, football and 107
    see also church-affiliated sports
        clubs
provincial newspapers see local
    newspapers
pub teams
    cricket 119
    football 121
    see also church-affiliated sports
        clubs; workplace teams
pugilists, as sporting heroes 141–2
Pullin, A. W. 146

quoits 20, 21, 22, 27, 28, 29

racism 9–10, 165–86
    see also Afro-Caribbeans; Asians;
        black sportsmen; British
        Movement; Leeds United;
        National Front; sectarian
        loyalties
radio
    Cup Finals and 92, 97–8
    football and 154
rational recreation 58, 73–4
    see also leisure
Read, Donald 87
recreation grounds
    local councils and 33, 36
    in mining villages 32–3, 36
    public parks 33
    see also sports grounds
Renforth, James 143
Revie, Don 152, 170

Rhodes, Wilfred 147, 161
Riach, Nancy 4
Richardson, Richie 166
Risman, Gus 95
road bowling see potshare bowling
Robbins, Keith 94
Robertson-Glasgow, R. C. 148
Robinson, Emmot 148
Ronson, Percy 153
Rosenfeld, Albert 159
rowing 20, 143
Rowlinson, Michael 64
Rowntree, Benjamin Seebohm 53,
    75
Rowntree, Joseph 62, 63, 72
Rowntree Cocoa Works 8, 61–76
    classes and societies 53, 63, 64–76
        competitive sport 69
        domestic crafts 53, 64–5, 72–3,
            74–5
        gender segregation in 63–4,
            69–71, 76
        Girl' Temperance Society
            65–6, 71
        gymnastics 67, 68, 69–70, 71,
            74
        incentives to participate 65, 71
        lack of interest in 70–1, 75
        numbers participating 70–1
        physical training 67–71, 72
        Swedish gymnastics 67, 68
        swimming and bathing 67, 68,
            75
        team games 68–70, 74
        Wednesday Club 66–7
    discipline at 75, 76
    marriage bar 64
    number of female employees 63
    sexual division of labour 63–4
    sexual politics 64
    wages 64
rugby league
    black players in 9, 159
    broadcasting of 91, 159
    church teams 116
    Cup Finals 7, 85, 86, 89, 95, 98,
        158
        see also Cup Finals

newspapers and 156–7
  local newspapers 89
North–South divide 49, 90,
    138–9, 157–60
Northern union 49, 116, 157, 158
social class and 157
sporting heroes 157–9
television and 92, 159
rugby union 3, 157

Sabbatarianism, effects on sport
  121
Saddique, Mohammed 167
Sadler, Joan 75–6
Samuel, Raphael 4
Sandham, Andrew 149
Searle, C. 9
sectarian loyalties 107, 130, 131
secularization 113, 126–7
self
  composition of 2
  constitution of 2
  language and 2
Shaw, Alfred 148
Shaw, John 141
Shrewsbury, Arthur 145–6
Slater, Ruth 70
Smith, Anthony D. 2
Smith, Chris 64
Smith, Dai 3
Smith, G.O. 140
Smith, Tommie 168
Snow, C.P. 150
Snowdrop Bands 58
social class
  church-affiliated sports clubs and
      114–17, 131–3
  class consciousness 2, 131–3
  football and 85
  identity and 2
  rugby union and 157
  social relations and 2
  working-class consciousness 2,
      131–3
socialism, sport and 132–3
sporting heroes 7, 137–64
  animals as 139
  black players 159

creation of 7
cricketers 144–50
female 4
footballers 150–7
gender and 139
knur-and-spel 142
masculinity and 7, 139, 147, 161
in mining villages 20, 21, 28–9,
    35, 36, 140
newspapers and 4, 107, 153,
    155–6, 161
  local press 146, 147
North–South divide 137–64
potshare bowlers 21, 28–9, 35,
    36, 142
pugilists 141–2
quoiters 28, 29
relationship with admirers 7
representations 7
rowing 143
rugby league 157–9
sportsmanship and 139
television and 155, 162
traditional sports 141–3
transfer market and 162
women and 139, 161
sports grounds
  church-affiliated clubs 117, 123
  house building and 123
  see also recreation grounds
sports history 3
  empiricist methodology 3
  reflectionist approach 3
sportsmanship 139
Stein, Jock 177
Storey, David, This Sporting Life
    11n, 157–8
Stoop, Adrian 141
Sugden, John 3–4
Sullivan, Jim ('Sully') 159
Summers, Bill 22
Summers, Will 20
Sunday schools
  annual celebrations 24–5
  sports clubs 117–18, 119, 124
    see also church-affiliated sports
      clubs
Sutcliffe, Herbert 147, 149–50

table tennis 116
team sports
  masculinity and 138–9
  North–South divide and 138–9
  women and 68–9, 74, 114–15
  see also cricket; football; hockey;
     rugby league; rugby union
Tebbit, Norman 167
television
  cricket and 150
  football and 106, 154, 155
  rugby league and 91–2, 159
  sporting heroes and 155, 162
temperance groups
  in mining villages 33
  Rowntree Cocoa Works 65–6,
     71
Tendulkar, Sachin 166
Thewlis, John 146
Thompson, E.P. 2
Thompson, Ethel 75
Thompson, Tommy 142
Thompson, William ('Bendigo') 142
Tomlinson, Alan 142
Townend, Kathleen 59
trade unions
  black footballers and 10
  Northumberland Miners' Union
     19, 34
  women and 54, 57
Trueman, Fred 150

unemployment, sport and 121–3

Vertinsky, P. 8

Wagstaff, Harold 158
Walker, Graham 4
Wall, Frederick 93, 94
Walton, John 6, 106
Waring, Eddie 92, 159–60
Watkins, David 89
Wesleyan Methodist sports clubs
     119, 130
West Indian Standing Conference
     165
Whannel, Gary 89
Williams, Gareth 3

Williams, Gwyn 11
Williams, J. 8, 9
Williams, Raymond 14
Wilson, Harold 85
women
  birth rate and 61
  as cheap labour 54
  church-affiliated sports clubs and
     7–8, 128–9
    women's cricket 114–15
    women's hockey 114
  cricket and 129, 147, 161
    women's teams 68, 114–15
  as domestic dependents 54
  domestic service 58
  education of 53, 61
    physical education 67–71
  emancipation of 8
  encouragement of domestic role
     53–4, 55, 56, 57, 58–9
  Girls' Friendly Society 58
  hockey clubs 68, 114
  ideology of motherhood 61
  'mandatory marriage' 54
  men's leisure and 53–6
  in mining villages 36
  models of femininity 53–4
  physical education for 67–71
    competitive sport 69
    team games 68–9
  recreational provision 58–60
    rational recreation 57, 72–3
    see also Rowntree Cocoa Works
  Snowdrop Bands 58
  social roles 54
  sporting heroism and 137, 161
  team sports 68–9, 74, 114–15
  trade unions and 54, 57–8
  voluntary associations and 58–60
  in waged employment 54–9, 60
  working-class 53–83
    in mining villages 36
    see also femininity; gender
Wood, Ray 155
Working Men's Institutes 14, 25
working-class consciousness 2,
     131–3
workplace teams 120, 123–5

colliery companies 124
cricket 123–5
football 121, 123–5
see also church-affiliated sports
    clubs; pub teams

Wright, Thomas 55, 57

Yorkshire cricket 119, 139, 140,
    146–8, 149–50, 160
    racism in 166–7